Also by
General André Beaufre

INTRODUCTION TO STRATEGY
1965

DETERRENCE AND STRATEGY
1966

NATO AND EUROPE
1966

1940

THE FALL OF FRANCE

1940

THE FALL

OF

FRANCE

by General André Beaufre

Translated from the French by
DESMOND FLOWER

WITH A PREFACE BY
CAPTAIN SIR BASIL LIDDELL HART

NEW YORK: Alfred · A · Knopf
[1968]

THIS IS A BORZOI BOOK
PUBLISHED BY ALFRED A. KNOPF, INC.

FIRST AMERICAN EDITION

© Copyright 1967 by Cassell and Company Limited. All rights reserved under International and Pan-American Copyright Conventions. Distributed by Random House, Inc. Published in London, England, by Cassell and Company Limited. Manufactured in the United States of America.

Library of Congress Catalog Card Number: 67–18628

Originally published in French as *Le Drame de 1940*
© Copyright 1965 by Librairie Plon

Grateful acknowledgment is extended to Captain Sir Basil Liddell Hart for permission to quote from his *Defence of Britain*, Copyright 1939 by the Modern Library, Inc.

PREFACE

by Captain Sir Basil Liddell Hart

I am very glad to see the appearance of an edition in English of
General André Beaufre's autobiographical volume on '1940', which
has been translated by another longstanding friend of mine, Dr
Desmond Flower, M.C. When I first met André Beaufre in 1935 he
was introduced to me as the youngest officer on the French General
Staff, and he made such an impression on me that it was no surprise
that he rose to the rank of *Général d'Armée*. He has subsequently
become recognized world-wide as one of the ablest military
thinkers of this era.

It is thus of great interest and historical value to have his views
on the fall of France in 1940, and its causes. This retrospect leads
him back, rightly, to the nineteen-twenties, the first decade of the
inter-war years, when complacency about victory in 1918 and the
methods by then evolved combined with the restrictiveness of
financial pressure to produce a state of stagnation in the French
Army. It was very marked by contrast with the eager search for a
new technique that was being pursued at the same time in the
German Army, where the consciousness of defeat in 1918 combined
with the restrictive conditions imposed by the victors to create an
incentive for new developments—while, ironically, freeing the
German Army of the burden of obsolete equipment that was, and
has always been in peacetime, a basic hindrance to progress.

The stagnation was, naturally, more apparent to outside observers than to the heads of the French Army, who were filled with the
complacency commonly induced by victory. In my 1927 book *The
Remaking of Modern Armies*, after a chapter comparing 'The Post-
War Doctrines of Germany and France'—which pointed out that
the Germans were seeking to revive mobility and flexibility
whereas the French favoured massive bombardment and extreme
deliberation—I devoted four chapters to an examination of the
'French Army Today' based on a visit to that Army the previous
autumn. Their conclusion, epitomized in a sentence, was that:
'Under the test of a future war the ponderous advance of such a

170234

machine might break down altogether.' The 'alternative course' I suggested was for France to exploit mechanization to revive mobility, and develop 'a mechanical striking force of highly trained volunteers, to form a spearhead to the national Army'— a theme taken up seven years later by Charles de Gaulle in his little book *Vers l'armée de metier*. From then on, he became the chief French advocate of mechanized forces, but received too little heed in his own country.

André Beaufre, too young to see service in World War I, became an officer in the French Army in the early nineteen-twenties. He entered Saint-Cyr as a cadet in 1921—'against the wishes of my father who thought there would be no more wars'. In a brief chapter he vividly conveys the toughness, idealism and mysticism of that famous institution. Captain de Gaulle was here his instructor in history and ever since has seemed to him 'a synthesis' of Richelieu and Mazarin.

From Saint-Cyr Beaufre went, by his own choice, to become a young officer of the 5th *Tirailleurs* in Algeria. In 1925 he was sent with one of their battalions to Morocco, to fight in the campaign, against the Riffs. Here he had some hair-raising adventures, and was then badly wounded, left to die but rescued by a party of Goums and decorated with the Croix de Guerre when lying on a hospital bed. After recovery, he took part in another campaign against the Riffs the following year, and this time was disabled by amoebic dysentery. The chapter finishes with some thoughtful reflexions on 'Colonialism'.

He was now urged to study for the *École de Guerre*, and although turned down initially as too young, he passed in the next year— which must have been soon after my second post-war visit to the French Army, in 1926. From acquaintance with the school I can endorse his criticism that it was a 'good secondary school' for the Staff rather than the *École Supérieure de Guerre* of its own exalted full title. Especially would I endorse his criticism that it was 'merely repeating a doctrine on the role of armour copied from that of 1918'. But I would differ from his recollection that in the teaching 'the defensive was to be the queen of war'. For I noted that the vast majority of the exercises here, and in the whole of the French Army, were devoted to the offensive—but an offensive strictly of the methodical and slow-motion kind, as in 1918—while hardly any-

thing was being done to develop new techniques of defence. That
trend continued to predominate until the eve of the next war.

I appreciate General Beaufre's testimony that his doubts of the
official doctrine were fed, and light came to him first, by reading my
book on the strategy of indirect approach, originally entitled *The
Decisive Wars of History*, arguing that 'war was not a game which
was won by sheer weight, but by the intelligence and finesse of its
leaders'. Presumably he read the French edition, published in 1933,
four years after the early English and American editions.

After a spell in Tunisia he was posted to the General Staff of the
Army, in Paris. Here he found the seniors 'were primarily concerned
with forms of drafting', and phrasing memoranda in a way so
'abstract' that their meaning was hard to perceive—which was a
help in avoiding the responsibility of taking decisions. In sum,
they were obsessed with trivialities. As to the modernization of
the Army, 'there was a lot of talk but no action'.

It was not long afterwards that I first met Beaufre—he was one
of a small number of the most promising younger officers who were
picked out for me by a discerning friend at the Quai d'Orsay. Most
of them were then more hopeful than they later remembered, and
were expecting that General Gamelin, who had become head of the
Army in place of Weygand, would hasten its modernization and
mechanization. But they were soon disillusioned. So was I, when
meeting Gamelin in 1937 along with Hore-Belisha, our new
War Minister. Gamelin certainly talked a lot about the need for
taking the offensive, and disparagingly about the defensive—but
it was all too evident that what he pictured was the old-style
offensive, with mechanized forces merely supplementing a mass of
slow-moving infantry divisions.

During the period of 'Munich' Beaufre was back in Morocco,
serving his time of active command as a Captain, but was recalled
to France, and to a post on the General Staff, in the spring of
1939—after Hitler had occupied the remains of Czechoslovakia.
At this point Beaufre's book gives an illuminating survey of the
military situation on the eve of war, which brings out vividly the
differences between French and German action. Although it somewhat over-estimates, as did most writers after 1940, the extent to
which German industry was applied and developed to war purposes,
its indictment of French inertia and out-of-date views is striking.

✳ PREFACE ✳

Towards the end of July 1939 Beaufre was appointed a member of the French military mission that was sent, belatedly, along with a British mission, to negotiate a mutual defence arrangement with the Russians. These missions, travelling by sea, only arrived in Moscow on 11 August! In a chapter of over fifty pages, Beaufre provides the fullest and most intimate account of these negotiations, which ended, ironically, in and with the Soviet-German Pact, settled on 19 August and announced on 24 August.

The next chapter of Beaufre's book deals with the 'Phoney War' —the opening nine months' phase of what became World War II. It is perspicacious, though inclined to press the facts into the frame of his thesis. Thus when he quotes nearly two pages from my last pre-war book, of July 1939, *The Defence of Britain*, to show that even I, a prophet of mechanized mobility, had changed my views radically since 1935, the passages which he quotes are not consecutive, as they appear to be, but taken in isolation and differing sequence from various pages, while omitting qualifying passages that would have shown that my views in 1939 had not changed anything like as much from those in 1935 and earlier as the selection suggests. Moreover, when he goes on to quote what I said of the French Army's prospects in 1939 he omits the key passages that show I was referring specifically to the heavily fortified Franco-German frontier, and not to its Belgian flank, when I spoke of an offensive starting 'with a heavy handicap'.

He is mistaken in imagining that this book of mine became 'the foundation of British thinking', but is still more mistaken in saying that my thinking changed in the years preceding the war until I 'reached a formula, as we have seen, which tallied with our own'. Gamelin would have gasped at this as much as I do! Moreover when he says that I made the same 'fallacious interpretation of the Spanish war', it is very evident that he has never read the chapter 'Lessons from Spain' that I included in the 1938 edition of my book *Europe in Arms*.

Even more surprising is his remark that in *The Defence of Britain* 'there was no more talk, as there had been earlier, of mobility or a revolution in strategy through the use of armour'. For there is repeated emphasis in almost every chapter on the need for mechanized mobility, and for 'armoured divisions', while a whole chapter (XX) is devoted to 'The Handling of the Army—New Tactics' and the revolution to be produced thereby with such new-type forces and methods.

He has, clearly, no intention to be unfair, or do anything more than reinforce his thesis, for he pays as high tribute as anyone could wish to my earlier views. But he is not a historian, as he frankly admits, and his 'object is only to show why we were beaten'—an object that naturally tends to forcing facts into a theoretical frame.

In 1939 one had to deal with the position as it stood, instead of as one wished it to be. Not having had to comment publicly at a critical time, André Beaufre may not realize the difficulty—a two-fold difficulty—of urging the development of a modern type of defence, the Western Allies' only remaining chance, while avoiding anything that might encourage the Germans to apply the new methods of attack that one had previously, and for so long, advocated. But the best proof of Beaufre's honesty of intention is the way he admits that by 1939 his own 'foresight had been progressively stifled' by his environment, and that he had come round to accept the official view.

In his final chapter he deals with 'The Downfall seen from GHQ'. Here his vividly recollected impressions of how complacency turned suddenly into panic, producing a paralytic inertia among the seniors, accord with the evidence I had soon after the war from other friends in the junior posts there. He brings out the atmosphere, and prevailing attitudes, even more vividly than they did—and with reflective sidelights. It is pleasant to read how Weygand, recalled to command when the collapse had gone too far to retrieve, showed a resolution, and receptiveness to new ideas, more worthy of French traditions.

With almost every point in André Beaufre's Epilogue, on the lessons of 1940, I emphatically agree.

B.H.LH.

CONTENTS

*

FOREWORD

*

THESE MEMORIES AND REFLEXIONS are centred around the drama of 1940, an event of prime importance in this century, the consequences of which are not yet finished.

This extraordinary collapse, which marked the end of an epoch, has sometimes had a veil drawn over it in the hope of forgetting the nightmare, and has sometimes been shamelessly exploited, with attacks upon one scapegoat or another, for emotional and political ends.

These attitudes are equally ill-founded. Bitter as this whole business was, no one has the right to ignore the facts or to distort them.

The difficulty is that there is always danger of finding oneself drawn into the polemics which still persist. In the hope of avoiding this pitfall I have held back these thoughts on 1940 for a quarter of a century. But the armistice still engenders the most violent partisan feelings, and the opposing protagonists of this denouement —Marshal Pétain, General Weygand and General de Gaulle— remain the targets of the bitter contradictory charges which still divide so many Frenchmen among themselves. Having had the privilege of living beside Weygand during the battle of 1940, then having been put in prison by him in Algiers in 1941 and condemned by a court-martial under the authority of Vichy, I feel myself to be above partisan feelings and in consequence the more free to bear witness to those things which I saw and understood. I have done so while trying not to pass judgement on men and events: that is the task of history. Rather I have endeavoured to recreate the atmosphere of the events through which I have lived. This is essential if one is to understand them. In addition, in the hard and difficult world in which we live, we have a duty to understand the phenomena to which we are subjected so as to try to bend them to our will, in however small a way, rather than be their plaything.

We shall see that in 1940 we were really the victims of a series of fatal events brought about by factors which had been apparent long before—from 1914 onwards—and of which the ineluctable consequences were not understood in time to grapple with them before it was too late. The great lesson of 1940 is that such maladies can only be coped with at birth, and only in the early stages is it possible to act effectively. Instead of the kind of fatal optimism into which we allowed ourselves to slip, there has to be a constant critical examination of the conjunction of events in order to isolate dangerous germs and deal with them immediately. In this objective and uneasy examination it is essential to avoid illusions or any temporarily fashionable views, which often are nothing more than a reaction against the excesses of the immediate past. Never must one lose sight of the broad principles which good sense dictates: to have a policy within one's means, to have an army to fit that policy, to safeguard the collective sense of survival which is called patriotism, to avoid the gathering storms by prudent and timely prevention—in fact, the opposite of what we did for twenty years.

After that it is too late; the march of destiny inexorably crushes those unfortunate people, whatever their abilities or shortcomings may be, who try to act at the eleventh hour.

The wind of history, when it rises, overwhelms the will of mankind—but it lies within the capacity of man to foresee these storms, to ride them, and, in the long term, to make them serve him.

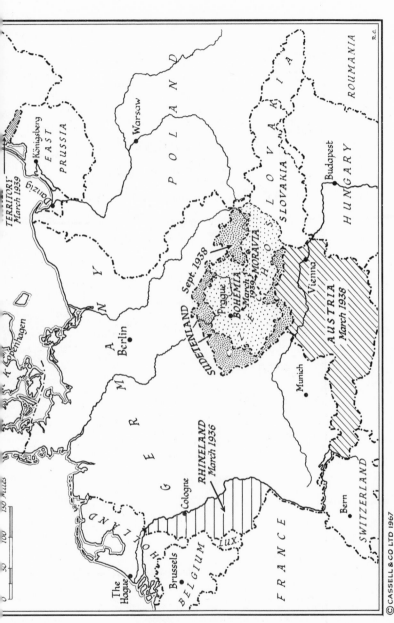

THE HITLERITE AGGRESSIONS

THE OPPOSIN

13 M

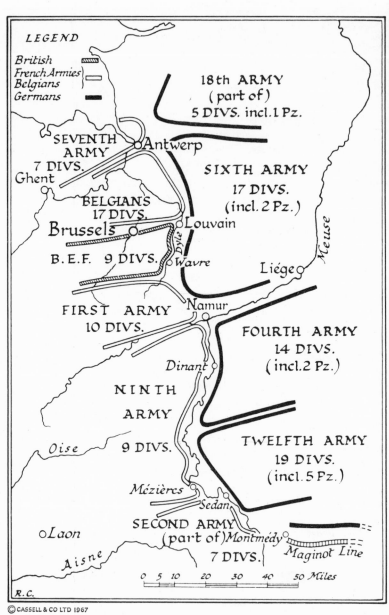

AREA OF OPERATIONS

MAY 1940

To My Son Roland

*

IT IS FOR YOU that I write this book, for you and your contemporaries in the twenty-first century. It is neither 'Memoirs'
nor 'Memories', even though the thread of it may be woven from
memories. For my intention is not to establish the truth of history
in all its complexity. This is not my line, and one does not suddenly
become a good historian after forty years of a life of action.

My ambition is at once smaller and greater: smaller because I do
not set out to give an overall picture of events which others can do
better than I; greater because I am trying to convey the real
feeling of events in which I myself took part or which my generation
has lived through.

I well know that each generation discovers life afresh and
realizes truths which appear new to them: each one of us must go
through his apprenticeship and must find his own way. What I have
tried to do may be in vain—that is a risk which I accept. But
perhaps you and your contemporaries may glean something from
this quick survey of a period which progressed from the horse to
the sputnik, from long dresses to tight trousers, from the *Café
Concert* to striptease, from European world dominance to the
hexagon—that is to say from the classic civilization to a new and
different civilization which is as yet ill defined. And precisely
because this civilization is not yet solid and is still seeking a firm
basis on which to establish itself, it is no bad thing to try to show
from whence it has emerged, how it has come about and where it is
going. In effect, the role of your generation is of prime importance:
it is up to you to settle the destiny of Western civilization by
choosing which of the various possible paths you wish to follow. If
your choice is a bad one, all is lost. To make such a choice is
difficult; I would like to help you.

What I would really like would be to write a book of philosophy,
because that is what it comes down to in the end. I may try it one
day if I have the courage—for it is a hard and thankless task, even
if one manages to avoid all the fashionable jargon. Here I am not

trying to 'instruct while entertaining', but rather trying to set
down what I feel I have to say in the least boring way I can
command. Hence the form of this book, a mixture of memories and
reflexions. Hence the lack of continuity both in the narrative and
the periods described because nothing could be more daunting—
or less realizable—than a complete and systematic review of the
last fifty years. To start with, one's own memory of them is patchy:
certain facts, certain scenes stand out clearly while the rest are
either clouded or forgotten. From a time which was once clear and
sunlit, interrupted solely by the diurnal advent of darkness, emerge
here and there faces, feelings and figments which in the mists of the
past made up some broader, well-lit pictures. It is these larger
pictures which I am trying to describe.

As to the reflexions, I shall try to keep them short and easily
understandable, confining them, as Bertrand Russell has put it, to
'the history of my ideas' and which I would further describe as a
'chronicle of my preoccupations'. I think that it is important to set
these preoccupations against the background of the moment when
they came about, because this shows the relative character and
contingency of thoughts, even when one is trying to be objective.
One must realize, too, that life is very short in relation to the time
which is needed for a careful elaboration of one's thoughts: during
four months in hospital or six months in prison no more than a few
solid conclusions came to me. At my age I feel that I would need
several lives really to get anywhere in knowledge and understanding. This is always one of the great difficulties of existence:
fate overtakes us before we have had time to analyse and appreciate
it. Therein lies the great danger for your generation because, as
I shall point out, you will have to make a major decision without
the time completely to comprehend its consequences. Perhaps I
may be able to point out some of the governing factors!

I have thought much about the range and duration of this
journey into the past. After all, evolution has to be taken as a whole
—beginning with *la belle époque* when I was no more than a child,
and coming forward through the two cataclysmic experiences of the
great wars which have given birth to the world we know today.

I will have much to say about the Army, even if this is not a
very fashionable subject today. For one thing, I spent forty years
in the Service—forty rich, satisfying and varied years, despite the

disappointments of history. Also the period through which we have lived was dominated by wars, great and small, and it is impossible to understand the trend of events without taking this into consideration and realizing, for example, the great effect which it has had on technical development. 'Battles' are not the whole story—far from it; but a clear understanding of history can only be achieved by a realization of the part which these clashes have played in the evolution of mankind. War has changed, but the struggle will continue—in new ways and in forms as yet undreamed of. The only hope with which we can comfort ourselves is that it may become less cruel.

To conclude, I can see that I am in danger of promising more than I in fact have to offer. I will do my best, my dear Roland, without, I hope, overplaying my hand or straining the reader's patience: with the constant thought that I am not preoccupied with the past, to which I will have to refer, but with the future which belongs to you.

PROLOGUE

Chapter 1
From Blue and Red to Horizon Blue,
1914–18

*

TODAY THE FIRST WORLD WAR seems a long time away. It has become as legendary as the wars of the First Empire, to which indeed it is perhaps nearer in spirit than it is to our present age. Looking back, one can say that this vast upheaval marked the end of the nineteenth century—wrongly called *la belle époque*—and opened the way to our rugged twentieth century, the century of rapid change towards a new form of civilization.

I grew up during this tremendous national drama; I knew no more of it than the reflexions and the shadows, but nevertheless I lived intensely with it: so much so that it dictated my choice of a military career and undoubtedly influenced certain elements in my character. What is true of me is true of France, which is still deeply scarred by this terrible experience, as the United States still is by its Civil War. That is why, although a modest witness, I think it is useful to set down the vivid, even if minor, impressions of those days which remain with me today. I am not writing history nor reminiscing, but trying to catch an atmosphere. It is this atmosphere which the legends that have grown up distort so much and which make the events of the past unintelligible to those who have not lived through them.

Everyone talks about the declaration of war in 1914 as if it were a bolt from the blue. Nothing could be further from the truth. The idea of war had been with us for years. Only those utterly lacking in any intuition can have been surprised. At any rate we children knew what was to come so well that when we broke up for the summer holidays in 1913, and again at the same time in 1914, we said: 'See you next year, if there isn't a war.' Péguy too 'knew' what was to be his fate and that of his generation, and he described it most movingly. It is possible that this collective premonition which I experienced was in itself one of the principal causes of the war. Certainly it gave to the 1914 mobilization a sense of national unity which no one who did not live through it can imagine. I was in Calais when it happened. It is impossible to describe the solemnity, the resolution and the enthusiasm with which the entire French nation answered the call to arms.

This army of 1914 was almost the army of 1870 about to take its revenge. It wore the same uniforms of blue and red which had charmed my childhood and which made such pretty splashes of colour against the green of the fields and were in fact just as much of an anachronism in war as the horse. In 1913 an effort was made to give the army a more modern appearance, to go over to grey or khaki like every foreign army. But French opinion rejected the idea and remained instinctively faithful to bright colours. All this was so far from the realities of war that I remember one uniform commended by Walter Scott, a fashionable designer at the time, which was actually tried out on a Paris unit; this consisted of a grey-green jacket, to be up-to-date—but with red trousers! Let us say that France had a naïve and old-fashioned conception of war, which we were to see again in 1939, and the recurrence of which gives food for thought.

✳

1914 was to become a succession of surprises: surprise at the reality of heavy fire-power, surprise at the breaching of the frontiers, surprise at the victory of the Marne, and eventually surprise at the digging-in and the stalemate. From my child's viewpoint I felt some of these surprises very close to me. At Calais everyone talked of the bloody fighting in Belgium and we heard suddenly of the occupation of Lille by the Germans. It was time to get back to Paris as fast as possible, and we took the train.

Today it is difficult to realize the role which the railways played at the time. Roads went for nothing, the permanent way was all-important. Troops, reinforcements, wounded, refugees, stores—everything went by rail. The stations were centres at which one could not only shower the troops with gifts and comfort the wounded, but stand in wonder watching the endless procession of Moroccans, turbaned Indians, kilted Scotsmen and French territorial troops with long moustaches like grenadiers of the First

Empire. All rolled slowly by in cattle trucks—'hommes 40, chevaux en long 8'—lined with straw and exuding an odour of smoke and red wine. The same trucks, lined with the same straw, but now soaked in blood, would return with the wounded, reminiscent of the horse-drawn waggons of the past but soon to be replaced by Red Cross trains which would make the horror a little more antiseptic.

Our train went quite well as far as Amiens; but there we had to get out in the middle of the night. The main station at Amiens was a microcosm of the frontier defeats. The troop trains going south were filled with wounded and the remnants of territorial regiments cut to pieces at Bapaume. In one dark corner a captain in sabots, a cane in his hand, was busy rallying about a hundred men round a furled flag; rumour had it that these were all that remained of an entire regiment. In another corner some khaki-clad English troops in shirt-sleeve order, with walrus moustaches, watched the confusion while phlegmatically drawing on their pipes. On the platform itself a mass of refugees squatted on the ground exchanging the most hair-raising news: the main line to Paris had been cut, the Moroccans carried strings of cut-off German ears in their haversacks, the Uhlans would be arriving at any moment. . . . An officer with a white band round his hat advised my mother to board a troop train. The one we took went to Rouen and we made the journey with soldiers of the supply services withdrawn from Lille.

The day after, at Rouen, we found ourselves in another world—that of defeated Belgium. The town was full of Belgian uniforms—tall *képis*, silver stripes and badges of rank which seemed both numerous and enormous to me, 'Guides' with light blue pipings. We were given permission to go on to Paris.

But when we got there we were told that the Germans had entered Meaux, which in fact was not true. So we took another train which jinked from station to station until several days later it reached the Midi. All the way, at every station, people were handing out food and drinks. At Nîmes a woman in black, whose son had been called up, expressed her astonishment that we should have with us young men of seventeen. As we went further, the mass of refugees gradually dispersed into the slumbering, sunlit towns. The war was far away once more.

The news of victory on the Marne reached us in a muffled way. Propaganda had already blunted our credulity. If I remember right, one merely had the impression, wrongly, of some extraordinary piece of good fortune which people were trying to make the most of.

What followed seemed even more incomprehensible: the German advance came to a halt, the front was held; and now no one talked about anything except the trenches. Our soldiers did not shave any more, moustaches blossomed into beards and gave rise to that historic name: *les poilus*.

We went back to Paris. There life went on in an atmosphere of patriotic fever. The Government winkled gold out of innumerable old family stockings by means of loans which were launched with all the advertising which today is lavished on the début of a new detergent. Manpower was totally mobilized. Those who were not called up designed for themselves some sort of para-military clothing, like the chauffeur's uniform which M. Poincaré wore; and already this proliferation of unsoldierly dress revealed the existence of a disease which was to spread: shirking. At the same time propaganda grew and grew without any relation to reality; what in those days the fighting men called 'eye-wash'. I remember at this time a performance at the Opéra Comique which was interrupted by an extraordinary patriotic tableau. It represented a scene in the trenches—trenches such as those who had never seen them imagined them to be like. It came straight out of *The Daughter of the Regiment*; it included the arrival of the Colours, the *Marseillaise* sung by Marthe Chenal, and so on . . . the height of nonsense performed with the best will in the world. The whole theatre reverberated with ill-informed and patriotic applause, which only underlined the growing division between those 'at the front' and those 'in the rear'.

The front, which I never saw, drowned in severe cold and a series of quite useless but costly operations. The rear knitted and showered its gifts on the soldiers, who were by now giving up their red trousers for a kind of navvy's corduroy—with coloured piping which theoretically qualified it as a uniform under the Geneva Convention. . . . Life settled into huts of branches as in the forests of ancient Gaul. And then suddenly, fairly quickly but progressively, there appeared the tin hat and horizon blue.

✳

Horizon blue was an astonishing psychological discovery which marked the vitality of France at this time. The colour was very pretty, although about as unsuitable for a mud-bound life as it was possible to be. When wet, it assumed the gentle tint of a clear spring sky. To the *poilu* it acted as a rejuvenation. Regiments in their brand new uniforms made a brave show in the landscape. Now poison gas arrived, and the mask which went with it meant the end of beards; luxuriant moustaches, too, shrank to toothbrush size. The generation of the Great War assumed a facial image which Hitler was to dishonour a quarter of a century later. With a new look the Army broke out from its chrysalis of 1870 and spread its wings of blue. And at the same time its equipment was brought up-to-date; now machine guns, heavy artillery, trucks and aeroplanes proliferated. The mass levy of infantrymen armed in 1914 with a rifle was gradually replaced by a semi-industrialized Army which Stalin later very accurately called the 'manufactured Army'.

At the rear the people, after their first burst of military romanticism, enthusiastically set about the manufacturing of equipment. The French flair for improvisation performed constant miracles: a factory designed to make teaspoons turned to the production of small arms ammunition, a bicycle works made shells. France as a nation was ruined, but private fortunes blossomed from the endless necessity for providing goodness knows what, from aeroplanes and spare parts to boots and saddles. Nevertheless there were still far too few pairs of hands. Women who had already revitalized their appearance by shortening their skirts and by wearing lace-up 'flying boots', went to work. One found them, with forage cap pulled down over one eye, as ticket collectors on the underground and as conductors on the buses. Others worked at the bench in factories, something which had never been seen before. Starving Kabyles appeared to sweep the streets. Then the Government recalled more and more soldiers from the front, and this in itself created a sense of irritation among the fighting men.

Meanwhile great battles were launched on their indecisive course, the far-away echo of some of them audible even to us in

Paris: Verdun, the heroic hell; the majestic offensive of the Somme
which was to lead to the throwing back of Hindenburg and a gleam
of hope: the victory of Brussilov in Galicia. The war had taken on
its new look of horizon blue and industrial efficiency. *Le Feu* by
Henri Barbusse exposed all the horrors of the struggle and killed
once and for all the conventional prints in the Déroulède style
which previously had captured people's minds. The casualty lists
grew longer and the war dragged on. Exhaustion began to make
itself felt.

Then the politicians took over. The Chambre des Députés
bedevilled the Government with so-called secret committees.
Lyautey, at one time Minister for War, fell. Joffre, who tyranically
insisted on his prerogatives as *generalissimo*, was sacrificed at the
very moment when he had at last regained the initiative in the
field. But people wanted a new look and they wanted victory. A
fresh supreme head of the armed forces was appointed: Nivelle,
who had succeeded at Verdun and who now promised rapid victory.

✳

Nineteen-seventeen was the difficult year. Nivelle made the
biggest nonsense it is possible for a general to make: instead of the
victory which he had offered, he bogged down in bloody defeat. At
the same time Russia collapsed in revolution. The morale of our
Army was broken, and that of the civilian population severely
strained. Defeatism, hitherto considered traitorous and unthinkable,
became rife. There were many supporters for the idea of a 'negotiated peace'. The example of the Soviet infiltrated through the
minds of the troops and of the country. Regiments mutinied and
contact was made with the Germans via Switzerland by members
of the left. The situation was so grave that the *Président du Conseil*
at the time, Painlevé, lost his grip. His son Jean Painlevé, a
fellow-pupil of mine at Sainte-Barbe, was mercilessly ragged by us
young patriots.

✳

Then Clemenceau came to power. This redoubtable little man
seized the helm in a grip of iron. In a famous speech which so
overwhelmed me that I can still quote it from memory today, his
leitmotive was 'I wage war!', and he ended with the words of the

✳ PROLOGUE ✳

Marseillaise: '*Allons, enfants de la Patrie, la France, le Monde libre sont avec vous!*' All contact with the Germans was broken off, directors of newspapers who had reached any understanding with the enemy were shot. At the same time Pétain exercised considerable tact in taking over control of the Army. The worst, that is to say the collapse of the country, had been avoided.

But we were only at the beginning of still more terrible trials. Germany brought her armies across from Russia to the western front. The war grew tougher. Paris was shelled and blacked out. The food situation deteriorated, bread was rationed, life was hard.

Next the Germans went over to the attack. For the first time in four years of fighting in France the front was broken. The British were talking—already!—of withdrawing on Dunkirk. Pétain wanted to cover Paris. . . . The one hope for France then lay in Foch, whom Clemenceau at this dramatic moment had put forward as Supreme Allied Commander. Foch drew into the battle the entire flow of the horizon blue Army, and the Germans were held before Amiens. Were we saved? By no means. Twice more the Germans were to break through, once by routing the Portuguese and once on the French front at Chemin des Dames. Each time they were held after days of knife-edge suspense. The war was taking on a breathless rhythm.

In Paris our nights were interrupted by air raid warnings. A heavy gun, 'Big Bertha', shelled the city monotonously, one round every ten minutes. At Sainte-Barbe we listened to each detonation, watched the clock, and greeted the next explosion on the dot with cries of 'Bingo!' We found it all very exciting. From the Montagne Sainte-Geneviève one night we watched *Le Bûcheron* going up in flames on the rue Sainte-Antoine. To avoid unnecessary congestion in Paris we sat for our university entrance exams at Easter in the dining hall of the college.

Then at Saint-Thibault I encountered for the first time the Americans—huge, ruddy, squeezed into khaki tunics, topped off with a Boy Scout hat, country boys rolling their shoulders, simple, strong, disciplined and efficient. I offered myself as an interpreter and lived with them throughout the following summer. Their arrival put new life into our weary war. But would there be enough of them and would they arrive in time?

At last the turning-point came: on 14 July 1918 a fresh German offensive in Champagne was flung back by General Gouraud's Army. And immediately there followed the riposte which Foch had been preparing for months: first the furious counter-attack by Mangin, taking thousands of prisoners, then an endless succession of hammer blows along the whole length of the Allied front. Foch had understood that with the military means of the time the initial break-through was possible, but the resources available did not allow for exploitation. Instead of seeking, like Ludendorff, for penetration in depth, he took advantage of the results achieved in the first few days of an attack, then switched the emphasis elsewhere. Pocket by pocket the Germans were winkled out, pushed back, and forced to watch, helpless, as their reserves dwindled into nothing.

One evening on the banks of the Saint-Satur canal, near where my brother was to be shot by the Germans twenty-eight years later, the Americans picked up a newspaper which announced the capitulation of Austria. The eastern front was finished. The end was near.

I settled down for my first year as a student in Paris.

November, 1918. A course of natural history, like any other. But it could not hold our interest. We had been told that the Armistice was probably to be signed later that very morning and would be marked by artillery salvoes. We heard the guns roar, but this time it was for peace. Afterwards there was utter silence. Then one of us jumped to his feet and shouted: *'Vive la France!'*

From that moment we all went mad. We walked out on our lecturer, leaving him like an emaciated and lonely bird; without permission we set off in a tumultuous crowd for the front gate. There we grabbed the flag which was always hoisted on Sundays and marched with it down the rue Cujas.

Everyone had the same feeling. Streams of students and schoolchildren were flowing in from all sides. On the boulevard Saint-Michel these streams converged into a river which swelled with every minute. We turned to the right, towards the Châtelet. I was in the front, marching next to the flag, shouting and singing at the top of my voice. Completely carried away as I was, my mind still registered the most extraordinary bits of childish lunacy. I remember one twenty-year-old youth who ran from one side of the street to the other whenever he saw a woman and whipped her skirt up, dropping it again to hurry off to another victim. No one seemed to mind.

By now people were pouring out of the houses and swelling the crowds on the pavements. Everyone was shouting anything that came into his head. The girls of course had a rough time but they laughed and put up with it.

Our ever-growing procession got to the Châtelet and turned left. The rue de Rivoli was black with people, mostly from the great market of Les Halles, and when we appeared we were greeted like heroes. The market women in their varnished sabots and shawls shouted: '*Bravo les petits! Vive la France!*' No one had any idea what he was doing or what he was saying.

We marched into the place de la Concorde and carved our way through the cheering crowd. Someone shouted 'Clemenceau' and at once we all chanted 'Clemenceau! Clemenceau!' We got to the rue Saint-Dominique. The gates opened and we poured into the courtyard, keeping on shouting, 'Clemenceau! Clemenceau!' After a few minutes a window was drawn back on the first floor, and there was Clemenceau—small, and deeply moved. He raised one stubby arm and shouted hoarsely: '*Vive la France!*' We shouted too, and I wept.

GENESIS

Chapter 2
Saint-Cyr

*

I ENTERED SAINT-CYR in 1921 against the wishes of my father who thought there would be no more wars. . . .

In spite of having schooled myself mentally for the experience, I found that Saint-Cyr was tough. The plumed shakos and white gloves of 1914 were the outward and visible signs of a venerable institution, part barracks, part college, part seminary, and riddled with tradition. In the School we were soldiers rather than students, dressed unbecomingly in horizon blue which we had to change six times a day for physical jerks and which was varied by the assumption of multi-coloured gloves: white for interviews with one's instructor, yellow for riding, and horizon blue (in cotton) for exercise. Badgered unmercifully by our seniors—who had all the power in the world over us—confined within a pitiless discipline which demanded always a kit properly laid out, a bed perfectly made, soles of boots perfectly dubbined and their studs perfectly polished, we existed through those first few weeks in a purgatory in which one asked oneself if the ceaseless round of disaster, punishment and chivying bore any relation to reality. Then things began to take shape; the training helped, and life became more bearable. As they said at School, we were beginning to fit in.

After the ceremonial parade on 11 November, at which we already managed to show up reasonably well, we were allowed out for the Sunday. Early in the morning we put on our walking-out dress, made up somewhat discordantly of an NCO's horizon blue tunic, red epaulettes, plumed shako and side arms. Duly inspected, we made our way in a body to the station where a special train took us to the Invalides. Thence in the early mist of a winter's morning the plumed shakos, slightly embarrassed by their get-up, scattered in all directions. In the evening a special train from the Gare Montparnasse got us back to Saint-Cyr just before midnight, not forgetting the traditional cheers for a certain Mme Dubois, notorious, it appears, under the Empire, as we rattled through Bellevue station. And so on to the next strict, implacable week.

I was happy and proud to be at Saint-Cyr. First time off I had achieved the object which I had been instinctively seeking.

I struck an even balance between intellectual and physical activity. The latter was severe, but I realized how important it was at this time for the toughening of my twenty-year-old body. The intellectual activity surprised me: we had first-class instructors and the courses were interesting.

But the heart of the matter lay on a higher plane. Without any verbal didactics, but by the sheer physical effort and the drill, and above all by virtue of the great military traditions which distinguished the whole School, we carried within us a sense of manly idealism. How far removed it was from the Latin Quarter, where I had lived for several years!

Looking back, I realize that this atmosphere met the real needs of youth, the sense of giving and the need for truth.

In this military induction we sought for one truth, one aim, one good example to follow. Patriotism swept all before it. Victorious France enjoyed an enormous prestige. We represented progress, we represented culture and we represented the grand tradition. Our elders had been heroes and we would drive ourselves to the end to be worthy of them. The marble plaques the length of the corridors bearing the names of those killed in action in every corner of the world inspired us with a sense of sacrifice and the highest sense of purpose. Here was a prize far beyond any prize this world could offer! We asked for nothing more than to take our place in an Order which recognized sacrifice as its aim and ideal, but accepted sacrifice with a certain elegance which shunned all thought of material or personal gain. It was a comfort and inspiration to us to know that we were dedicated to the general good and set upon entering a profession which was as interesting as it was admirable.

Of course all this represented the theoretical ideal; sometimes the hard facts did not live up to it and there were disillusionments. I was genuinely surprised to discover that there were some of my companions—perhaps no more than a handful—who were not so starry-eyed as I.

In the trivialities of daily life and the infinity of tasks to which we had to turn ourselves, the ideal to which we looked up drove us on to cope with anything.

Our instructors, some of whom were naturally better than others, set an example and imposed upon us a sense of total discipline. Some of our teachers were remarkable. In geography the instruction which Commandant Lucien gave us on the implications for Europe of the Treaty of Versailles was far ahead of most university courses at that time. In history Capitaine de Gaulle—young, elegant in yellow boots, breeches and pastel blue tunic, already a figure of dignity—held forth to us in rolling periods on the policies of Richelieu, Mazarin, and the Treaty of Westphalia. I was profoundly struck by this course which cut across everything which I had learnt before. The character of the man showed itself in what he had to say to us then and I have never been able since to think of him except as a synthesis of these two great Prime Ministers.

There were weaknesses. The one which I thought most marked was the course on tactics. Was this really the 'military art'? I remained unsatisfied and it was not until much later that I came to understand the reason for this shortcoming.

Looking back, I realize that another lacuna was the absence of any political education. The Army's rule of avoiding any link with politics left us with the superficial ideas drawn from our family circles. When the crunch came, this ignorance was to prove fatal both to the nation and to the Army.

But in our enthusiasm and our confidence in the future, we never questioned our ability to surmount any trials which might one day face us. Our ideal of the perfect officer was modelled upon Galliéni and Lyautey—at any rate mine was. It was an ideal combining courage with impartiality, and culture with action. The life opening before us seemed rich in possibilities. With our youth and our unshakeable faith we were impatient to be on our way.

The old School, founded originally by Mme de Maintenon as a girls' home, was destroyed in 1944 by the American Air Force in one of those haphazard and useless raids which were fashionable at the time. The ruins, retaining their own imposing dignity, have been left as they were. Cocteau used them as the setting for the underworld in his film *Orphée*. The Americans offered to rebuild the School, but in our impecunious dignity we refused, and the School moved to Coëtquidan. I have only been there once, for a reunion, and I was struck by the complete severance from tradition which this move brought about. Today there are the same splendid young men, but the link with the past has gone. I found them more juvenile and, shall I say, more ordinary than we were. Cut off from Paris, deprived of its historic buildings, the School has lost its elegance. The move, logical from the practical point of view, was a psychological mistake. The wise decision would have been to spend the winter at Saint-Cyr and the summer in the field at Coëtquidan or some open space in the Midi.

But I realize that the ethical problem of these young men is more difficult to resolve than ours was. To us, victorious France with a vast empire represented a clear duty without a cloud in the sky. Since then the tragedy of 1940, Vichy, the reverses in Indo-China and the frustration of Algeria have left wounds which can be healed only with the utmost difficulty. For these wounds my generation cannot escape some responsibility, despite our initial hopes and our devotion. That is why we owe to those who come after us as complete an explanation as possible of the chain of circumstances which brought about these events of the not too distant past, so that they may at least have some chance of avoiding the same mistakes.

Chapter 3
Light Khaki

*

I OPTED FOR the 5th *Tirailleurs* in Algeria.
Duly equipped, I at last embarked upon the life which I had always desired.

Algiers came up to my expectations. In those days it was still a colonial town, a jumble of picturesque streets and white villas smothered in bougainvilia under a blue sky, with palm trees and eucalyptus silhouetted against the blue of the bay. What struck me at once was the sweet scent of the carob stocked in the harbour, the gentle warmth of autumn and the sense of an ever-changing scene. It was not really wild, of course, but a beautiful door opening onto the open country. Like every new boy, I was overwhelmed; I studied Arabic, and with Loti felt deeply the power of Eastern civilization growing over me. Would that it could have been 1830, or, better still, Cairo in 1796. . . .

My first contact with the Army was more mundane. The Army of Africa at that time was far removed from the ideals of Saint-Cyr! The regiment, clad in any old uniforms left around in store after the war, run by officers commissioned from the ranks who remained NCOs at heart, was nothing more than a drafting body for regiments in the Armies of the Rhine, Syria and Morocco. Under the pressure of punctilious administration with next to nothing to provide, the shambles was complete; the troops were occupied in guard duties and trivial chores, instruction was reduced to a useless routine quite out of touch with what I had been taught at Saint-Cyr. I tried in vain to introduce a few indispensable reforms (for instance, dividing the company into platoons). But the company commander, who never got out of his office, said it was hopeless because the sergeant-major was against it. . . . For a time I lost interest in the job, biding my time until I could get to one of the various theatres of operation which existed then.

Quite soon I was given the task of taking a reinforcement draft to Syria. A long voyage though the eastern Mediterranean with four hundred men under my command. Sicily, Cyprus, and then

Beirut. Syria at that time still bore a markedly Turkish appearance: the fur hats of the police, the peasants' boots, the German trams. The country interested me but did not enchant me: the architecture seemed less attractive than that of Algeria, and the general Europeanization had gone too far for my taste. Baalbek, Damascus and the desert did not strike me with the same powerful impression as Algeria had done. I would never ask for a posting there.

When I got back to Algiers, there was an exciting prospect: the regiment had been ordered to send one of its battalions to Morocco in a few months' time. I volunteered but had to wait all winter in the little garrison town of Aumale which dominated a pass in the Tellien Atlas. By the light of a pressure lamp and warmed by a smoky wood fire I read mountains of books. In due course the battalion was brought together and training began. Life suddenly became good.

We entrained early in the morning at Algiers, with new equipment. At the main railway station we were greeted by the bands of the other regiments: the 1st *Tirailleurs* at Blida and the Legion at Bel Abbès. At last the 'adventure' of which I had always dreamed had begun.

At Oudjda, Morocco cast its spell over me at once with its white houses, the close cropped beards, the turbans pushed back off the forehead, the geometrical designs, the vast space. We were put on to the Draizina, a rather unlikely little narrow-gauge train running on a straight track which we could see going on and on into the distance. After four days on trains, of which two were spent on the Draizina, we got off at Fez in the middle of the night and camped outside the minute station which was all there was in those days. But we were soon told that we were being thrown in at the deep end: while we were entrained, Abd el-Krim had called out the Spanish Riff and under his leadership the tribes to the north had determined to make war: Fez, garrisoned by no more than one company of the Legion, needed every man it could get. Trucks picked us up at the station and we were to be deployed at once to cover the northern approaches to Fez.

This moment was wonderful: Fez at first light was the Thousand and One Nights which I had always dreamed about, but which I hardly believed could still exist: a sprawling city from the Middle Ages with its hundreds of minarets, its embattled walls, its swarming populace, sitting in the midst of a bare, denuded landscape untouched for centuries. I was overwhelmed. We pressed on to the north, bumping and banging in our trucks driven by unsafe Indo-Chinese drivers over a bad road. We detrucked on the bank of a wadi and formed our first fortified camp looking out over the low ground. That night we were harassed by the enemy. This was war.

I do not want to go through the whole period step by step, but merely to record the deep impressions which left their most profound mark upon me because the world has changed since those days and what seemed so near to us then can appear almost unbelievable today.

We formed part of a column under the command of Lieutenant-Colonel Freydenberg. A 'column' was a small self-contained Army, the form of which has been standard since the days of Bugeaud; it was made up of several battalions of infantry, spahis, partisan irregular troops and artillery, which advanced in a square formation. The guns and the baggage train were in the middle, the battalions formed four sides of the square while the cavalry and the partisans deployed all round the outside. This human square, alone in hostile territory, kept its formation up hill and down dale—the baggage following the track while the flank guards plodded on endlessly under a blazing sky.

I can still see the partisans wheeling round us, the caïds at their head, uttering shrill cries as they galloped past, then climbing up to the crests of the hills. They employed the traditional Moroccan tactics, setting fire to the villages after a few shots, looting quickly and withdrawing equally quickly.

We, the regulars, plodded on over the uneven ground, through scrub and meagre corn and soya fields, worn out by the heat of the sun and the draining of constant perspiration, the men bowed under the weight of their kit and ammunition, their feet agonized in their heavy boots which filled up with water every time we forded a stream. Not in the best of condition to start with, we were soon at the last limits of exhaustion.

Then the column halted at the foot of a hill from which the partisans had just withdrawn. The advance guard had made contact.

The hills ahead of us appeared deserted, but soon the air was filled with shrill cries which echoed from rock to rock, and sporadic firing broke out. In front a battalion of the Legion in their white *képis* deployed as regularly as though they were on an exercise. The artillery (four 65 mm. mountain guns!) opened up. We had to attack through the legionaries. We clambered over rocks and through olive trees, bullets whistling past us; then there was nothing except a few dead Riffs lying in their holes. We climbed on, out of breath. Then a deserted village—a poor village smelling of rancid oil, the sole sign of life a flurry of scrawny chickens destined for the pot that night. We reached the crest, regrouped and called the roll: a handful of wounded, one man killed. But there was not much time left before nightfall. We made camp, built up some small walls for cover, looked for fresh water, unloaded the animals, pitched the tents, sited our machine-guns, arranged the guard roster, lit the fires, made soup—we were by chance in a small bean field which was quickly harvested.

At sunset we ate a supper of chicken and beans cooked in rancid oil with bread a week old. Dead tired, each of us tumbled into his tent while the sentries called across to one another in the old tradition of the First Empire, to keep awake. Suddenly our sleep was rudely interrupted by the unwelcome shout: 'Stand to!' Firing broke out, every man leaped to his post. The darkness round us was punctuated by the flashes of enemy rifle fire. What was going on? Sometimes no more than shadows in the night; sometimes an enemy group had infiltrated into the camp. Eventually the firing would die down and we would go back to sleep till the next alarm, and so on through a night too short in any case to relax our weary bodies. In Morocco everyone had to stand to before first light, for that is the most dangerous hour when a surprise attack can come in. Exhausted, pulling our swollen feet back into our boots, we drank scalding coffee, buckled our equipment, loaded the animals, folded the tents, stowed the kit and, as the day broke, set off on another day just like the last.

This Riff campaign of May 1925 in the Ouergha valley was exceptionally hard. Newcomers like myself did not realize this, but Moroccan veterans shook their heads: we were up against trained fighters who manoeuvred skilfully. They surrounded our small frontier posts and reduced them one after another, thanks to the few pieces of artillery which they had captured from us. Our three or four columns, spread over some hundred and twenty miles, could not be everywhere at once. Each day we relieved a post, brought out the garrison or reinforced it, but the actions were always difficult, sometimes indecisive; our casualties were serious and physically we were at the end of our tether.

One day as we were attacking a height, from which we had a wide view behind us, the enemy drove in our rearguard and reached the convoy which had to defend itself as best it could. Happily Freydenberg was able to get a message to a group of partisans a few miles away who arrived at full gallop through the already standing corn and took the Riffs in the rear. It was an extraordinary spectacle.

On another occasion my battalion was trying to relieve a minute post held by a sergeant and twenty-five men. Deployed facing the ridge, but too far away and with an ill-protected right flank, the attack began with an interminable approach march through the crops, which was greeted by a hail of fire, shaking the *Tirailleurs* and causing a certain amount of alarm and despondency among all ranks. At this moment we found in front of us a narrow ravine forming a natural trench; everyone went to ground and momentum was lost. The men fired without aim, rifles held above their heads. There were orders to advance but no one budged. Amidst all this I saw Commandant Lemaire coming by—boots polished, silk scarf round his neck, a monocle in his eye. Modest second lieutenant as I was, I ventured to suggest that we should reform under cover before we tried to advance any further—which was the wisest course. He replied: 'Young man, war is a shambles. Take what men you have and get up there.'

Without a second thought I shouted 'Advance!' and, as no one moved, I mounted the bank of the ravine myself and started to climb with the uncomfortable feeling that I would get a bullet in my back at any moment. After about thirty yards I paused to look over my shoulder and saw that five men had followed me: this was my 'Army'. Further back there was a constant exchange and the

machine guns kept up their covering fire over our heads. With my
five men I worked from rock to rock; each time we paused behind
cover I violently waved my scarf to let the machine-gunners see
where we had got to. By leaps at last we were at the top of the
ridge and the post. A bearded sergeant appeared cautiously and
offered me a mess tin of salty water. Below, groups of *Tirailleurs*
were now working their way forward following their officers.

But the post on the ridge was dominated by heights on either
flank and these were still held by the Riffs, who kept up an accurate
fire. The Commandant was among the first to arrive; he congratu-
lated me and then said, 'Take the men who are here and clean up
that height on the left.' So I set off once more with my same five
men. We had first to go down a long slope and were greeted by a
hail of fire. We were able to take cover in a small grove of fig trees
and I ordered my men to return the fire, only to find that between
them they had just one round left! I took it and fired at a silhouette
between two rocks. At the same moment I was hit and bowled over
like a rabbit. My 'army' picked me up, each by an arm or a leg, and
carried me back to the post, where the Commandant embraced me
and I found myself the centre of a miniature court trying to assess
the seriousness of my stomach wound.

They put me in the sergeant's mud hut, the walls of which were
covered with indecent pictures and photographs. Outside, firing
continued. I learnt from the wounded lying beside me that the
Riffs had counter-attacked our exposed flank in the plain and taken
the battalion in the rear, overrunning the machine gunners and
some men who were lagging behind. The artillery was now firing
to cover the disengagement of the column, leaving us on our
ridge. . . .

Soon, into this improvised First Aid Post, they brought a
Captain with two bullets in him and the Commandant himself, who
was in a bad way. The situation was becoming critical; there was
no more ammunition, very little water, and we were surrounded.
The Captain, who had taken command of the battalion, decided
under cover of darkness to bring everyone into the post behind the
wire, for, having no ammunition, he feared a night attack. But the
post was too small. The men were packed in the courtyard like
the Underground at rush hour. They lay on the corrugated iron
roofs in rows like sardines. Pushing through to us with difficulty,

a few of the surviving officers came in to give us a handshake. 'We shall all be dead tomorrow. You're a good scout; see you in heaven!'

The night in our mud hut was alive with groans and delirious babble. I was in great pain. My neighbour—my Quartermaster-Sergeant—kept up an endless rigmarole, largely about my wound. From time to time there was the odd shot; the roof squeaked under the hobnailed boots of the men crowded there; but no attack came. I slept.

I was woken by the sound of shells bursting not far away; the column which had come to look for us was neutralizing the heights dominating the post. The Captain in temporary command came to see the Commandant, who lay still and deathly pale, and made the sign of the cross.

'I'm not dead yet,' the Commandant managed to whisper.

'I have come to tell you my decision,' the Captain said. 'The battalion will withdraw as best it can, but we must leave the wounded behind.'

'You have no right to leave us here,' said the Commandant.

'If I can find volunteers to carry the wounded, well and good; but I am not prepared to slow the whole battalion down if they can't keep up.' (He finished up as an officer in the gendarmerie. . . .)

Then they took us, for better or for worse. Everyone pushed and shoved to get out through the gate and the wounded came last. I was being carried in a canvas tent; all of a sudden the slope became so steep that they had to slide me down on my back. It was naturally a slow job. Everyone just marched on past me. I saw the last section coming, led by someone I knew. I asked him to detail some men to relieve those who were carrying me, because they were exhausted. 'Sorry, chum,' he replied, 'I haven't got time.'

The rearguard passed us; my men kept on dragging me down, but we were way behind the battalion which was rapidly disappearing. Bullets crackled round us. I felt that the men carrying me were going to abandon me. I had a pistol. Should I threaten them with it? Finally, in a little hollow, they put me down and vanished. There I was alone, stark naked, a hole in my stomach and a pistol in my hand. I had seen the body of my sergeant Meddah after he had been tortured by Riff women; when the first Riff came within sight I would see him off first and then shoot myself. I was extraordinarily calm; the sky was blue and time stood still.

Then I heard marching feet. This was it; I was ready. In the patch of sky above me, I saw turbans' with red braid: they were Goumiers! I called out, and three of them jumped down into my little hollow. No doubt they had stayed behind to rifle the corpses; they looked at me without interest. Happily I could speak a little Arabic. 'I am an officer,' I said.

'What, they are abandoning their officers now! How low can you get!'

Everything changed. They picked up the tent by its four corners and we set off on a crazy course. What men! Holding the tent with their hands and their teeth, I heard their rasping breath, punctuated by the Riff bullets around us. They pressed on for several miles without stopping, as I had seen the partisans do. The bullets became fewer and further between. Then we reached a wadi through which I was dragged like a bag of dirty linen. On the far bank we caught up with the rearguard of the battalion. They wanted to take over from my Goumiers, who indignantly refused and took me on to the First Aid Post.

I was in a bad way and I hoped that they would operate, but they had not got what they needed for this. It was arranged to fly me out, but this meant first a three mile shaking in a litter on mule-back to the airstrip. I screamed and had a haemorrhage. We got to the aircraft, which was guarded by partisans. The pilot was jumpy and wanted to take off as quickly as possible. Still naked, I was put on the upper stretcher, open to the air. The Captain was below me. The cold caused me to have another haemorrhage and the blood poured down all over the Captain; when we landed at Fez he was drenched in blood. As for me, naked on my stretcher—a soldier, a modern Saint Martin, spread his cloak over me, the loss of which no doubt earned him eight days' detention, and led to my being accepted into hospital as a private.

✳

On the operating table I told the surgeon my rank. 'Goodness, so you're an officer? Would you like a glass of champagne?' he said. The panache—that indefinable word—of this unexpected welcome in such bizarre circumstances touched me. They operated without an

anaesthetic and then I found myself in a small room with a painted
ceiling, walls lined with faience tiles and doors of carved cedar, in a
dream palace which whispered with the sound of running water.
In my feverish state, the cry of the hundred *muezzins* of Fez
summoning the faithful to prayer sounded in my ears like the
clamour of battle echoing round the hills and calling us forward
into action. My mind revolved round and round this hard and
terrible world of war into which I had been initiated, the crushing
physical effort, the cruelty of the actual fighting, the endless
suffering of the wounded. The danger which I had so far completely
ignored now seemed to me intolerable. Every single incident went
through my mind again and again, and I lay there certain that
every rifle shot I thought I heard was aimed at me. . . .

When I awoke I found that a rose had been laid by my bed. I
was asked if there was anything I wanted. What sweetness after
the trials we had been through! They had gone in to decorate the
Commandant in the next room to me; he summoned up enough
strength to say that he would not accept unless 'that young Second
Lieutenant next door is decorated as well'. On to my unbelieving
chest they pinned a borrowed cross. From that time on, against all
the odds I started to get better. I had setbacks, one leg was
paralysed, but I had no doubt of the outcome. More wounded were
still pouring in, the hospital was full, and I was evacuated to Rabat
on crutches.

Rabat was a fresh paradise. Above all, I got to know Lyautey,
whom I had once seen in the hospital at Fez. Every day Lyautey
went round the hospital, no doubt to get some feeling of the morale
of his troops. He arrived on horseback, with a guard of Spahis;
but he had in fact driven to the hospital and mounted his horse just
around the corner: a proper sense of how these things should be
done. His approach was absolutely direct: 'Good morning. How
are you feeling? Bad news today; forty killed at Colombat. . . .
We've got to fight our way out of that one. See you again.' One
day I remember he suddenly spoke personally to me; he said; 'All
that gang in Paris and the Government have got it in for me. It's
no fun being Resident General here, I can tell you. As for Doriot
[already a Communist], if I could get my hands on that shit, I'd
do him. 'Bye now!' One felt he was a friend, one felt there was a
basis of understanding. His presence was imposing but never

overwhelming. I do not think that I have ever met any other human being who brought to me quite the same sense of contact between man and man.

I began to get about a bit on my crutches. Rabat at this time was still centred round the Casbah des Oudaïas but was beginning to grow in the Lyautey style, which became known in France through various exhibitions. The town was congested with two-wheeled carriages driven by Moroccan orderlies and drawn by their officers' chargers. The church was still built of wood as were most of the administrative buildings. It was an elegant and old-fashioned capital in a setting which was rapidly changing into something far ahead of its time.

A further intake of wounded led to my being posted to Casablanca, then still an underdeveloped city of streets which led to wide open spaces. Thence on to Oran, Algiers, and so home. With my brand-new cross gleaming on my uniform and my health returning, I felt that somehow I had come through a tremendous adventure.

After convalescing in France and spending the next winter in the Atlas Mountains at Aumale, I asked for a posting back to Morocco. There I was in my element; that was what I had always hoped for. I went back with another battalion of my regiment; but this time I was not only blooded but also physically fit and no doubt mentally more developed than a year before. The campaign, which took us from the Spanish Riff to Tache de Taza, in the Moyen Atlas, seemed easy, even pleasant in spite of the 'element of real danger', and much less adventurous than the previous one.

Our commander, General Dosse, had evolved a tactic of night operations, leap-frogging from height to height. I was given an independent group, rather like a modern commando. Thus I learned to take my bearings at night, to march soundless through the mountains in the dark without tripping over, to know how to listen, to avoid making dogs bark, to surprise without being surprised. After one or two successful operations we developed great self-confidence. The nights under the brilliant canopy of stars were fresh and dry. Life was good!

We were working with the Spanish, with their new army restyled by Primo de Rivera. I was struck first by their new equipment which was better than ours and then by their old-fashioned tactics which nevertheless seemed better suited to the matter in hand than ours; we were too closely based on the 1914–18 way of doing things. One day I was at the junction between the two forces, where the Spanish, sleeping in close lines with piled arms like Detaille's *Le Rêve*, were being bothered by a 75 mm, which the Riffs had captured. At first light it was a magnificent sight. On my left the French advanced in small groups in open order interspersed with Renault tanks moving at walking pace. On my right four squadrons of cavalry charged as cavalry had charged under the First Empire: the Alcántara Dragoons in the lead, followed by mounted *Regulares*. The Riff gun engaged them over open sights and tore great gaps in them. But after half an hour the cavalry had recaptured the gun, while our slow-moving tanks had barely advanced more than a mile.

Abd el-Krim, hitherto kept going by foreign adventurers and deserters, quickly folded. After a fairly tough operation near Targuist, where we had come up against his personal guards, he sent in a party to open negotiations with Commandant Montagne and eventually surrendered to the French. Overnight, life returned to normal. We came down from the hills and camped by the streams and the olive groves—without defence works; the sudden peace seemed strange, and never once did our erstwhile enemies break their truce.

I had put in an application to serve with the Goums. I was detailed to take part in the disarmament of the Riff tribes in the Spanish zone. Those were marvellous days, riding through the mountains, with sumptuous meals at the tribal headquarters and long-drawn-out parleys sitting on a carpet facing one another. The conversation always went the same way: 'You have fifty rifles.'

'No, ten.'

'Come now, in the engagement at X. . . there were sixty of you.'

'Yes, but most of them were unarmed . . . and in any case how do you expect us to drive the Spanish out if you take all our arms away?'

Curiously enough, we were not the real enemy, and, believe it or not, on several occasions people in Riff villages volunteered to help us if and when we were attacked by the Spanish! I was to find the same sort of thing in the Moyen Atlas where the people, traditionally opposed to the Sultan, regarded their opponents as not the French but the Maghzen, even though it was we who had come into Morocco to unify the country in the Sultan's name. I discovered that local politics could be very tortuous and unpredictable, and sometimes misunderstood in Rabat.

These men whom I now met face to face were magnificent, noble, elegant in their hand-woven *djellabas*, sensitive and full of humour, covered with scars of old wounds from which only their hardiness had enabled them to recover and which they showed with pride. They led the bucolic life of ancient times, preserved by some miracle into the twentieth century. In some valleys no European had set foot before us. In one valley, even, our horses created a sensation because they were the first which had ever been seen! I admired the terraced gardens irrigated by a system of well maintained canals which sometimes brought the water from over a mile away. This was the golden age, in its elemental simplicity.

A signal recalled me to my battalion which was leaving the Riff for a further campaign. We were going south to the snowy peaks of the Moyen Atlas. This new operation, short but very violent, was to take us up to 9,000 feet and to bring us up against the white Berbers (the Ait Seghouchene), a race even more elemental and even more formidable. These warriors, in a class by themselves because of their physical strength and their complete contempt for death, specialized in surprise attacks with the knife from dead ground. General Freydenberg's column had been badly mauled. We went to its help, marching through magnificent cedar forests and greeted by the whistle of bullets discharged from ancient rifles. We had three engagements, in one of which our General was very nearly put in the bag but was just got out by the muleteers of the Legion who were escorting him. We were four days in the mountains without rations, the men chewing on an occasional ear of rye; then we wound our way up goat tracks for twenty-five hours without a halt, only to find that it was all over and the Ait Seghouchene had asked for an armistice. The whole battalion raced down into the valley to drink from a clear stream, indifferent to the efforts of one unco-operative character who loosed off the last of his ammunition at us.

Interminable road-building, guards, patrols, building forts, mixing the lime ourselves, the German axes of the Legion felling tall cedars, steaming in the heat of the day in wide open spaces, mysterious horizons still unconquered, pack mules falling into deep ravines, sweet smelling ashes covering the *mechtas*, the gradual re-opening of the markets, at first timidly and uneasily—the whole of this colourful, intense, masculine and worthwhile life took hold of me at twenty-one: I made up my mind I would stay in Morocco.

But fate decided otherwise. Clouds of flies followed us wherever we went and dysentery set in. I went down with it in due course; three days of fever and delirium, with my batman trying to keep the flies off me with a leafy branch. As soon as I could I mounted my horse, made what seemed a very long trek down into the valley, and took the first truck I could find back to base. I finished up back in the hospitals where I had been the year before. In those days amoebic dysentery could be a very nasty business. I spent three months in various hospitals and then found myself once again in Algiers.

Today, looking back, I feel a profound sense of melancholy. What sacrifice, devotion and enthusiasm were poured into that colonial adventure of which I lived through the last phase!

To the younger generation today which has been taught that 'colonialism'—as it is called—has been at worst a crime and at best a mistake, I would like to say this. I would like them to understand what made us act as we did and to realize that in each generation the prevalent ideas are produced by the spirit of the time. I do not believe that the ideas which are current today are necessarily any more justified than those which we held years ago. In matters of this kind fashion changes constantly and is generally more powerful than any individuals. We think of ourselves as free and reasonable human beings, but in fact we are little more than jetsam before the great waves of ideas which sweep us along.

We fought these colonial wars with a clear conscience, sure that we were bringing with us civilization and progress, certain that we would help these people to emerge from the backward state in which they found themselves. We respected the men against whom we fought and believed that tomorrow they would be our friends.

Never in Morocco did I see a prisoner or a peasant, however suspect, maltreated. Our troops, our Goumiers, our partisans, with whom we shared this hard life in manly mutual confidence, had been our enemies yesterday. Their loyalty knew no bounds and we loved them, simple as they were, for their courage, their primitive strength, their age-old wisdom, their good manners and their sense of honour which no trials could ever tarnish. I am convinced that they submitted willingly once they were satisfied that one was a leader, and a courageous leader. Thereafter they showed us a thousand little attentions and a touching tenderness. Those who were still our enemies also had some respect for us. They fought for their honour, but they knew that we represented the future for them. When we were the stronger, it was because Allah was with us; the fighting over, they rallied to us without any reservations, curious to know about this new civilization which was coming to them. Administered by officers of our *Affaires Indigènes*, which Lyautey had had the foresight to form into a hand-picked body, they were not slow to appreciate the benefit of what we were doing: justice was seen to be done, peace reigned between the tribes, there were more roads, markets, money and medicines. Year by year, according to Galliéni's formula, tribe after tribe got the message. The 'wind of history' was blowing from the west.

Why has all this been thrown away so soon? Was it really indeed all thrown away? Basically it has been a magnificent achievement: Morocco in fifty years advanced from the Middle Ages to a modern civilization; it was the most positive result imaginable. Algeria on the eve of independence was developing fast. Tunisia, more slow-moving and less rich, had made material progress in forty-eight years. We awoke these people slumbering in the margin of history. The most fanatical North African nationalists cannot deny the benefits brought to them by our intrusion and today the populace in general looks back with regret to the 'time the French were here'.

But there is no denying that we had to go; there is no denying that here a statue of Cardinal Lavigerie has been pulled down, there those of Lyautey and Bugeaud; that the streets have been renamed—even that called after Maréchal de Lattre who led the Moroccans to victory; that our language, still spoken everywhere, is challenged by a return of Arabism, that the Algerian army wears

Egyptian uniforms while the Moroccan officers, curiously enough, wear Spanish kit. In heaven's name, why this divorce?

It is too soon for an accurate accounting, but it is already possible to strike a trial balance.

We did many good things, but their effect was cancelled out by our mistakes. The basic cause of all was the divided state of Europe and the two world wars which not only drained the substance but also ruined the reputation of irresistible strength which the western people had enjoyed. The second, more specifically French, was the defeat of 1940. Our prestige was shattered: Allah was no longer with us. That is why everything which bears upon this defeat is so important.

In North Africa itself we made numerous mistakes. Foremost without question was the endeavour to mix conquest with liberalism and thence, like Bainville's formula for the Treaty of Versailles, to take too harsh a line where we were in fact weak and to be yielding where we should have been strong. The difficulties arising from this basic contradiction led us into a perpetual oscillation between opposing formulas and a constantly disordered attempt to reconcile them: paternalistic military government which held tribes back in their primitive state; a laissez-faire development of education and finance without planning; theoretical assimilation into metropolitan France accompanied by the intrusion of the most sordid politics; the dreams of Napoleon III and Lyautey of an 'Arabic Empire'; a wide use of the grand principles of Liberty and Equality; a civil service administration which was efficient, but at the same time meddlesome and sometimes tyrannical; the invasion of colonists from the homeland and the dominance of private interests.

All these contradictions were by-products of the nineteenth century and without question it was difficult for us to escape from them. Nevertheless today, more clearly than ever before, one can see that the biggest single element of evolution and instability was the introduction of our liberal and capitalist economy into a patriarchal structure. Under its pressure the old ways of life broke down far and wide. A large part of the population, accustomed to living hard in accordance with ancient tradition, found itself a new proletariat inextricably mixed with a European population at a level of life artificially inflated. The population explosion, helped along by the introduction of our efficient medical services, considerably aggravated this state of affairs: we had built up all the makings of a revolutionary situation. It only remained to produce the men ready for revolution, and this we did by providing education without responsibility: no senior positions open to native officials, no jobs for the thousands of graduates and the hundreds of lawyers whom we turned out every year: and yet, on the other hand, a constant invasion of 'petits blancs' who monopolized the administrative and middle class business positions. Looking back, one can see that even by the 1930s a situation had grown up the future of which was limited.

Could these mistakes have been avoided? This would certainly have been difficult. Every nineteeth-century colonial system— French, British, Belgian or Dutch—has suffered the same fate, by whatsoever principles it sought to govern, and these of course differed widely. The same applies to the Spanish and the Turkish Empires. One asks oneself if indeed there can be any 'colonial' formula which is not doomed to failure. History shows us a number of successes, some too cruel to be cited as an example today, such as that of the United States where their *'pieds noirs'** simply suppressed their *'arabes'*; some too far back in history to apply, such as those of Prussia and the south of Spain. Nearer to our own time, Russia has put together a vast colonial empire which she still controls, but of which the future is uncertain. Nevertheless the survival of that empire today brings one thought to mind: in this example there has been a combination of very firm authoritative direction with a certain federal flexibility and socialist modernization—all effected for the public good and not for any private interest. If to this there is added the prestige of the USSR, arising from its material and ideological strength, confirmed by its victory in war, it is apparent that these conditions are very different from those which affected us.

I would like to add one more thought. The successful colonizers of the past (such as the Normans or the Franks) were feudal. The conquerors infiltrated the conquered and established themselves hereditarily among them. Thus there was continuity and a common

* *'Pieds noirs'* is the phrase used for European Algerians while the *'arabes'* are the natives. There are no English equivalents of these two words, to my knowledge (trs.)

interest. Our military conquest produced no barons, but only a number of masters, big and little, frequently replaced and always looking towards metropolitan France where they knew their ultimate future lay. Furthermore the capitalist economy led to the introduction of big impersonal companies which had no local attachments, and also to the divergent and necessarily selfish interests of the settlers. The system had neither coherence nor logic. Either the administrative authority should have been vested in the settlers, or, better still, it should have been run for the good of all by a body dedicated to this task. Neither the one nor the other was possible in the early twentieth century; the second is perhaps the scheme from which a rational 'African socialism' could emerge.

Whatever way one looks at it, the unhappy ending of this great colonial endeavour shows how blind men can be in their own obsessions, and points up their inability to foresee the future or even to understand what is going on around them. There exists a vast library of books and papers on every aspect of our colonial activity, but amongst all those thousands of volumes there are not ten which attempt to get to the heart of the matter. We went in for colonialization because it was then the thing to do. We pulled out even more quickly for the same reason, thereby creating havoc which may well be irreparable. Is the 'wind of history' an irresistible force, or is it rather the psychological result of a chain of obsessions?

Whatever the answer may be, those who, like myself, took part in this work have today no remorse: very much the opposite. The misguided ingenuousness of Gide and Mauriac had no effect upon us because we knew what the creative enthusiasm of a man like Lyautey meant, faced by the task of awakening those vast lands and unspoiled peoples. We knew because we lived with it. We were conscious of having been the active agents of history, long before Marxism pretended to be its guiding force, because the world has always been made up of such marriages—part rape, part consent— in which civilizations and races come together and give birth to a crossbreed which carries the torch on into the future. This is the way Europe came about. Perhaps the seed which we planted in the lands of Islam may yet bear fruit, despite all the mistakes and despite its unhappy ending.

Remorse, no; but still many regrets. . . .

Chapter 4

The General Staff

✳

GENERAL BOICHUT, who commanded in Morocco and whom I had met in hospital, gave me a piece of advice (which I later discovered was inspired by my father). 'You have the Croix de Guerre and three citations. That is enough fighting,' he said. 'Get yourself ready now for the École de Guerre.'

This piece of advice awoke many echoes in me. At the time I was still sick and would be unable to leave until long months had passed. But I had always been attracted above all by the intellectual aspect of warfare, an attraction which Saint-Cyr increased; furthermore my experiences in Algeria and Morocco had made me aware of the evident shortcomings in military thinking. The Army of the Twenties was obviously run on ill-conceived and outdated lines. I was eager to understand, to take to pieces the machinery of which I had so far blindly been a part. At Aumale already, during my long evenings alone, I had tried to analyse the immense problems which faced us, as much in Africa as in Europe. There was no question but that this possibility appealed to me. I had not thought it likely to come so soon, but since it was suggested. . . . I would return to Morocco after I left the École de Guerre.

I studied for the École de Guerre in a charming small garrison at Dellys, in Kabylia, on the shores of the Mediterranean. A correspondence course, extremely well worked out, deluged us with papers and different types of work. All this I did in the evenings. The days were devoted to training the company I had been given. Independent, in a strong position because of my recent combat experience, I was able to apply my own ideas, and I kneaded this rich dough of French and Kabyles with gratifying results. With organization and effort, one could get what one wanted.

At night, I swotted away at my notes, set my ideas in order and, not without difficulty, taught myself to draft. I found a mass of things which I ticketed like separate files: the evolution of tactics, the complexity of battles and campaigns, the great problems of the contemporary world. I came to the conclusion that the war of 1914–18 was no more than a clumsy first draft, that we were entering the mechanized age and that everything which we had been doing was outdated. I devoured military reviews but found even in their pages nothing but timid and half-baked suggestions. I was a rebel. Everything had to be relearned and reconstructed. What a wonderful task!

If I dwell on the psychological aspect, it is because it shows the reaction of a fresh mentality faced by the problems of the hour. Almost everything which in due course came about passed through my mind at that time. Later, under the mental yoke of the École de Guerre and the General Staff, this ingenuousness which gave me such clear vision disappeared. I was more perspicacious in 1929 than in 1940. . . . This is a lesson which should be remembered. Youth does not possess all the good qualities; but, on the other hand, experience can be a burden which may sometimes impede clear thinking.

The first year I was refused permission to sit for the École de Guerre because I was too young. I was desperately disappointed. I immediately applied for training as an air observer, which meant three months' hard living in wooden huts at Avord, primary training and uncertain flights in primitive aeroplanes which would appear prehistoric today. The French Air Force at that time, as I later realized even more, was still in its infancy, both technically and mentally. It was decidedly not my kind of atmosphere. I had applied for training as a pilot, but was told that I would have to transfer to the Air Arm. This I refused, and went back to Dellys.

In the following year I was finally given permission to sit for the École de Guerre and I passed.

The École de Guerre enjoyed great prestige. The victors of 1914–18 had all taught there. The General commanding the school greeted us with a solemn discourse on its title: École *Supérieure* de Guerre, with heavy emphasis on the '*Supérieure*'.

In fact, it was a good secondary school for the General Staff, with occasional sorties into the '*Supérieur*.' But above all, the

shortcomings of the School sprang from the teaching of a restricted
doctrine in which tactics, basically one-sided, were made to appear
like a quantity surveyor's estimate. The war of 1914–18 as codified
by Debeney, and Pétain, had reduced everything to a mathematical
sum worked out with a ready reckoner—troops, ammunition,
stores, casualties and time equated with the number of kilometres
involved. This convenient technique seemed reassuring, but was
functionally unsound—as one was to see in 1940—because it left
out the human element. The slightest consideration of the fronts in
Russia, Salonika or Palestine would have exposed the inanity of our
thinking. But these secondary fronts were of no interest to the
French Army, as was made plain to me when, several years later,
I arrived on the General Staff; the head of the 3ᵉ Bureau put his
finger on a map of north-east France and said to me: 'Never forget
that no ultimate decision can be achieved except here. . . .'

This narrow, even blind, thinking on military matters sprang
from a general inability to consider war as a whole, and even less
to consider the problem of strategy. Preoccupations of this nature
had been the hobby horse of the school in the years before 1914.
There Foch taught an operational strategy well founded and, by
its abstractions, leading towards fundamental truth. There Colonel
Grandmaison presented a theory, much less crazy than was thought
at the time, on the importance of the initiative and a basic determination which his detractors described as Bergsonian. These ideas
contained many good things, but they fell down through a tragic
misunderstanding of the technical realities of war, because 1870
was too far away and because—a frequent French weakness—we
failed to appreciate the lessons of the Boer War and the war in
Manchuria, just as we were in due course to fail to appreciate the
lessons of the Spanish Civil War. Hence in 1914 Plan 17 (drawn up
by Foch and Joffre) was technically unsound and as a result the
first battles were tragic and bloody defeats. Joffre, tactically
defeated but enjoying strategic superiority owing to the rigidity of
the Schlieffen Plan, won on the Marne a purely strategic victory
which he could not exploit for technical reasons.* These were
appreciated by neither side, and as a result the extension of the
front to the sea and then trench warfare were imposed upon both
sides.

* See my book, *Introduction à la Stratégie.*

This apparent setback to the pre-1914 strategy struck the Army forcibly and produced the erroneous idea that the strategy itself had been at fault. Colonel Pétain, who in his infantry course at the École de Guerre had taught methodical and prudent tactics in opposition to the 'strategy' of the period and who commanded a division with efficiency on the Marne, was to embark upon a late but startling career which took him to the head of the French Army. For this sceptical and down-to-earth realist, the whole of the pre-1914 spirit was wrong. No more panache, élan or grandiose abstract conceptions: one must limit oneself to present experience and concrete problems. Everything must be based on technique and limited to tactics. The war of 1914–18, which in fact was nothing more than an unfinished sketch of things to come, seemed to him the alpha and omega of the new art: for him experience showed without question the inviolability of a continuous and fortified front. True, there were breakthroughs in 1918, but these were always pieced together again. Hence the defensive was to be the queen of war. France was to cover herself by a fortified line, the Ligne Maginot, which fitted in well with the ideas of a pacifist France worn out by her unprecedented efforts over four years. No one will attack us, but if they do *'on ne passera pas'*—as at Verdun. If that did not prove efficacious, the whole world would support us, the blockade would stifle Germany and, as in 1918, after several years of war and a total effort by the entire nation, the enemy would collapse.

This falsely reasonable line of thought reveals an astonishing inadequacy. But this did not occur to people in those days, dazzled by the victory of 1918 and charmed by the appearance of a concept which was not 'adventurous'. At the same time Foch the strategist, who was separated from the French Army by his 'Interallied Commission', and Berthelot, the Foreign Office Secretary General, had drawn up a security system for the application of the Treaty of Versailles and the subjugation of a defeated Germany, the masterpiece of which was the 'Little Entente', grouping together the new countries of Poland, Czechoslovakia, Rumania and Yugoslavia, the issue of the dismembered Austro-Hungarian Empire. These countries came into the French orbit and it was obvious that one day we would have to defend them against a reborn Germany. That meant an offensive Army, capable of going forth beyond its own frontiers. But Pétain did not believe in these vast combinations: as he showed in 1940, he had but one belief—the hexagon, and the defence of the hexagon. As defence was the be-all and end-all, our Allies had no option but to follow our example and build their own little Maginot Lines.

If I dwell upon these lines of thought, which I am sure I have not misrepresented, it is because they show up the tragic errors of the victors of 1918: a fallacious doctrine drawn from precepts too narrow, and a complete divorce between foreign policy and the organization of the Army. In sum, two grave mental errors' caused and hidden by a complacency and an extraordinary dogmatism, the poisonous fruits of victory.

All this was more or less clear to some of us, but we were impressed at the same time by the prestige of the great war leaders, plus their imposing appearance (that of Pétain was extraordinary) and the intellectual *brio* of their statements (Gamelin for example was most impressive), expressed both coldly and clearly.

Nevertheless certain things kept feeding the doubts in our minds. First, for me, there was the reading of Liddell Hart's *The Decisive Wars of History*, which revealed a comprehension quite different from that which we were taught. War was not a game which was won by sheer weight, but by the intelligence and the finesse of the leaders. The essential factor in defeating the enemy was not force, but deception: it was necessary to delude him, to worry him, to disorganize him by an unexpected approach, and having thus created a weak point to exploit it to the full. In a word, the game of strategy is essential. Tactics, which the French doctrine regarded as the basis of everything, should be no more than the handmaiden of a higher strategy.

These basic truths, the ignorance of which shocked me, clearly added to the malaise which we felt at seeing the high command refusing to take any steps towards modernizing the Army. The Air Arm stagnated in a miasma of obsolete ideas; the armour, the future of which seemed obvious to us, remained hamstrung by narrow and fruitless conventions. The cavalry had the worst task of all: to become motorized and at the same time to try to work out a solution to an insoluble problem—how to use horses and machines together. One of our professors, Colonel Bruneau, the father of the B tank, opened up some vistas which excited us. But in the final lecture, duly approved, Colonel Dame bitterly disappointed us by merely repeating a doctrine on the use of armour copied from that of 1918. We suffered this disease, but we hoped that we would be able to overcome it when we in turn reached the General Staff.

In the midst of this stifling military conformism there were nevertheless at the School some more rewarding courses expressing wider views: Rivaud on Germany, France's eternal problem; Siegfried on economics and the United States as the key to the twentieth century; Colonel d'Argenlieu on military history, in which we saw in detail the incredible atmosphere surrounding the beginning of the war in 1914; Colonel Menu on war industry in which, in 1932, he predicted the coming of the atom bomb.

These two years, when at the same time I followed extramurally the courses of political science, were richly rewarding in the amount I learnt. Without question I gained in mental agility, but, in the military sense, despite the harvest of knowledge which I had garnered, I remained unsatisfied. We had before us the hope of taking part in the rejuvenation of the Army, to cleanse it from the mud-bound gangrene inherited from trench warfare. It would be a difficult evolution, but we were full of confidence.

Naturally I applied for Morocco, but was posted to Tunisia. I was very put out, since I regarded the time spent with the General Staff merely as an interlude, and I was furious that the pacification was going on without my being there. But chance, which governs everything, perhaps knew best: the man who got the posting I wanted was disabled in action and perhaps Morocco would have lulled me to sleep, as it has so many, with its simple delights.

Tunisia had more agreeable attractions: light, sharply marked horizons, a blue sea and endless beaches, a countryside more charming and less brutal, with small cafés in blue and white shaded by vines, houses decorated with ancient tiles, its *ghorfas* so picturesque as at Medenine, its innumerable Roman ruins and the huge forests of Kroumiria. But that was not the life we led in the field. . . .

The main military object in Tunisia was defence against Italy. Here I saw at first hand the marked weakness of our military thinking. The General Staff occupied a cool and ancient palace where we conscientiously tried to deal with the mountains of paper which surrounded us. As for the 'Defence of Tunisia', it existed only as a few illusory plans, but nobody seemed to mind. On the shore, under orders from Paris, the Admiral flying his pennant at Bizerta commanded up to the moment the enemy set foot on land. The troops, ridiculously inadequate for the defence of a hundred and twenty-five miles of coast-line, were deployed by him on the beaches and quite incapable of any serious resistance. There were practically no reserves (this was apparently the 'lesson' of Gallipoli). The moment the enemy landed, the General was to assume command of a situation which was none of his own making. . . . As for the defence of the southern frontier, this was taken care of by *one* battalion and a handful of cavalry which firmly awaited the enemy in an already prepared position about a mile and three-quarters in extent. Not only was it presumed that the enemy would make a frontal attack, but, after having been engaged, this solitary battalion was supposed to withdraw and go through the same lark all over again further back—three times in all! It was very depressing. To improve this situation, the solution chosen was to build a small *ad hoc* Maginot Line—the Mareth Line, for the defence of which the necessary troops could not be deployed in under two weeks. I took part in the laying out of this line, and none of us imagined that one day it would be held by the Germans and broken by the British.

The only information we had about the Italian forces in Libya came from a bunch of poverty-stricken agents and was largely useless. I got permission to visit Libya at my own expense and was able to bring back proof that there was not one division there as we thought, but two. . . .

When I returned I found waiting at the frontier a telegram offering me a post at the General Headquarters of the Army in Paris. It did not take me long to make up my mind. I had to get out of this depressing situation, however great the charms of Tunisia itself at that time.

After the statutory number of visits, I was received at the Headquarters of the Army, complete with sword and white gloves, by my opposite number, Captain Zeller, the future resistance leader and Governor of Paris, the elder brother of the man unhappily involved in the Algiers *putsch* of 1961. After having explained the routine and the hours of work, he added one remark which I have never forgotten and later often had occasion to recall: 'There is one thing, my friend, which I think you ought to know. You know General Gamelin?' (then Chief of the General Staff). 'Well, let me tell you, the General has no guts.'

It is difficult for me to express more thoroughly the atmosphere of the *État-Major de l'Armée*, where there was the greatest freedom of expression and of mentality, both political and military, a trusting and straightforward friendship which contrasted strangely with a direction which was finicky and lacking in real standing.

I saw very quickly that our seniors were primarily concerned with forms of drafting. Every memorandum had to be perfect, written in a concise, impersonal style, and conforming to a logical and faultless plan—but so abstract that it had to be read several times before one could find out what it was about—the 'Cactus style' of Pétain, described so amusingly by Loustaunau-Lacau in his *Mémoires d'un Français rebelle* with a solemnly wise sense of suggestion—'I have the honour to inform you that I have decided . . . I envisage . . . I attach some importance to the fact that. . . .' Actually no one decided more than the barest minimum, and what indeed was decided was pretty trivial.

The first task given to me brought me at once to the heart of the matter. I was told to make a study of the possibility of reducing the period of military service to eight months. I just didn't understand; with Hitler already Chancellor of Germany, the existing year's service was manifestly insufficient. On the other hand, the crypto-fascist *putsch* of 6 February (to which I will come back) had brought into power a Cabinet under Doumergue which appeared to have a more patriotic appeal than that of Daladier, and Pétain was Minister for War. . . . It was explained to me that the directive came from the Marshal himself, who wanted, apparently, to make some gesture to the left. Furthermore a few days later he stated to the Army Commissioners that he was opposed to any lengthening of the terms of service which was without question contrary to our military requirements at that time. Thus at one fell swoop we were in the middle of a parliamentary manoeuvre which was directly opposed to the interests which had expressed their confidence in Doumergue and in Pétain. This small incident stuck in my mind so that in 1940 I was not imbued with too much confidence in the 'Saviour of Verdun'.

Well, so be it. If I was required to study the means of reducing military service to eight months, I could but carry out my task according to the provisions and wishes of the General Staff. What was to be the 'programme'? My chief at that time, Colonel Verneau, who died heroically in a concentration camp in 1943, gave me this extraordinary reply: 'My poor dear boy, anybody can see that you are new. I can assure you that there is no programme, and there never has been a programme. All we can do is to go through the motions as best we can.'

Thus I was inducted into the profound philosophy of the General Staff, a body of potential leaders deprived of all constructive thought by years of exhausting struggle against the negative nepotism of the Treasury, the niggling of Parliament, and the nonsense started all over again by each successive Minister for War. Gradually a drill, born of experience and obstinacy, was worked out for dealing with each of the enemies: with the financial pundits the form was to take what had been granted and never seem to ask for a supplementary budget (even if it was in fact badly needed); Parliament one blinded with an impenetrable mass of detail; with a new Minister one seemed at first to agree entirely and then one went on to bury him under an avalanche of technicalities. All these ploys were unhappily purely defensive and nothing constructive came out of them. But at the time it seemed a victory to have saved the Army on any terms. As General Schweisgut, first Deputy Chief of the General Staff, said to me later: 'All right, no one could change anything in our Army, which may have been a pity; but don't forget that it is because of this very fact that we survived at all.' Thus defence triumphed throughout and it did not take long to discover that this was one of the unexpressed principles of the Third Republic, masked under the equivocal title which the jurists gave to it—'the equilibrium of power'. At the Ministry for War the General Staff was theoretically in command, but had no money, no administration, no personnel and no stores; the Secretary General had the money and the administration without any responsibility for command; the senior officers had the men and the stores, but no authority. The Minister himself sat on top of the heap but could do nothing without getting all the instruments in this extraordinary orchestra to play the same tune, a complication which deadened initiative. The whole affair had only one common element: inertia.

Thanks to this system, the Army survived but became more and more run down. Everything which I had seen in Algeria now became understandable: the skeleton forces tied up in trivial chores and guard duties, individual instruction rushed through in four months and then everyone dissipated into one vast 'tail': cooks, orderlies, orderly room clerks, grooms, drivers, storemen, etc. . . . no battalion could put more than one full-strength company into the field—or at best two below strength—and they never went into action properly trained. The hard core was either tied up in administration or in instructing raw recruits. Those called to the colours had too often the idea, as Marshal de Lattre expressed it later, that military service was a waste of time on the threshold of their manhood. The Army dissipated its substance by flopping about in a uniform too big for it, and the cinema with its sick jokes only underlined this decadence. It was a long way from 1914 and 1918!

The reasoning behind this—the comeback, as it were—was to be mobilization. According to the ideas then current the war had been won by the reserves. There was a certain element of truth in that, but the terrible shock of 1914 had been absorbed mainly by the regular Army; furthermore, and most important of all, it was the stalemate of trench warfare which gave us time to indoctrinate our reservists and even our territorials for this type of warfare which was so new to us all. According to this conception the peacetime Army was not to be an Army at all, but a school for training reservists. Cover was provided, or so it was believed, by the Maginot Line and its interlinked fortresses. As no one thought in terms other than a continuous front, the Army when mobilized would have to be enormous (over a hundred divisions in 1939). In consequence the peacetime organization was regarded as a hard core for the mobilization of the *Grande Armée*—and this is why its establishment, reduced to derisory numbers by cuts in the length of service, was split up into so many units.

This transfer of interest from the regular Army to the conception of the nationally mobilized Army, together with the poverty of immediate resources, led to the worst kind of intellectual poverty, the bogus mystique of size for its own sake. Instead of planning for genuine possibilities, one tried to bridge the gap between the dream and the reality by the artifice of forecasting mobilization: but there was a lack of all stores, equipment and uniforms. No doubt at one time there had been enormous stocks of material but they had all been used up or become obsolete. To re-equip an Army of several million men would cost an astronomical sum which it would be quite hopeless to ask for from a Parliament which had already considerably trimmed the military budget. The showdown —imaginary—was to be the mobilization. There were no horses, no trucks, no men: all right, *when the time came,* they would magically appear by requisition and call-up. There were no boots, no shirts: but a single notice in the mobilization papers would take care of that. If the Army needed new tanks or mobile mortars, digging designs out of the files and placing orders would do the trick —on mobilization. Unhappily I am not exaggerating, and this state of affairs existed through every branch of the Service.

It is this mental approach which explains why the manifest deficiencies no longer worried anyone. By the magic of mobilization France would find itself possessed of a dream Army, the shortcomings of which the hypothetical possibilities would hide. Wanting too much and able to achieve too little, the Army slipped away into a bureaucratic fairy tale. 'The late French Army', a Cassandra used to write from 1928 onwards and not unnaturally what he wrote was misunderstood. In fact the new Army was even worse than it looked; the edifice of French security was founded upon two piles of paper: treaties and mobilization.

As to the modernization of the Army which was announced at the time when I left the École de Guerre, there was a lot of talk but no action. My colleague charged with the study of the mechanized brigade or division, Captain de Virieu, drew up a fresh scheme every fortnight, while his initial enthusiasm was drained away in fighting vested interests. Meanwhile Major de Gaulle had published his little book postulating the formation of a mechanized force which went along with everything we had wanted for several years. But by an error of tactics, which Paul Reynaud told me later that he had pointed out at the time, the book was entitled *Vers l'Armée de métier*, and that started trouble. The left saw in it a return to the Praetorians. General Weygand, Commander-in-Chief designate, who was fighting hard to get the length of military service extended, was afraid of what effect the arguments for a smaller Army might have. The General Staff too was against it, which was unfortunate because we remained saddled with a set of out-of-date ideas.

Meanwhile Great Britain had established an armoured brigade, and in France motorization and mechanization were fashionable subjects in the reviews and in garrison discussion. I had met Liddell Hart who convinced me with his new ideas. Could not something be made out of this mess?

There then occurred an apparently minor event which produced extraordinary, long-term results. General Gamelin, who had just succeeded General Weygand, uttered an ukase the sense of which was as follows: 'There is widespread discussion of motorization and mechanization. I wish it to be understood that the sole authority for the establishment of doctrine is the General Headquarters of the Army. All articles and all lectures on these subjects will therefore be submitted and authorized by the said authority before they are published or delivered.' Everyone got the message and a profound silence reigned until the awakening of 1940.

Meanwhile I had been charged with the organization of the African Army, which placed under my control the troops in North Africa as well as the African troops in metropolitan France. It was an enormous task, involving more than half the entire Army. I had seen conditions in Algeria, Tunisia, Morocco and even Syria at first-hand; I was in my element.

My first task was to try to relieve the disorganization of the regiments of *Tirailleurs*, which I knew so well, by welding them into properly constituted units. What a business! I had to attack a host of authorities step by step. At last I managed to get approval from all the relevant authorities and my project, approved by the General Staff, was submitted to General Gamelin. The General consulted his deputy—who was taking the waters, and this man in turn took advice . . . from a captain of *Tirailleurs* who was taking the waters with him. The captain said no, on the grounds that it might mean getting out of Algeria! This was the setback when it seemed as if we were home and dry.

But North Africa was beginning to pose more serious problems.

A pogrom against the Algerian Jews had caused trouble in Constan-
tine and the numbers involved showed that it was the beginning of
more serious disturbance. Already when I was in Tunisia we had
had to restore order and arrest Bourguiba. So we found ourselves
faced by the question of the future of our colonization in North
Africa. For me it was not a new question and I had frequently given
it considerable thought when I was there. While I was in Morocco
there was much talk of a memorandum from Lyautey to the Government in which he gave the Protectorate a life of twenty-five years
because, he said, this formula must lead to the creation of a state
which when it was formed would wish to become independent. A
century and a half before, already, Necker had said that colonies are
like fruit which drop from the tree as soon as they are ripe. This
time element, which became somewhat extended, did not surprise
us and many of us felt the necessity of foreseeing the future and
getting things into perspective. Algeria remained a different problem because there was no Algerian State. On the contrary at the
time one saw among the European population some of those elements which might lead to a Dominion, like at that time South
Africa or Australia. The demographic Muslim explosion had not
yet come about and there remained many possibilities.

Having reached the centre where decisions were made, I was
curious to know what policy for North Africa had been worked out
and how one could help orientate its evolution. I was in touch with
the Ministry of Foreign Affairs which controlled Morocco, Tunisia
and the Levant, and with the Home Office which was responsible
for Algeria under the curiously mixed heading of 'Couteutieux *and*
Algeria'. The more I looked into things, the more I discovered the
incredible truth: France had no North African policy!

In 1935 I accompanied General Georges to a conference of what
was called the Haut Comité Méditerranéen, presided over by Laval.
Each territory was represented by its Resident, Governor or High
Commissioner. The meeting brought out the absence of policy to
such a degree that it was almost like a caricature. Peyrouton for
Tunisia said that there would be no political problem if a market
could be found for their surplus corn and oil. The Governor-General
of Algeria, Cardes, said that in his opinion all the trouble sprang
from the political activity of the Ulemas—then, Laval interjected,
strengthen the police. Ponsot, for Morocco, blamed the Treaty of

Algeciras for all the diplomatic and economic difficulties which had followed. The Director of the Levant, M. de Saint-Quentin, representing Syria, thought the difficulties in his territory were purely electoral. Laval, like any politician, summed up the contradictions but decided nothing. . . .

Meanwhile Laval had just reached a vital point in his foreign policy. By the Rome Agreements he had succeeded in aligning Italy on our side against resurgent Germany. In the event of war one French Army Corps was to be moved to the Brenner pass to link up with the Czechs. At the same time a compromise was reached on Tunisia, which the Italians had always claimed. This considerably changed the situation in North Africa. I was sent by special plane—most unusual in those days—to discuss with the civil and military authorities on the spot what the consequences might be. I received various opinions, sometimes unexpected. General Giraud summoned me to tell me that it would be necessary to introduce tanks into the *Tirailleurs* Divisions. General Catroux at Marrakesh advised me to do away with the Algerian-Moroccan border territory, while General Trinquet at Tiznit, in bed with severe otitis, stressed to me the necessity for maintaining it. But apart from these individual opinions, it became obvious that security was the major problem. In the absence of any positive policy, happily there still remained the armed forces of which the prestige was as yet still unimpaired.

From all this I drew up a plan which to my great surprise was adopted without argument. Africa should have two types of troops: the security forces (the Legion, Zouaves, Senegalese, *Chasseurs d'Afrique*) forming one division in each territory and charged with the maintenance of law and order (seven divisions); and fighting troops which on mobilization would be formed into North African divisions of which one echelon (five divisions) would be moved to France if the necessity arose and the other could either follow the first or if required remain in North Africa and cover Tunisia. Further, in the event of war, there would be appointed a single commander for the whole of North Africa, and General Noguès was nominated for this role. This was the plan which was in operation in 1940.

Alas, the Rome Agreements enjoyed a very short life: in Mussolini's view—and more clearly in the secret clauses agreed to

by Laval—these agreements were intended to cover the Italian
expedition against Ethiopia. Great Britain, which still believed in
the 'route to the Indies', came out in opposition—somewhat slowly,
but with resolution. We were caught on the horns of a dilemma:
either to abandon the Italians whose aid in Central Europe was so
valuable, or abandon Great Britain, our traditional ally in the
great crises. There was a moment of hesitation (I was myself
having, with some disquiet, to study the effect upon our overseas
territories of a possible war with Great Britain!) then we came down
on the side of the English and agreed to economic sanctions against
Italy. Mussolini countered with the Rome-Berlin Axis, to which
he remained faithful until his own death and the ruin of his country.

But the clouds were gathering on all sides: Spain first in revolution and then civil war aggravated by foreign intervention; the
rearmament of Germany. The showdown was visibly approaching.
One Saturday morning we learnt that the military reoccupation of
the left bank of the Rhine was imminent and we were to return that
afternoon (we used to observe the English weekend) and again the
following day. Next, that same afternoon, we learnt that Hitler had
renounced the Locarno pact and Part Five of the Treaty of Versailles. The Government, strong in the understanding recently
reached with Great Britain over the sanctions crisis, threatened
immediate military action. General Gamelin consulted the specialists: the reply was precise—it was impossible for us to put an
effective expeditionary force into the field, that is to say with the
necessary manpower and equipment, without starting full mobilization, about a million men, and requisitioning vehicles.

Justly alarmed at the magnitude of such measures, the political
aspects of which could be prejudicial to us, the Government called
for a study of a more limited mobilization, something similar to
the call-up of one age-group which Mussolini put into operation at
the time of the assassination of Dollfuss. We started a discussion:
would it be possible to improvise an expeditionary force by amal-
gamating the regular regiments so as to make best use of the troops
available and bring them up to strength by calling up one class of
reservist? The amalgamation of the regular regiments was possible—and I myself supported this—but one would be committing

in hostile territory a vital part of the skeleton of the totally mobilized Army. If war resulted, our entire mobilization—the famous
mobilization—could be compromised, an idea which produced
shrill cries of horror from the specialists. As to the call-up of one
age-group—that was *impossible*: the individual papers were filed in
each mobilization centre by units and in order of release; to call up
one age-group would mean a gigantic riffle through the entire files
which could not conceivably be carried out in a few days. Furthermore the vehicles necessary for even one Army Corps could not be
provided from the resources of the Regular Army, which would
mean requisition; but General Georges pointed out that the studies
undertaken at Geneva to define aggression had concluded that a
nation which first authorized requisition showed by this very act its
willingness to become an aggressor. . . . Sunday passed in frantic
studies, trying to patch up in one day the mistakes of fifteen years.

At the Council of Ministers on Monday Gamelin voiced his conclusion: not knowing what was to follow, we could not jeopardize
our entire mobilization plans for the sake of putting one improvised
Corps in the field; the only sensible thing to do was to carry out
the plan and mobilize a million men. So positive the night before,
the Government now hesitated in the face of such radical action;
London was not against us, but we would have to go it alone; the
opinion of the ruling classes and of the best informed was not in
favour of the adventure (at a dinner that same Monday a financier
said to me that the essential thing was not to stand in the way of
'economic recovery'!). We drifted from Monday night into Tues-
day, but already we were faced by a *fait accompli*; the Germans had
attained their objective on the left bank of the Rhine. It was decided
then . . . to protest to the League of Nations!

The die was cast. We had let slip our last chance of stifling at
birth the rise of Hitler's Germany. This conclusion, so obvious
today, was apparent to me in 1936, and I was not alone. But this
not very difficult foresight was far from general. Through idleness,
stupidity, political blindness, or simply frivolity, general opinion
lived through these grave events, the result of which was to be a
great and catastrophic war, in a sort of somnambulism on which it
is necessary to dwell at some length, because it shows how fate
deals the cards of history and lulls to sleep its chosen victims.

The leaders first. In June or July 1936 I was appointed interpreter to General Gamelin who was to use the occasion of the
unveiling of the Canadian memorial on Vimy Ridge by King
Edward VIII as an opportunity to have a private talk with the
British Chief of the Imperial General Staff, Field-Marshal Deverell.
It was the first meeting of its kind and one had come a long way
since the previous year's tension over Ethiopia. I was certainly
going to hear something interesting. Gamelin, covered in decorations, and myself in sky blue and red dress uniform with gold
stripes and sword, together boarded at the Gare du Nord the
special train put on for the King, the President of the Republic and
their guests. A compartment had been reserved for us. Deverell
entered, a much decorated giant, a typical Colonel Bramble, and
immediately asked in English what the latest score was in the Davis
Cup; as it happened, I was able to tell him. Gamelin sat silent in
his corner; I tried to draw him into the conversation. Deverell
looked towards him and said: 'Ask General Gamelin what he
thinks of the German tanks in Spain.'

To which Gamelin replied more or less in these words: 'All our
information indicates that our policy is the right one. The German
tanks, too lightly armoured, are scrap iron.'

When I had translated this reply, Deverell gave an inarticulate
grunt and seemed to be thinking with some difficulty. Gamelin,
encouraged, touched upon his preoccupation with his left flank in
Flanders, but my transmission of this did not seem to interest
Deverell.

'Ask the General what is the greatest lesson he learnt from the
last war.' When I translated, Gamelin swallowed at this difficult
question and went back into his shell. 'Well, the biggest lesson I
learnt,' said Deverell, without waiting for an answer, 'is that the
next war will be short.'

I quickly translated to help Gamelin in giving his reply; this
declaration was a body blow to him and he rapidly started to think.
Then Deverell said: 'Yes, the next war will be short because it
must not be allowed to be long!'

Gamelin ignored this last sally; his reply was ready. In his most
professional tone he said: 'The greatest lesson which I learnt from
the last war is that the high command must at all times keep a firm
hand on the operations. In a word, battle must be controlled.' When

I translated this Deverell seemed surprised, grunted again . . . and went to sleep.

It would be difficult better to sum up the abyss which separated our two Armies. I was shattered. Gamelin remained quite calm and to pass the hours before us I tried to draw him on one subject and another, and finally I was bold enough to ask why he had refused to move in the previous March. His reply was straightforward and revealing: 'I was faced by a Germany which mustered a million men (this was not true, that figure included police, the S.A. and the militia; the Wehrmacht, as we know today but did not realize at the time, was unfit for war and Hitler had made up his mind to take his own life if we intervened). I asked for a million men. The Government did not consider this possible, so there was no alternative but to wait for another time.' I thought again of the judgement which Captain Zeller had expressed to me at the Headquarters of the General Staff. How could one entrust such responsibilities to a little man like this, more professor than general, manifestly out of his depth? How in these conditions were we to meet the terrible test which he so calmly announced?

The irony of it all was that Gamelin—whose prestige abroad was high, as was that of the French Army—complained to Duff Cooper, then British Minister for War, that Deverell seemed too old. Deverell was relieved of his position a few months later and was succeeded by Gort. One wishes to heaven that Deverell had likewise complained and got Gamelin removed!

Let us now look at the country. It is a difficult analysis, which others have already done well: Fabre Luce with his *Journal de la France* and various memoirs, Jouvenel in a remarkable little book which he published in 1942. Here I only want to touch upon the most important points.

By 1930 France had not yet succeeded in reaching stability after the glories of the immediate post-war period when she saw visions of a new *belle époque* in the rosy clouds of victory.

Ostensibly the façade of 1918 still stood up—that is to say, the Little Entente; but Germany was gone—no more reparations, no more occupation. Germany had regained her liberty and was mounting a monstrous revival under the sign of the swastika. Great

Britain and the United States were partly responsible for this rebirth which was already worrying a French-dominated Europe.
The USSR emerged from the shadows of revolution and came back
into the European picture, feared and misunderstood. Further away,
China was experiencing the difficult labour which Malraux described so well in *La Condition Humaine*. On our doorstep Italy,
which we had thrown back into the arms of Germany, had under-
gone a revolution more spectacular than genuine and was goose-
stepping away while the Ministers, under Mussolini, ran around
gaily jumping through burning hoops to the plaudits of the crowd.
Spain, deep in an implacable civil war, was liquidating Communism
in the name of Christianity. In the defeated countries, in Vienna, in
Budapest and in Germany, the ruin had been total. Mustafa Kemal
had been able to save Turkey— partly thanks to us—by a victory
over Greece, and then by a real revolution, brutally Europeanizing
his people. There could be no doubt that a new world, hard and
distressing, was growing up.

Meanwhile France, unaware, was dancing the Charleston and
simply trying, after the torment of 1914–18, to be happy. England,
in rather the same mood, had returned to its imperial politics and
the extension of its colonial system, the old game of playing one off
against another—opposing France in a minor way because she was
supposed to be strong, supporting the Germans, the Riffs, the
Syrians. It took the warnings from Italy and a reborn Germany to
revive, even to a small degree, the Entente Cordiale. This minor
Anglo-French war sprang more or less from an incredible blindness
and total lack of appreciation of what was to come.

But internally the desire for peace and quiet was offset by a mass
of problems which appeared insoluble. First the economy: the franc
was unable to stand up to the terrible cost of the war. Poincaré had
been forced to devalue by seventy-five per cent. With the monetary
balance restored, France rejoiced once more in a strong currency
until the financial crisis in the United States started the great
depression and unemployment mounted dangerously.

On the other hand France did hear the distant echoes of the
dramatic changes taking place in the world, of the reverberations
which, softened by our surroundings, produced a political situation
which was relatively mild but nevertheless disorganizing. France
hesitated between three solutions which somewhat unequally split

up the country: to go along the more or less bourgeois road of radical liberalism, to turn towards an ex-Servicemen's neo-fascism coloured with Maurrassisme, or to try Communism. The Communists had been defeated in 1919, but were now rapidly gaining in strength, thanks to the economic crisis. The radicals, returned to power in 1924 under Herriot, were stultified by the manoeuvres of politics and were clearly unable to cope with the ever-mounting difficulties. It was in these circumstances that the fascist *putsch* was made, occasioned by chance by the affair of 6 February 1934, but quickly brought to naught through subtle manoeuvring by the radicals. Nevertheless my generation, tired of the parliamentary impotence of the Third Republic and fascinated by the remarkable progress made in Italy and Germany, retained a hankering after fascism. Laval, brought up as a socialist, thought that he was the man for this sort of political game: he flirted with Italy, attempted to re-establish the economic scene with a fierce deflation—and opened the way for the huge wave which carried all before it in the 1936 elections under the name of the *Front Populaire*. It was a combination of radicals, socialists and Communists.

It was believed that there would be a revolution. But this was, once more, no more than a warning. After several days of somewhat romantic disorder, the socialists under Léon Blum triumphed over the radicals and reduced the explosion to more reasonable French terms: some necessary social legislation was hurried through, the intervention on behalf of the Republican Government in Spain was cancelled, and everything went back to normal.

The major change was in foreign policy, which now became openly 'anti-fascist'. The German threat was at last being taken seriously, which could not fail to reassure those who, like myself, saw with concern that we were running out of time. But France was far from its old Jacobin traditions. The devotion of the *Front Popu* to a national policy was compromising in the eyes of a large section of public opinion. The French crypto-fascists were making warlike sounds, which the veterans of 1914 understood only too well. Thus was born and steadily developed a divergence of understanding which was to have the gravest consequences: the old 'nationalists' became pacifist while the dyed-in-the-wool pacifists were forced to play the role, quite new to them, of intransigent patriots. The result was a splintering of opinion which, touched off by yet another devaluation of the franc by Auriol, led to the return to power of the radicals under Daladier. We fell back into an era of half-measures, and war was approaching fast.

This imbroglio left France divided and disorientated, the only common sentiment being a desire to live in peace and enjoy the evening twilight. A German had considerable success with an optimistic little book entitled *Dieu est-il français?* But another German wrote more cruelly: 'France is the arch-type of a dying nation. She is a nation without purpose or importance . . . the people have lost the fire, the pride, the thirst for glory of classical France . . . they are a small nation with a great spiritual heritage, a minor power on the edge of Europe, cast out from all the streams of dynamic development, cloistered on the defensive . . . the French people can be left to themselves, for time irrevocably is against them . . . France is no longer the main concern of Germany, she is the main concern of nobody and can be left to fall into the footnotes of history.'

This severe judgement, alas, was to receive in 1940 an ominous confirmation.

As war came nearer, it was time for me quickly to serve my time of active command as a Captain. I returned to Morocco, of course, and chose the 2nd *Tirailleurs Marocains* with whom, after several weeks at Agadir and the extreme south near Ifni, I found myself back in Marrakesh. I felt quite clearly that this was the end of the line. But the magic of Marrakesh made this particular end of the line a paradise before the torment to come: the dry atmosphere, the clear sky, the snow peaks of the Atlas rising beyond the palm groves, the motley town in which I had rented an enchanting little palace, the vast countryside across which in spring one galloped through the short-lived flowers, the glorious sunshine, the star-filled nights, the deep siestas within the heat of a tent, all these things which I recalled with regret during the years to come left with me an unforgettable memory of a golden age now vanished for ever.

My command, in spite of the poor state of our military affairs, was richly rewarding: good troops, good NCOs and the joy of handling and training a first-class body of men in a heavenly setting gave me a great feeling of richness.

But I knew that the truth lay elsewhere. I worked hard and to good purpose. I carefully analysed *Mein Kampf*. In it I discovered with the greatest misgivings a doctrine which, while false in itself, was nevertheless terribly logical and efficacious. The Munich crisis, which I followed on the radio, confirmed my apprehensions (no one who has not heard the broadcasts of a Nuremberg Rally can understand the explosive force of those rantings!). The backing down which followed a token mobilization (when I had to put my battalion on a war footing) seemed to me the ultimate mistake, the mark of destiny. I drew upon those reflexions for an article which the *Revue des Deux Mondes* published in due course . . . 15 August 1939. I called it 'The Peaceful War or the Strategy of Hitler' and in it I analysed what was new then—the methods which we now call the Cold War. My theme was that we had no option but to go into business and find out how to win the cold war, otherwise we would find ourselves drawn into a shooting war with all its consequent calamities for Europe. The idea was right, but to carry it out required both realism and energy, virtues which, as we shall see, remained in abeyance until the awakening of 1940.

I went on with an investigation of tactics and made a considerable study of the possibility of breaking a defensive front by the massive use of armour. I reached the *certain* conclusion that the tactical resources of the period made an operation of this type on the one hand possible but on the other unpalatable. It was essential to work out a new type of defence based on armoured counter-attack. Could we do it in time?

The storm was gathering visibly. When Czechoslovakia was occupied by the Germans the moment of drama was at hand. I received a telegram posting me to the General Staff of the Army. The interlude in Morocco was over and I was conscious of entering upon the decisive phase of contemporary history.

In Paris my surprise and my disappointment were profound: the headquarters of the Army was still living in the same old way. None of the problems which had been posed two years before appeared to have been resolved: it reduced one to despair. Furthermore, on the personal level, I had not been posted in to undertake any important task, as I had hoped, but merely as a routine development in my career by giving me a period in the section called the Legislature. The idea that on the very threshold of a great war I should spend my time learning the art of drawing up laws and decrees seemed to me as farcical as it was distasteful, as indeed did the whole attitude of headquarters, of the government and of the country. I felt more and more as if I were living in a paralysing nightmare. I experienced moments of genuine despair, I remember, as I daily walked across the lovely Place de la Concorde and my agony was increased by the feeling that so few seemed to share my views.

One morning as I was walking down a corridor I was suddenly asked if I would like to go on a mission to Moscow. I accepted with enthusiasm. Fate had lifted me out of the rut of routine to throw me into the very centre of real problems.

This privilege I have now enjoyed for more than twenty years.

Chapter 5
July 1939

※

BEFORE STARTING ON the events of 1939–40, I think it would be useful to review the overall picture of the situation which the evolution of events had produced, so that the explication of what followed may be clearer.

If I enter here upon this slightly theoretical study, it is because such a vital subject has far too often been shrouded in pious omission, or passionate, politically-inspired fables. In fact nothing is more important than to reach a precise diagnosis of these events, the long range consequences of which are still by no means over. To lay bare the causes of our incredible defeat is not to take upon oneself the right of judgement, or the apportioning of praise or blame, and even less to revive the sterile arguments of Riom or those which followed the liberation on the apportioning of 'responsibility' for the defeat. Rather, one should try to relive objectively a vital chapter in our history in order to reveal the complex mechanism by which fate decided our lot.

It is apparent that the sequence of events had produced a mental and material paralysis in the victors of 1918, so that the vanquished benefited from a whole host of favourable circumstances.

This lesson must never be forgotten.

On the French side, we have seen, through my own personal experiences, some of the essential causes of my country's weakness: the exhaustion of a country drained of blood after four long years of war, the sclerosis which stultified a victorious army, the grievous fault of having deduced from this victory an erroneous and too dogmatic way of thought and, possibly even more harmful, the basing of the army organization on concepts totally different from those of the nation's foreign policy. To top it all, the disarray and division of public opinion on political matters made impossible the structural reforms which alone could have given back to the State the vigour and the efficiency which circumstances demanded.

This last reason was decisive because from 1936 it made the obviously much-needed military overhaul quite impossible. It has been fashionable, ever since Vichy, to lay the responsibility for our lack of preparation on the *Front Populaire*. What I have said already must make it plain that 'responsibility' goes back far beyond that—in fact to 1921. That mistakes could be made at that time is understandable. But that it subsequently proved impossible to put the mistakes right is a much more serious matter. This perpetuation of mistakes was certainly based on the erroneous conclusions drawn from 1918, in spite of the lessons learnt from Spain, and encouraged by the promotion to leadership of officers brought up to this way of thought. But there was, furthermore, the extreme apathy of the nation.

A few illustrations of this apathy: the decision to build the Maginot Line was made *in 1928*. By 1932 only a few constructions were anywhere near completion; in 1936 the armament was still incomplete. It was not until 1938, *after ten years*, that the fortified system as originally planned was completely finished. The extension towards Belgium was still on the drawing-board. It took the Germans eighteen months to build the Siegfried Line.

It was decided *in 1924* to adopt a new light machine-gun and at the same time to alter the small arms ammunition of the infantry. The new light machine-gun was brought into service between 1926 and 1932, but the design for a rifle which could use the same ammunition was not chosen for another twelve years—in 1936. In 1939 we had only a few hundred thousand of them for an army of several million men, and our total production capacity was 10,000 a month.

The Air Arm was given its autonomy in 1930. It drew up its plans for an establishment of 1,000 aircraft. Despite the fantastic rise of the Luftwaffe, this programme was adhered to until 1939. The first formula established by the independent Air Arm under General Denain was based upon aircraft carrying a considerable crew, slow and heavily armed; this formula, drawn up in 1930, did not see the light of day until 1936—by which time events in Spain had shown it to be quite ill-founded. It was then decided to copy the fast planes of other countries. In 1940, four years later but—what is more important—after six months of war, we possessed a total of 500 fighters and ninety bombers which were really modern.

At the same date the Luftwaffe, created in 1932 and given the go-ahead in 1936, mustered 7,000 first line aircraft.

These are not the only examples; the same situation existed in all departments: heavy artillery, anti-tank guns, heavy machine-guns, ack-ack defence, machine-gun carriers and tanks. The point was reached in 1939 that when we wanted to double the number of our armoured units, all we could do was to divide those already in existence in half!

It was not lack of money, although this was handed out parsimoniously enough—nor by Parliament which from 1936 onwards always voted the military budget without discussion, but by the stop imposed by the Ministry of Finance during the preparation of the budget. It was simply paralysis, an impotence of achievement which was by no means confined to the Army. We are an ancient country, the institutions of which date from the age of the horse and plumes; we had not succeeded in adapting ourselves.

One must consider why the Germans had adapted themselves better.

When one looks back on the manner in which destiny dealt the cards during the period preceding the last war, one cannot fail to be struck by the difference which existed at the time between the French military forces and the young German Army. It is certain that historians of the future will be astonished to see two future adversaries proceeding along such divergent paths. I have described what we were doing, and why. I will try to show why the defeated enemy of 1918 embarked on a line of thought truer than our own.

Beaten, the German Army received from its defeat the stimulus which gave it a desire for revenge. We had felt the same after 1870. This stirring into action, the source of all real success, is undoubtedly nature's way of re-establishing the balance of power. The first beneficial effect of defeat is a concentration of energies. Another less obvious one is a severe examination of one's conscience and a revision of all values. This lively attitude contrasts with the mental security which we enjoyed; when one is passionately searching for truth one is usually not far from discovering it.

To the advantages common to all defeated peoples, there was

added in Germany's case the fact that we had destroyed her entire military machinery. The creators of the Reichswehr were able to start practically from scratch, which gave them the opportunity of building on hitherto untried lines: they were not lumbered with stocks of obsolete equipment, nor with obsolete generals. Relieved by us of all the old rubbish which every ancient institution accumulates, they found themselves obliged to start again with a new framework.

The disarmament imposed upon them served them well in another sense: there was no obligation to follow the military theories of 1918. These theories postulated a military wealth of men and equipment which was out of the question for them until about 1937 or 1938. Our way of making war in strength which presupposed a continuous front had no interest for them, in spite of our prestige. In circumstances completely different from our own, the Germans were bound to reject our line of thought and to seek a new formula, consonant with their means and their aim. Untrammelled by the past, they were free to work it out as they wished.

Their new formula took fifteen years to achieve, but from the start the German General Staff found some basis in the thinking behind the 1914 campaign. At that time Germany had been within an inch of victory: had it not been for the Marne, the Schlieffen Plan would have split the Allied forces before they had had time to coalesce. It was the long war which beat Germany, because it gave her enemies time to mobilize their military and industrial power, and to impose a successful blockade. The lesson of the 1914–18 war was that it should have been won in the first August, which was quite possible; therefore a short war, *a lightning war*, had now to be envisaged. This theory comes out in various writings, notably in those of von Seeckt from 1921 onwards. It gave German military thought a definite orientation.

Open warfare postulates the primacy of manoeuvre, contrary to our own beliefs. We had come to the conclusion, based on the thoughts of 1918 in France, that manoeuvre had become extremely difficult. The Germans did not fall into the same trap because their experiences were not limited to the western front: most of their officers, including Hindenburg and Ludendorff, had fought on the eastern front; there they experienced a modern type of warfare in which the possibility of movement remained ever present. Furthermore it was in this type of action that they gained their only important victories, so it is not surprising that they were convinced and that they sought always to reproduce the same conditions. At a time when we were seeking what we considered the necessity of stabilization, the Germans had no thought in their minds but movement. The same reasons which made us seek a reproduction of the battles of Malmaison and Montdidier drove the Germans into thinking of a modern Tannenberg and a new Schlieffen Plan.

It remained to find the means. The problem was not a simple one; it is evident that in a theatre of operations vast in comparison with the forces engaged, which was the case in Russia during 1914 to 1918, a campaign of movement was always possible. But on a front stiff with troops, as would be the case in a campaign against France, there was the danger of returning to trench warfare, miles of barbed wire, a machine-gun every fifty yards, bringing with it the enormous difficulty of the slightest manoeuvre. The armistice in 1918 came too soon for a positive result to have been reached and it is not unreasonable for us to have drawn the conclusion that there could be no answer but another stalemate. There again the Germans were saved by the situation in which they found themselves: they knew that a stalemate could bring them neither victory nor revenge. There was no question of accepting the inevitability of trench warfare; on the contrary some means of avoiding it had to be found at all costs.

To this end the Reichswehr, proud of its youth and high quality, believed in the swift attack, that is to say a major offensive launched before the enemy had time to mobilize. By this means there would not be the time in which to gather the manpower necessary for the stabilization of a continuous tenable front. As Jouvenel wrote: 'The heads of the Reichswehr were experienced soldiers, airmen, commanders of assault groups, and plain adventurers. They appreciated the virtue of surprise which stuns and paralyses the enemy. Why could not principles which had succeeded for a handful of partisans be applied on a vast scale to a nation in arms?' Thus the two essential virtues were quality and speed. But this conception, however well taught and understood, carried with it considerable risks when attacking a known adversary, such as ourselves. The slightest hitch could lead to complete disaster. Furthermore the Maginot Line and our plans for early mobilization might render it too difficult, if not impossible. For there was no getting round the problem of breaking a fortified front: this could only be achieved blow by blow.

In seeking a solution, the Germans were once again favoured by chance, since defeat always brings advantages to those who know how to use them. A fighting man is always more impressed by what he has had to suffer himself than he is by what he has dished out to his enemy. We remained haunted by the absolute hell of shellfire at Verdun, the gas, the tenacity of the German machine-gunners and the discovery that it was impossible to break the enemy's front: the Germans retained only the sharpest memories of the novelties which 1918 had brought: the armoured attacks and the bombing by vast air fleets. Since they had borne the brunt of it all they drew a lesson from it more clearly than we did, and therein lay the germ of their return to manoeuvre. Because we had used these methods more or less successfully, we were, so to speak, disenchanted by the subject. But because the Germans had been on the receiving end, they took a serious view of it to which no practical answer had been forthcoming.

Furthermore we had after the war prevented them from having any modern arms; this merely served to concentrate their thoughts on the subject. We had 2,600 tanks for which we foresaw no more than a modest use, but the Germans exaggerated the potential of this armour if employed in mass and were forced to apply their minds to what they considered a major danger. Exercises, manoeuvres carried out with dummy tanks and anti-tank guns served to turn them more and more towards the possibilities of armour. While our obsolete Renaults rusted in the tank parks they felt powerless, and dreamed endlessly of the moment when they would have in their hands the equipment of which they were at that time deprived. Since there was nothing they could do themselves, they learnt all that they could from what was going on elsewhere—in England, Russia, France and Italy, and from the writings of Liddell Hart, Fuller, Douhet and de Gaulle. From all this came one undeniable conclusion—a desire for total modernization.

As soon as the political climate made it possible, their rearmament was to be based, with all the squandering of new-found wealth, on the latest machines. The next war, the ultimate target was to employ a massive use of armour and aircraft. The Spanish war was a useful corrective (the tanks had been built too quickly and were not heavily armoured enough), but nevertheless broadly confirmed the theories of Guderian. Now Germany possessed a complete military blue-print which could only lead to the long-desired revenge.

Here we have the nature of things which led Germany to the solutions which were to bring victory and which broadly, sank us in moral and intellectual paralysis. There is only one lesson to be learnt from this: it is the losers who learn; while victory on the other hand contains within it the seeds of death.

But the doctrine of *blitzkrieg* was really only one aspect of the military thinking which the Germans drew from the years between 1914–18. It ties up with their insistence upon the necessity for rapid victory. They refused to recognize that their army had been defeated: their downfall they attributed to the blockade, to the revolution, to economic and moral collapse.

This thought haunted the military leaders, such as Ludendorff, who at the time had considered themselves powerless with Germany crumbling behind them. It haunted also the fighting men themselves who, like Hitler, had in 1918 seen the troops become more and more indisciplined the further back they were from the actual front. It seemed to them that the country could not face the terrible test of another war, even a swift one, if it were not already forearmed against these internal dangers. From this fear came the knowledge that preparations for war must be completed in every walk of life, which Ludendorff set out specifically in his book *Der Totale Krieg*.

Preparation for war was to be on a moral basis. Every conceivable method was to be employed to give the country a sense of 'togetherness'; any disruptive element—were it revolutionary, ideological or religious—had ruthlessly to be eliminated. A German way of thought needed to be created, based on the needs of the race itself and capable of standing up to the rigours of war. This task was one of the most important facing both army and State. Thanks to this canalization of energy, which Ludendorff considered had been best achieved in France between 1914 and 1918, the people could be persuaded to put up with any privation, and a maximum effort could be extracted in men, money and production; it became possible to orientate and converge every activity towards the idea of war. By means of this total mobilization, war became the sole idea and intention of the nation.

But achieving this unity was not sufficient in itself; it was necessary also to take precautions against any blockade in the economic field. To this end the army had to control and reshape the economy so as to render it independent of the foreign market. Dumps of stores were laid out, *ersatz* materials were used wherever possible and consumer goods were rationed in order to conserve resources. As complete an autarchy as possible was imposed—indeed by widespread planning life became as strictly governed as it was at any time during the war.

Thus the German army drew from the war of 1914–18 the conception of total mobilization which so denied the normal way of life as to constitute a new type of State. The State which Ludendorff visualized in *Der Totale Krieg*, and which as Commander-in-Chief he supported, was a State absorbing every private activity and directing it to one end—war. Contrary to the Communist totalitarianism which had the avowed intention of improving the economic situation for the general good, the German doctrine appeared as a Spartan super-totalitarianism having as its end the sole purpose of giving the country its greatest fighting potential.

This extreme military concept might have been banished to the museum of military thought if the State had enjoyed at the time a stable Government. But the concept came to life when the country was going through a series of crises. From 1923 onwards Germany was moving towards an anti-liberal revolution somewhat on the Italian pattern. This movement came from the republic's inability to restore Germany to her previous position, from the disgust felt at their 'collaboration' with their previous enemies and from uneasiness in the face of the growth of Communism. But the wave which really swept Weimar away was caused by the fact that the principles on which they had based their policy were foreign to the German spirit, avid as it was for strength and grandeur, and that the bourgeoisie who should have supported the régime were crushed by inflation. Defeat and ruin sowed in Germany the seeds of a revolution the purpose of which was to give some body to the dreams of the common man: revenge, a sense of order, and unlimited power.

This renewing of the passionate personal feeling which Keyserling had described as 'the instinctive and indescribable drive of the masses' found in the theory of total war an idea made-to-measure. Hitlerism grew from a conjunction of this revolution, arising from the depths of the German soul and the movement of the nation towards militarism.

It seems useless to try to analyse which of these two tendencies appeared first. It is doubtful if the Reichswehr created National Socialism from the elements which it found to hand, despite the presence of Ludendorff at the Munich *putsch*. It is more reasonable to suppose that the two movements were born spontaneously and separately from the conditions following defeat and that they marched along with the same ends, because although they enjoyed different intentions—and I do not intend to go yet again over the history of Nazism—they finished by coming together as one and the same.

The doctrine of National Socialism, when one strips it of its political clap-trap, is essentially the imposition of revolutionary tendencies turned towards militarism: because the purpose is revenge. The military tendencies likewise turn towards revolution through abuse of technique in achieving their acknowledged ends.

The target was to give the nation all the strength of which it was capable in order to face up to the war which would bring world power. Hitler expressed this view quite clearly in *Mein Kampf*: 'Germany will either become a World Power or will not continue to exist at all.' 'The Movement must find the courage to organize our national forces and set them on the path which will lead them away from that territorial restriction which is the bane of our national life to-day, and win new territory for them.' 'For flaming protests will not restore the oppressed territories to the bosom of a common Reich. That can only be done through the might of the sword.' 'The plough is then the sword; and the tears of war will produce the daily bread for the generations to come.' This philosophy, quite different from ours which depended on Geneva, was based upon a total acceptance of war. The affirmation of a dynamic transcendentalism at the highest level made war the sole purpose of the new order.

In consequence everything was geared to the use of force. I must return again to *Mein Kampf*: 'The forging of this sword is a work that *has to be done through the domestic policy which must be adopted by a national government*. To see that the work of forging these arms is assured, and to recruit the men who will bear them, that is the task of the foreign policy.' The method was the total and permanent mobilization of the country, thus directing the whole civil population to one end. In accordance with the ideals of Ludendorff the nation would be galvanized morally by the National Socialist movement which would turn once again to the ancient Pan-Germanism, the ideal of imperialism presented under new colours. The energies thus harnessed would be exploited by a *technical dictatorship*. Jünger and Niekisch sketched out plainly the extreme conception which needed to be applied: it was concerned with 'shaping the world to a technical plan . . . The modern State has no constitution; in place of a constitution there exists merely a work programme, and the tasks arising from this programme.' 'The technical and objective direction of industry must be developed until it becomes the norm throughout the world.' The worker must become 'a new figure of prime importance'. Yet 'the submersion of the individual is a consequence of his total integration into the programme . . . There is no longer any division between combatants and non-combatants, nor between a state of peace and a state of war; and total mobilization becomes a permanency.' This theory is pure militaristic bolshevism. It tended to turn Germany, in Göring's words, into 'an unique factory, fortress and kitchen'. But it tended, as Rivaud pointed out, 'to give unlimited authority to the best technicians. Germany was put together again by the soldiers, her administrators and bankers much more than by the Nazis. But the man of genius who prompted the national movement and directed the masses in which he had aroused a feeling of fanaticism, was the man who made possible this union of demagogy and technical ability which alone made Germany's return to power possible.'

Hitlerism was the expression of a whole bundle of tendencies. It was the dream of strength through joy, that is to say the dream of the young, the adventurous, the intense in opposition to wisdom and moderation. It was also practically the same expression as the Pan-Germanism of pre-1914. But at the same time it was a method of governing and a way of economic life totally opposed to liberalism. These techniques, born of necessity, brought a positive solution to the economy of the country without, as in the case of Communism, abolishing capitalism: it was in fact the adaptation of a capitalist structure to a Communist purpose. But if one looks at the sum of these tendencies, it is clear that their purpose was a moral, intellectual and economic *militarism*, a total mobilization with an Imperial Germany as its sole end.

This was the concrete form, the whole end of the philosophy of Hegel and Nietzsche. It was the Iron Age which the latter had prophesied when he made his appeal to the 'barbarians of the twentieth century'. It was the escalating to a national level of the biological concept of selection by the strongest: that is to say that military strength was to be the only factor between the rise or fall of a nation. To survive, the German people had to identify themselves totally with the State, which planned everything to give them the maximum power. Never has a more complete or more intense expression of militarism been given than that produced by the Nazi party.

This formula was a specifically German interpretation of the ideas current at the time. Each of the dictators had produced a formula suitable for the needs of his people: Kemal and the modernization of Turkey, Lenin and the construction of a new Russian economy, Mussolini and the virile education of his people. Hitler himself saw conquest 'guaranteed by the triumphant sword of a people endowed with the power to master the world and administer it in the service of a higher civilisation'; it is a wild, Wagnerian dream, lost in the wastes of Valhalla.

Thus their defeat had imposed on the German Army the necessity for a *blitzkrieg*, and the Nazi revolution made possible the total effort which would be required for this military *coup*; all that remained was the need to find an occasion—first to opt out of the Treaty of Versailles and then to strike for the domination of which they dreamed. This became Hitler's main task. This man, with the masses behind him, was to use every connivance of diplomacy and strategy to raise himself, for a time at least, to the highest peaks of conquest.

Later, no doubt, this phase in the history of the Reich will be taken as a model.

The German renaissance, unlike most historic phenomena, was deliberately planned and carried out with astonishing sureness. Hitler thus occupied an almost unique position: that of the prophet allied to the man of action.

The development of events during this period, in spite of the deliberate smoke-screen of propaganda, shows clearly the two ideas which brought them about.

The first was that Hitler pursued one end: to bring about a political and strategic situation that would make possible the violent conflict which he considered indispensable. The Germans were conscious of having failed in 1914 because good military preparations were compromised by a faulty political set-up: they were determined not to make the same mistake again. This time the political situation should bring military action its just rewards. This was Hitler's broad theory, specifically set out in *Mein Kampf*. At the same time one conception was unavoidable: that Germany was weak and isolated, surrounded by enemies relatively strong and linked by treaties of alliance. This postulated that she would have to gather sufficient strength to break the net of mutual guarantees woven round her by France; and this in turn meant eventual military action, to be preceded by a period of preparation which would make success inevitable. This was Hitler's objective in the period 1934–40.

The second idea which dominated the politics of these six years was that this period of preparation was to be brought about by new methods which constituted the first application of what the Germans called *Wehrpolitik*.

What was this new method? Our lack of curiosity as to what was going on on the other side of the Rhine left us in complete ignorance until the very eve of Munich. We then discovered the true meaning of the studies made by Professor Haushofer and Professor Banse: namely, that total war was to be expanded through all its international implications; since war was no longer to be limited to military operations, it should be possible in peacetime to apply the principles of total war. By this means a state of war could be distinguished from a state of peace only by actual shooting, and thus there was evolved a state of undeclared war.

This kind of war is waged through the paralysis of the enemy's will to fight, by encouraging at one and the same time a belief in one's ultimate success and in the virtue of one's cause. It is the total application of a psychological concept of war. In order to whittle away their enemy's resistance the Nazis had recourse to new methods of political and propaganda infiltration; they used these with diabolical ingenuity, at the same time appearing to offer a threat of military and economic power which bore no relation to the truth. Advancing on several fronts with a co-ordinated plan, they were able to exert irresistible pressures, applied now here, now there, in order to produce the best possible conditions for the military action which was eventually envisaged. The method was the same in each case: the diplomatic isolation of one potential opponent, an instillation of doubt in the mind of the public in that country, constant pressure even to the point of a *coup d'état* in order to produce an element of hesitation in the opposing government, followed by a show of strength: the whole amounting to a monstrous campaign of intimidation. Generally capitulation followed without recourse to arms; if not, the military action which followed was more a summary execution than a battle, because of the favourable strategic situation which had already been set up and because of the *blitzkrieg*.

This complicated German manoeuvre succeeded five times in succession, giving to the simple facts of geography a new vocabulary—geopolitics and psychopolitics, which took into account firstly the strategic meaning of the map and secondly the moral standing of their eventual enemies. Both were founded on a biological and political concept, and they imposed a close examination of the real strength of neighbouring powers; this revealed a fatal weakness which was ripe for exploitation. The conclusions which they could not help but reach on the weakness of England and the hopeless decadence of France formed the basis and the justification for Hitler's grandiose plan.

A little earlier I cited the pitiless criticism of France written by one observer: 'France is the kind of nation which dies. . . .'

No wonder that Hitler drew from such judgements great encouragement for embarking upon his extraordinary enterprise.

We have seen that the political situation in Europe in 1933 imposed on Hitler the necessity of not risking any major conflict until he had been able to turn to his own advantage the gifts which lay to hand. This preparatory phase bore two aspects: internally it was necessary to create the strongest possible military force, while abroad it was essential bit by bit to destroy the political system which Foch had constructed. Rearmament on the one hand and the splitting of one's potential adversaries on the other: such was the plan on which Hitler embarked and in which he succeeded, thanks to the incredible blindness of his future victims.

Germany's rearmament, undertaken when she felt she had regained her power, was masterly. The Reichswehr understood that military might could not be accomplished without industrial backing of a high order; the problem therefore was not, as with us, one of creating huge armed forces, then at a given moment switching private industry to a war footing, but on the contrary of preceding any visible military action by the undertaking of a vast material programme. A plan was worked out which not only equipped the new army quickly but also provided the means for a great immediate productive capacity in the event of war, in the knowledge that their potential enemies would need one or two years to gear themselves to anything resembling the same rate of production. Germany's answer to our timorous attitude to stock-piling was a gigantic plan of equipment which would give her a two years' lead over us at the outbreak of hostilities.

This policy, fashioned in 1932, was spread over every branch of industry: metallurgy, chemical products, transport and aircraft. The extent of the effort can be made plain by a few figures: the number of man-hours worked in the country per month rose from 620 million in September 1932 to 1,535 million in September 1937; the number of skilled workers in industry which was 3,706,000 in 1932 rose in five years to 7,187,000. But this general stepping-up of industry by more than 100 per cent was applied specifically to the needs of the Army: the automobile industry, for example, which employed 66,000 workers in 1933 had by 1937 expanded to 210,000, an increase of 300 per cent, which reflected clearly the recognized need for mobility in the *blitzkrieg* to come. I have not been able to obtain the figures for aircraft but I am sure that they would speak for themselves equally clearly.

Such an effort constituted at one and the same time not only the best preparation for war, but the best policy of internal economy: the Hitler régime, thanks to rearmament, recruitment and industrial increase, completely absorbed the unemployment problem; while by artificially stifling the crisis which was hanging over German industry, it pleased those who had given financial backing to the movement.

But this kind of programme postulates inexhaustible funds and every modern State has at one time or another bowed beneath the fantastic burden which it finds itself forced to undertake. Ever since 1918 France had drifted from crisis to crisis without finding any solution to the problem which obsessed her political life and paralysed any chance of military rehabilitation. Hitler did not suffer from the same difficulties because his Government was made up of the best technical brains available and its economic policy was placed in the hands of a financial wizard: Dr Schacht. This man, who had already triumphantly put to rights the affairs of the Second Reich, now succeeded in imposing an even more rigorous policy: putting into effect the theories laid down by Havenstein in 1910, he financed the enormous cost of the rearmament programme by means of an internal clearing house, while supporting the value of the mark abroad by a most rigorous exchange control. By these means, which had already appealed to the financial autarchy of the USSR, Schacht was able to release Hitler from the shackles of normal budgetary control and give him unlimited means for his purpose without damaging the financial image of the State in the world market. A genuine *deus ex machina*, he gave Germany financial autonomy at a time when her aggressive policy would have cut across the world money market which had up to that moment kept her going. He was in effect the real architect of Germany's rebirth. Thanks to him, Germany could pay for her armaments, pay her soldiers and her civil servants, plus the cost of her social development and propaganda—thus making possible the total mobilization which the General Staff desired.

During this time new cadres, new pilots, new technicians were phased in, perfectly synchronized with the manpower and production plan, so that the Army expanded exactly in tune with the demands of foreign policy and the rhythm of production from 1932 to 1936—these four years were needed for industrial development and the training of military cadres. In 1936 the main clauses of the Treaty of Versailles were repudiated and in the three years thereafter, with a speed which must cast an element of doubt on its genuine strength, the little Reichswehr grew to the point at which it could absorb and use the industrial potential of the whole of Germany. By means of this extraordinary forethought and organization Hitler forged the weapon which he needed to have in his hand for the achievement of his foreign policy.

In foreign policy the general design of renascent Germany yields so easily to study that it is simple, while tracing the general outline, to show the plan followed and each step of its realization.

The initial plan is easy to see, for it is described clearly in *Mein Kampf*: 'People of the same blood' should be in the same Reich. . . . When the territory of the Reich embraces all the Germans and finds itself unable to assure them a livelihood, only then can the moral right arise, from the need of the people, to acquire foreign territory.' Therefore 'as a State, the German Reich shall include all Germans. Its task is . . . to lead them slowly and surely to a dominant position in the world.' Thus are set out from page one of the book the bases of the policies of 'racism' and 'living space'.

The living space vital to Germany is to the East: 'in Russia and [in] the border States subject to her', and Hitler set down his famous phrase: 'We put an end to the perpetual Germanic march towards the south and west of Europe and turn our eyes towards the lands of the east.' This conception was none other than the old

Prussian tradition, conquering the Slavic territories; it fitted in even better with the anti-Communist ideology of the Nazi party.

But to undertake this conquest, Germany had to avoid tangling with a powerful coalition: 'The German nation . . . must not fall into the errors of the pre-War period and make the whole world its enemy. But it must ascertain who is its most dangerous enemy, so that it can concentrate all its forces in a struggle first to beat him.' [In fact the main adversary is France which must be knocked out before any march to the East can be undertaken.] 'France is and will remain the implacable enemy of Germany', but 'today we are all convinced of the necessity of regulating our situation in regard to France; but . . . it can have significance for us only if it serves to cover our flank in the struggle for that extension of territory which is necessary for the existence of our people in Europe.'

In view of this definite statement concerning France, Germany had to avoid the same dangers of blockade and war on several fronts which had occurred in 1914–18. She hoped to avoid them in the future by keeping open maritime communications and by successively isolating her adversaries.

To achieve this aim Germany had to practise a policy of alliance: '. . . nothing really great in this world has ever been achieved through coalitions, but . . . is always due to the triumph of the individual.' These alliances are forged 'under the prospect of common gain and conquest'. Who were to be Germany's partners in this struggle for supremacy? Hitler analysed the situation and concluded: 'Taking this point of view into consideration, only two states remain to us as possible allies in Europe—England and Italy.'

England would bring maritime security and eliminate any risk of a blockade. This end appeared to Hitler to be of capital importance and justified the greatest circumspection; in criticizing the policy before 1914, he traced the broad outline of the conduct which he envisaged: 'No sacrifice should have been considered too great if it was a necessary means of gaining England's friendship. Colonial and naval ambitions should have been abandoned and attempts should not have been made to compete against British industries. Only a clear and definite policy could lead to such an achievement. Such a policy would have demanded a renunciation of the endeavour to conquer the world's markets, also a renunciation of colonial intentions and naval power. All the means of power at the disposal of the State should have been concentrated on the military forces by land.' On the other hand he thought that England had doubts about France from the very day after victory, would readily fall in with his European projects, and would be interested in the carve-up of the French colonial empire.

With a free hand once more on the Continent, means had to be found of dividing Europe, so far united against Germany by France. Here the logical move seemed to be the reconstitution of a *Mittel Europa* with Italy, which was justifiably revisionist, discontented, imperialist and the cradle of fascism. Thus it can be seen that against France there would be set 'the most powerful of flanking movements', which would constitute a continuous screen from the Baltic to the Sahara, behind which the Little Entente would find itself isolated and easily broken up.

For all that, this manoeuvre could only succeed if it were wrapped up in ideologies with the object of encouraging national energy and disguising from the enemy the real objective. These smoke-screens were first the campaign against the Versailles '*Diktat*' and the 'equality of rights', then the Wilsonian theory of the right of peoples to choose their own fate as applied to the extension of the Reich to all German-speaking peoples; then the less idealistic theory of 'living space'; later Pan-Europeanism; and lastly the anti-Communist crusade. But at each step 'It is important that the leader succeed in making the masses believe that each partial step to be attained, or conquered, is an end in itself and the only target worthy of their attention.'

Thus this plan, so clear and of such remarkable architecture, appeared in its execution as a series of surprises delivered in unexpected directions.

Such was the initial plan, written in 1923. What was the realization to be? The main lines are well remembered today: the division of Europe, creation of the Greater German Reich, the crushing of France, conquest of the Ukraine and the Eastern Marches. At first sight everything seems to have gone off as expected.

But one can at once see a capital difference, which is that the plan set out in *Mein Kampf* rested vitally upon an alliance with

England. It is fair to say that Hitler did everything to realize this essential part of his programme: following his seizure of power he sent Ribbentrop to London with the object of bringing about a *rapprochement*; later, in 1935, he himself succeeded in concluding a naval pact—much more in the spirit of the *Mein Kampf* policy—by which he undertook to limit the German fleet to 35 per cent of the British. He hoped thereby to lull rising misgivings. But despite this he failed, not only because Ribbentrop was clumsy in London, but above all because English complicity in his designs was just not in the nature of things.

In effect an alliance with England was only possible if France remained a threat to the British Empire, as those in power in Downing Street had feared immediately after 1918. In fact France showed absolute friendship towards England; there was no clash of interests between the two peoples; on the contrary from Herriot to Blum, through Tardieu, French policy continually evolved along the lines of understanding. Indeed the imperialist policy of Italy in the Mediterranean controlled which of the two would be the eventual ally of Germany; for a moment Hitler hesitated—if France sided with Italy, it would be Germany which would provide the armies for England on the Continent. But at this decisive moment France opted resolutely for England. Then, the German tendency being always to take the line of least resistance, Hitler played the Continental card of the Berlin-Rome Axis, instead of the world card which an alliance with England would have been. Thus fatally the initial plan was upset.

This plan was without doubt impossible of realization, for it seemed out of the question to associate England, the pivot of Versailles and of Geneva and a profoundly democratic nation, with a policy both revisionist and fascist. Hitler consoled himself by listening to Ribbentrop—who assured him that England would let him have his way out of weakness and lack of understanding—and above all by reading the geopoliticians who saw in England 'an Empire in decline', a colossus with feet of clay. England, occupied with her own worldwide difficulties, so slow to understand and to realize, would be faced by a *fait accompli* before she would have time to rearm. In any case, if war did break out, would not Germany's aerial supremacy allow her to outclass the British fleet?

Thus Hitler's attitude towards England evolved. Even in 1939 he thought that he was right: once, twice, three times England remained inconsistent, at least in appearance. But the seizure of Czechoslovakia in March 1939 opened the blindest eyes. England with her proverbial tenacity began to move, clumsily, slowly, but surely. From then on she was to be the enemy of Hitler everywhere as she had been of Napoleon, an enemy irreconcilable and impregnable in her island. And the whole plan of *Mein Kampf*, its patient preparation, its successive successes in preventing a world coalition: all went for naught. Hitler was caught in an infernal circle and found himself driven into precisely that which he wished to avoid: war on several fronts and a blockade. By having misunderstood the possibilities in the English question, Hitler was forced to face a problem of a magnitude which he had never expected. The day on which, in 1935, he played the Continental card, he lost the war to come.

But let us go back to examine the development of his manoeuvre.

The essential factor of his European policy was the Axis, that is to say the strategic and geographic division of the Continent; it was the reproduction, more efficacious because it reached the central Mediterranean, of the *Mittel Europa* situation, or rather the empire of Charles V, and also of the ancient Guelph tradition of the Germanic Holy Roman Empire which he proposed to reconstitute. To form the Axis two objects had to be attained: the Italian alliance and the Anschluss with Austria, which formed the pivot and the point of contact of the eventual Germano-Italian fronts. But in 1932 these two objects seemed inconceivable since Italy sought to assure her security to the north by means of a buffer in the shape of Austria, where she exercised her influence through the Dollfuss government.

Logically Hitler needed the quickest possible agreement with Italy on the grounds of fascist solidarity and the unity of revisionist views. Immediately he came to power he went to see Mussolini. But the Venice meeting was a setback: Mussolini distrusted this too young partner; and furthermore his Ethiopian projects made an understanding with France and England essential, while a still feeble Germany had nothing to offer and appeared solely as a beggar.

Hitler then tried to achieve the Anschluss first, for this project was particularly dear to him: a sentimental and personal matter, described from the very first lines of *Mein Kampf*, it would be the first application of the *'Ein Volk, ein Reich'* doctrine, and a great success for the internal policy of the new régime. The Anschluss would seem readily acceptable to the democracies, covered by the principle of the liberty of peoples to choose their own fate. It would be not only most rewarding but also the easiest line. As Germany was not yet strong, the operation would have to be subtly mounted, with no external pressure, by means of an internal *coup d'état*. But the *coup d'état*, politically ill-prepared, failed: the assassinated Dollfuss was replaced by Schuschnigg, Italy mobilized, France roused. Hitler realized that nothing would be achieved without serious political and military preparation.

The Four Power Pact allowed him to re-enter the European political scene beside England, France and Italy. But Italy, occupied with preparations for her Ethiopian adventure and warned by the *coup d'état* in Vienna, went into an accord tending towards stability in Europe in exchange for a blank cheque in Ethiopia. England, unaware at the time of the German menace, hesitated; France, on the other hand, took advantage of the occasion and, by the Laval agreements of January 1935, as I have said earlier, mounted a military consortium against Germany which effected a liaison with the Little Entente by acquiring the right to send a French expeditionary force through Italy to the Danube. The Vienna failure had had disastrous consequences for Germany which found herself more encircled than ever.

Hitler drew back and bided his time. From the recent events he reached the conclusion that the Anschluss could only be brought about with Italy's agreement and with good military cover on the French frontier. In order not to run the risk of exchanging Austria for the left bank of the Rhine, this cover postulated possession of the Rhineland.

The trouble brought to Europe at the end of 1935 by the conquest of Ethiopia gave him the chance he was waiting for. England, so blind in Europe, was more sensitive to anything impinging on her Empire and its communications; when she saw Italy committed, she unmasked her batteries and believed that she could bring her to a halt, a miscalculation which led to sanctions. Germany then kept aloof, with the result that Italy was drawn nearer to her, while the bridges between Italy and France and England were broken— the dangerous Laval agreements were nullified and England was preoccupied in the Mediterranean. The moment had come to strike the first blow.

The prime move in the game which enabled him finally to snuff out Austria was the renunciation of the Locarno Pact and of Part Five of the Treaty of Versailles—that is to say the remilitarization of the left bank of the Rhine and the proclamation of equality of rights in military material. Thus he achieved three objectives: morally he affirmed Germany's revival, materially he opened the way for his own rearmament programme, strategically he improved his cover against France in case she found herself constrained to denounce the Anschluss. It was an impeccable move.

The realization was no less good. The manoeuvre was to be the first in the new style: based on secrecy and speed, it was carried out with extraordinary audacity, for his forces were insufficient and mobilization impossible. Furthermore the German General Staff were opposed to the idea, as they did not consider themselves ready, but Hitler judged better, he knew that we would not move. At the same time he covered his action with a thick layer of political equivocation: he made out that he was interested solely in the honour of Germany and the elimination of all that remained of the infamous Versailles *Diktat*, which constituted the last obstacle hindering an understanding with France. From the height of his tribunal, before electrified crowds, he offered France a twenty-five years' peace and proposed to 'bury the hatchet of war'. Hitler was right: we did not move, despite England's passive argument (we would rather she had helped us) and we have seen why. Hitler triumphed, he had demonstrated his strength and shown up the weakness of the French scarecrow. He had only to exploit this success to pick up the winnings from his gamble.

It is true he was favoured by the Communist agitation which was brewing in western Europe. Playing his ideological anti-Communist role, he could afford to wait until his rearmament was completed, while dividing and isolating France and while tying up more closely his interests with those of Italy in the Mediterranean.

There was no difficulty about the division of France: since 6 February 1934 France had been made up of Nationalists and Reds.

The set-back to Laval's policy of deflation, and above all the action on 6 February considered as 'provocative', led to a wave of 'anti-fascism' which was supported by England (who feared at one moment that Laval would pursue a policy favourable to Italy and thought that a Blum government would be solid Democrat), and by Russia (which wished to control the Western governments by Communism in order to build up an ally behind the back of the German danger). The elections naturally put in power the *Front Populaire*, the excesses of which soon brought a violent national reaction. Hitler aided this reaction which gave him a foot in internal French politics, the consequences of which were to be seen during the war. By a sad change of position, the anti-German parties of the left became militaristic and were accused of being 'bellicose', while the nationalists became pacifists at any price: from this moment the traditional unanimity towards Germany was broken.

As to the isolation of France, he had only to pluck the fruits of Germany's anti-Communist position, strengthened by the prestige gained through his success in March. The *Frente Popular* in Spain had given Hitler the opportunity of helping Franco's military revolution. In giving aid he gained in several ways; he further strengthened his ties with Italy in the Mediterranean, he prepared for himself a valuable strategic platform against France and England, finally and above all he gained an important ideological position. The 'fascist solidarity' would permit him to appear as a maintainer of order and brought him the sympathies of the reactionaries who exist in every country: Yugoslavia drew nearer; Belgium, which was no longer shielded by the demilitarized Rhineland, returned to neutrality; Japan signed the Anticomintern Pact, theoretically an anti-Russian gesture but which under the guise of anti-Bolshevism gave her the possibility of a powerful diversion in China and in the Pacific to paralyse England; Poland, fundamentally anti-Russian, signed an accord and separated from France. Then on 24 October the German policy attained its first highly desired objective: Hitler and Mussolini concluded in Rome an alliance based upon their ideological solidarity, on their friendship born out of sanctions—confirmed upon the battlefields of Spain—and on the existence of common interests in the Mediterranean and the Far East. The Rome-Berlin Axis was born, the first step was completed.

However, the agreement was still precarious and perhaps would not stand up to the Anschluss. Hitler did not lose sight of his objective but, learning from the previous annoying experience, he waited until he had every trump in his hand, the German strength organized, the ties with Italy strengthened by success in Spain, and France still further weakened by internal division (he had great hopes of the CSAR, an extreme right-wing organization, at this time). Meanwhile he made some play with claims for the return of Germany's colonies which, as he had said in *Mein Kampf*, were quite contrary to his real views.

A year later, in September 1937, the Axis began to harden, Franco-Italian relations grew considerably colder, Mussolini paid a visit to Hitler. Seduced by the gigantic parades and grandiose views of the future, he was won over and acquiesced in the project. The Anschluss was under way. But the military commanders hesitated once more: Hitler dismissed Blomberg and Fritsch in February 1938 and organized his definitive military team with Brauchitsch and Keitel. France was wallowing in internal troubles. Everything was ready. On 11 March he launched the operation against Austria, a combination of internal agitation and military pressure. Schuschnigg gave way; the Anschluss was completed, the second objective achieved; the cutting up of Europe was now plainly realizable.

Now Hitler could move into the second phase, the pressure on Central Europe and the break-up of the Little Entente. This, by its position, constituted the most dangerous bloc; it was also, by its division into new countries, riddled with massive minorities, the weak link in the Versailles chain. Faithful to his principle of taking the line of least resistance, he made no move other than the organization of his plans, which required no more than one year.

For this the obvious objective was Czechoslovakia, soul of the Little Entente, the Slavic *avant-garde* in Central Europe and ally of the USSR with a frontier which drove like a wedge into the flank of the Reich. Three-quarters encircled by Germany since the Anschluss, her military defence thus became unviable.

But, made prudent by experience, Hitler carefully prepared the way: first he succeeded in the disunion of the Little Entente by various means. Now he was playing upon the anti-Communist complex in Yugoslavia and Rumania (where a tentative *putsch* by the

Iron Guard had recently failed); now he created links of economic solidarity by fruitful agreements with the agricultural countries which were delighted to find a buyer for their excess production; now he was asserting that France was out of reach of these neighbours—and French influence was certainly declining; at the same time he suggested that a parting would be fruitful and would also bring in Hungary, Poland and perhaps also Rumania. But this was not all: when it came to the test the going would be hard and it was absolutely necessary to paralyse the slightest offensive ideas remaining in France. The showpieces, at once military and psychological, were the construction of the Siegfried Line, and the invitation extended to General Vuillemin, in order to impress him, to visit the young Luftwaffe.* Then there remained the usual camouflage of his intentions by able propaganda: the affair was presented to the world as a purely German matter and concerned only the oppressed Sudetens who were rightly coming to a point of revolt: Czechoslovakia itself was not the target and only the Reich and all Germans were in question.

The action, magnificently orchestrated by the manifestations and the speeches at the Munich Congress, began. Czechoslovakia, undermined from within by a fifth column and the Henlein party, was subjected to strong diplomatic pressure by the Allies, impressed as they were by the Siegfried Line (not yet finished at that time) and by Göring's Luftwaffe, they preferred sacrificing the strategic frontiers of a country to the threat of general war for which they were not prepared. Finally Hitler raised his voice and massed his forces concentrically round Bohemia. The feeble, soft Chamberlain and the hesitant Daladier gave in. It was Munich. The military ally of France, the cornerstone of Foch's strategic system, was dismantled, and this with the help of the great democracies. The success was enormous. Hitler had succeeded not only in knocking out Czechoslovakia, but primarily in causing France to lose face before her one-time satellites: the Little Entente was completely broken up; the USSR, remote from the negotiations, was rejected from European politics; Poland and Hungary, beneficiaries from the carve-up, became a solid part of the new order.

* With the same intention, unprecedented disclosures were made to Captain Stehlin, our Assistant Military Attaché in Berlin (see *Témoignage pour l'Histoire*).

It remained to exploit the reduction of Czechoslovakia to impotence. With diabolical ability Hitler equivocated once again: the day after Munich he pretended to inaugurate a new policy based on the maintenance of the *status quo* in the West and a free hand in eastern Europe. Then he talked about the Ukraine, a vague term by which everyone thought he meant the USSR. This policy was sanctioned by two agreements with England and France, culminating in a visit to Paris by Ribbentrop, the preparations for which were fruitfully made by Abetz who formed certain useful intelligence links and distributed a good deal of money.

In the first beautiful days of March, by surprise Hitler flung his troops into Prague and forced President Hacha to recognize the German Protectorate. Almost simultaneously the Italian partner laid hands on Albania, an operation which was some recompense for the Anschluss, and which above all closed the Adriatic to any aid which might be needed by Yugoslavia.

Germany was now mistress of the Danube and overshadowed the Balkans. Allied prestige was ruined, the Little Entente dispersed, and the USSR profoundly disappointed. At the military level the profit was immense: forty divisions of Czech prisoners with their stores, which meant equipment for forty German divisions—a turn-around of eighty divisions, equal to the army of France. The remaining central powers in Europe were depressed to see weighed against them something like the 130 divisions which Foch had foreseen, and still the German power was increasing day by day.

Hitler could now risk the next phase.

After having dislocated and digested central Europe, would Hitler now turn against France? No, not yet, for he might find himself once again in the position of 1914–18 and be obliged to wage war on two fronts, which he had to avoid at any price. The Allies in fact had reacted to the occupation of Prague by guaranteeing Poland, Rumania and Greece and by opening negotiations with the USSR. It was necessary at all costs to speed everything up so as to prevent the formation of an Eastern bloc.

For this two operations were required: to snuff out the Allies' alliance with Russia (more about that in the next chapter), and then to destroy Poland without risk. The preparatory phases would then be completed and Germany could embark upon the great test, 'the final settling of accounts with France', before extending her domination over the territories of eastern Europe.

I will there end this study of the development of the extraordinary manoeuvre of *Wehrpolitik* which Hitler developed from 1934 on. A marvel of precision, preparation and logic maintained in the midst of the known movements of policy, it constituted a masterpiece of a kind the like of which will not be seen again for a long time, either for its cynicism or its efficiency.

The comparison with our hesitant and vague policy, with our limited and gutless doctrines, shows that our defeat was written in the results achieved by Hitler. In 1935, at the time of the Laval agreements in Rome, the military system conceived by Foch made possible the bringing together against Germany a minimum of 280 divisions (French, Belgian, Italian, the Little Entente and Poland) to which might be added the forces of the USSR (110 divisions) and of England. After the constitution of the Axis Germany gained eighty divisions (Italy, Hungary, Bulgaria) while our forces declined by almost the same amount. After the destruction of Czechoslovakia, Germany, deploying 130 divisions, could count on a further seventy-five divisions from her allies, making a total of over 200, whilst we were reduced to fewer than 200 divisions (France, England, Poland, Rumania). This is why we logically sought the balancing weight of Russia and considered that this was our last chance of entering the conflict with more or less equal forces. After the destruction of Poland, the balance was finally broken: 132 Allied divisions (France, England, Belgium, Holland) had to face 270 in 1940. Nothing can make clearer than these two figures the frightening success of Hitler's undertakings.

Meanwhile something big with consequence had come about to make all his initial calculations false: the fact that Great Britain ranged herself among his adversaries. Today one is torn between admiration for the success achieved, and astonishment that such a change caused no modification of the elaborate projects. Germany went on to the end of 1940 just as if the plan laid down in *Mein Kampf* was her unique destiny, as if the war must be won on the Continent, as if Great Britain were not among her enemies. Great Britain was thus given a respite in which to improve her insufficient preparations, and when Germany finally saw that she would have to conquer the island, the hour had passed and a landing was impossible.

What a lesson—that such rigidity of execution can bring to nothing a plan the earlier stages of which were realized with such complete mastery!

FATE

Chapter 6
Mission to Moscow

*

O<small>N</small> 4 A<small>UGUST</small> 1939 the French military mission left Paris for London, seen off at the station by M. Maisky, Soviet Ambassador in Paris. There they were to join the British mission and proceed to the USSR by sea. The idea was to use the time on the voyage in order to establish a common Franco-British approach, for hitherto little had been done in this field.

The French delegation was led by General Doumenc, a subtle and imaginative polytechnic graduate who had shown his ability by organizing the motor transport during the battle of Verdun, General of Aviation Valin, brother of the present Inspector General, a Captain of Corvette, a Major as interpreter, the General's ADC and myself.

The task before us was vital. Our repulse in the end was complete and led to the beginning of the Second World War. This repulse, we shall see, resulted from the incredible contradictions of our policy. I think it is not without interest to give a fairly detailed account of these vicissitudes, so serious in their consequences, in which were clearly revealed the vagueness of our conceptions and our complete inability to settle on a line of conduct.

The invasion in March 1939 of what was left of Czechoslovakia crowned Germany's Danube policy and left her hands free to go on to the next stage. On the Allied side, this *coup de force* opened even the blindest eyes and showed the necessity for an energetic diplomatic recovery if there was to be any chance at all of avoiding the next conflict.

As we have seen in the previous chapter, German policy had succeeded in upsetting every construction and all the guarantees which French policy had built up in Europe against the day of German recovery. Now it was necessary—and under the threat of imminent war at that—to go into fresh combinations which might be able to hold Hitler's projects, that is to say to re-form a bloc of states attached to the Entente, destined to constitute an eastern front, a front in rear of the enemy which French policy had always tried to establish and which would replace the action of the Russian Empire during the previous war.

But the constitution of this front, instead of being carried out as of old by alliances and military treaties, took the form of post-war treaties on the basis of legal formulae grafted on to the Pact. Moreover it was a question of unilateral guarantees which Britain and then France gave for the maintenance of the frontiers of this country or that; but, even if unilateral, these guarantees were not given without the agreement of other interested countries and required negotiations as difficult as a treaty of alliance.

This policy of guarantees brought with it the greatest possible inconvenience. It made the peace of western Europe dependent upon the whole of eastern Europe at a time when it was obvious that the latter was tumbling in ruins, and that no organized groups could be formed strong enough to make the enemy think again. Besides, this policy contributed to inflaming the conflict and made it certain that Germany, which could not now stop without grave difficulty, was bound to react. Thus on 18 April Hitler renounced the German-Polish pact in reply to the British guarantee given to Poland; and almost immediately the disgrace of Litvinov, known for his Geneva sympathies, gave some indication of a possible reversal of Russian policy vis-à-vis Germany. In fact on 7 May the French Ambassador at Berlin sent a signal that Hitler had decided to settle the Polish question, and it was for this reason that he felt the need of Russia, with whom he contemplated the fourth partition of Poland.*

From this moment the German attitude towards Poland became more and more aggressive; incidents multiplied and the tension mounted from day to day. It is true that on their side the Poles, superbly unaware, would not give way on any point and appeared determined to settle the Danzig question by force of arms.

The German-Polish tension, which poisoned the second quarter of 1939, gravely affected Franco-German relations. On 13 July, in reply to a note from Georges Bonnet, Ribbentrop sent to the Quai d'Orsay a personal letter in which he said that Germany rejected any French interference in her vital spheres of influence and concluded with these words: 'If conditions are such that the French

* See General Stehlin, *Témoignage pour l'Histoire*.

Government wishes war, it will find Germany ready at any time.'

Faced by the menace of war, which grew more acute from day to day, I have said that the Allied policy was to construct an eastern front. But this front was still very fragile. The forty Polish and twenty Rumanian divisions were spread over a front of several thousand miles which the Germans could penetrate where and when they chose. It was necessary to strengthen these divisions with considerable forces and above all to give them the possibility of holding out by providing them with the space and the necessary resources to prevent an almost immediate collapse. These forces, this space and resources only the USSR was in a position to provide. Thus the Allies themselves were led to seek the aid of the Soviet. This aid, we have seen, was indispensable from the military point of view; to obtain it was the sole chance of preventing war—at least so far as 1939 was concerned.

Negotiations with the USSR had been opened. In spite of all the good reasons which we have enumerated, it was necessary to overcome much repugnance both in France and England; the Soviet by its meddling in other people's internal politics had become a bugbear; furthermore official relations, which for a while had been excellent in 1935 at the time of the Laval-Potemkin agreement, had grown markedly colder after the Munich agreement when Russia felt bitterly hurt at being totally excluded from the negotiations.

For these reasons the *pourparlers* with the Russians by the ambassadors accredited to Moscow had no success. This procedure was not a happy one because it gave the Soviets the impression that France and Britain took them no more seriously than to act through intermediaries at a secondary level. On the other hand there seems no doubt that the French and British Ambassadors at Moscow did not carry enough weight with their own Governments to prevail upon their seniors to follow the policy directions which were obviously logical. The result was that these negotiations dragged on for five months and very quickly degenerated into sterile discussions on niceties of wording.

Public opinion, which confusedly gathered the importance of what was at stake, was astonished and impatient to see that no substantial results had emerged from several months of discussion.

It was obvious that a new approach was required: the Soviets had asked on several occasions that top level representatives should be sent to them, and at one time there was talk of Lord Halifax's going to Moscow. At the last moment he was taken ill, no doubt diplomatically, and replaced by Mr Strang,* a civil servant, whose departure and return by aeroplane served no useful purpose except that it provided a few news photographs.

By the end of July the negotiations had arrived at this point: the Soviet Government was ready to conclude a pact of mutual assistance in the event of German aggression, to include all the States the frontiers of which had been guaranteed by the Allies. But the Soviet Government wished the treaty explicitly to take cognizance not only of direct aggression but also of indirect aggression, and to the latter they gave a very wide interpretation. Furthermore the USSR was not prepared to guarantee the frontiers of Holland or Switzerland until Poland and Turkey had concluded pacts of mutual assistance with themselves.

When one reads today the text of the projected Franco-Anglo-Soviet treaty, one asks how diplomacy could get itself to such a blind and finicky point and let an agreement of so great importance slip through its fingers because of minor differences.

Let there be no misunderstanding. Under these anodyne formulae, the question was nothing less than the independence of the Baltic States. The definition which the Soviet put upon 'indirect aggression' would have allowed her to seize them at any moment, and we did not wish to see them abandoned to the USSR. This attitude would have been valid in itself if it had corresponded to any positive conceptions. But in fact since we were asking for something from Russia, it was necessary to admit that they had the upper hand. Further, it was quite obvious that we would be totally unable in any case, short of allying ourselves with Germany, to prevent the USSR from taking the Baltic States whenever they wished.

M. Naggiar, our Ambassador in Moscow, sent word that the Russians asked that the negotiations be reopened by means of military missions. It seemed possible that this could be a psychological shock which might lead to a result. No one saw that to reach

* Now Lord Strang.

military agreement without political agreement was to put the cart before the horse and that all the problems which one had been trying to avoid would appear on the table with a new and sharper edge.

Everything now depended on the instructions which our missions had received. But these were vague on essential points and terribly negative on the points which were bound to become crucial in the course of the negotiations. They must be examined with care.

The instructions were elaborated in the course of Franco-British conversations on 13 July 1939 and at the meeting of the Chiefs of the General Staff on 17 July.

At the Franco-British reunion of 13 July 1939, there was largely an exchange of questionnaires. That proposed by General Gamelin was as follows:

I   Communications with Europe:
     by sea : Murmansk, Archangel
     by air : through Scandinavia

II   Action in the Baltic against Germany's sea lines { Aircraft / Submarine } { Attitude of Finland and the Baltic States. }

III   Polish and Rumanian fronts { Security of the eastern frontiers of these States. / Provision and servicing of warlike material. / Provisions of basic materials (corn, coal, metals). / Supply of aircraft. }

IV   Turkish front { Seaborne action in the Aegean by warships, merchant ships and transports. / Action of the Army in Thrace. / Aircraft action: co-operation in action against the Dodecanese. / Various supplies. }

It will be seen that so far as the Polish and Rumanian frontiers were concerned, the only question which arose was important aerial support from Russia; the use of Russian troops was never envisaged.

The conclusions of the Chiefs of Staff when they met on 17 July took up much the same points. Nevertheless so far as the Polish and Rumanian theatres were concerned the formula became somewhat enlarged: the mission was to examine the following questions: 'Reinforcement of the Polish and Rumanian armies with mechanized units, and eventually land forces [sic] if *Poland and Rumania so require*. Reassurances to be given to the two countries so far as their eastern frontier is concerned.'

In this case the provision of Soviet land forces for the benefit of Poland and Rumania was envisaged, but only by agreement with each country. What this agreement should be or how it could be brought about was never considered.

Finally on 27 July General Gamelin in sending to General Doumenc the conclusions of the 17 July meeting set out the instructions for the mission to Moscow in the following terms:

'The question of sea communication between western Europe and Murmansk is to be agreed with the British who have the command of the waters under discussion: moreover ports of departure will be in Great Britain.

As to the Mediterranean route, this poses the problem of command of this sea and well may not be, at least early in the conflict, a safe route.

As far as communication by air is concerned, the possibility of flying over Germany must not be ruled out, but it would seem that regular traffic should be re-established by civil aircraft flying a route over the neutral countries of northern Europe.

For naval action in the Baltic it would be interesting to have details of the possibilities of the Russian fleet which has fifty-two submarines in this area.

The Poles cannot officially admit, at least not in peacetime, the principle of intervention by Russian troops on their territory in the event of war; but there is no doubt that in a moment of danger they would accept the presence of Soviet aircraft, and perhaps also mechanized units. The possibility of their opening their frontiers to Russian armed forces of all kinds appears remote. On the same subject it appears that the Rumanians would be equally guarded, but the Turks might be more amenable.

Action in the eastern Mediterranean requires a settlement as quickly as possible of the Dodecanese question. This should be an operation undertaken by the Turks with the support of the British Navy and by Allied Air Forces to which Russian aircraft must be joined at the first opportunity. It is to obtain this force of Russian aircraft in the Dodecanese that you must be at your most tactful. This force will also be indispensable should Bulgaria's neutrality be untenable and should she find herself attacked either by the Turks based on Thrace or Greco-Turkish forces advancing from the region of Salonika. In these circumstances what would be the extent of USSR co-operation?

The delivery of basic materials—foodstuffs, armaments, munitions and machine tools—by Russia to Poland, Rumania and Turkey would evidently be well received by the powers concerned. It is very desirable to see the USSR furnish what France and England cannot supply, at least in the near future. The attached note enlarges on this question.

The Turks only envisage any substantial operation in the eastern Mediterranean and the Balkans once they do not consider themselves menaced by the Russians in the Caucasus; you will no doubt have an occasion to make this known to the Russians and to draw from them a desirably friendly reply.'

GAMELIN

Thus these instructions contained not a word about the political difficulties which had been raised concerning the Baltic States, and they sought to avoid completely the far more vital question of Polish-Soviet co-operation. When one rereads this text and when one looks for the idea behind its drafting, there is the impression that Russian co-operation was simply an accessory to be used with profit in any of the problems which confronted our diplomacy and our strategy and that not once had an agreement with Russia been considered as the cornerstone, the foundation of this fragile eastern wall by which we were trying hastily to avert the march of war.

It seems that this conception was as much that of the Quai d'Orsay as it was of the boulevard des Invalides. The least one can say is that there was no over-fulness or clairvoyance: simply an inventory, a catalogue of questions had been drawn up to put before the Soviets. By no means had an understanding been reached on the two essential problems—to know the policy vis-à-vis the Baltic States and on Polish-Soviet military co-operation—the examination of which imposed itself on the negotiations from the start.

The British instructions were no more satisfactory. Received in Paris during the night of 31 July–1 August, they consisted of a printed document about an inch thick which examined every facet of the problem without producing any ideas as to directive. All the same, certain passages of the text remain in mind, passages which revealed the tendencies of British diplomacy towards the problems which were going to arise. It was recommended that we should proceed only with the utmost prudence, never pass over any interesting information, bear in mind constantly that German-Soviet collusion was possible, and above all to spin out the negotiations as long as we could. It appears that the British had no illusions as to the outcome of the conversations which were about to open and that they were above all anxious to gain time. All this was far away from the dreams of public opinion.

Be that as it may, the news of the dispatch of the military missions brought a breath of hope. One newspaper wrote: 'At last the work of the military experts will give real sense to the diplomatic negotiations and will show exactly how much value may be placed upon the agreements which will be signed. Let us therefore wish them well in their work which will be to fulfil tasks as necessary as they are difficult, let us hope that their work will be swift and successful, and enable the diplomats then to bring matters to a close.'*

On 31 July M. Daladier saw General Doumenc and said to him: 'Bring us back an agreement at all costs.'

The general idea was evident; it remained to determine the means necessary to obtain such an objective. It was a particularly difficult task, especially for military representatives.

---

* See in Appendix I, page 143, the text of a telegram sent at this moment to Berlin from the German Ambassador in Paris.

At Victoria Station in London the British delegation had turned
out in force to meet the French mission for the benefit of the Press.
The first meetings in London were purely formal; serious work was
to be got down to on board ship. On the 5th, after the short train
journey from London to Tilbury, the delegations embarked before
a battery of cameras.

The *City of Exeter*, an old Ellerman ship used on the South Africa
run, chartered by the Admiralty for the occasion, was a perfect representative of the old British merchant marine. Solid, her comforts
already a little passé, capable of standing up to the worst weather,
her crew entirely Indian, she was a silent witness to the Empire.
This 9,000-ton ship, with her twenty-six officers, became for six
days the scene of a conference which was perhaps the first of its
kind.

In the course of the conference the French delegation got to know
its opposite numbers a great deal better. The senior British officer
was Admiral Reginald A. R. Plunkett-Ernle-Erle-Drax, KCB, DSO,
Naval ADC and equerry to the King, tall, mild in expression,
courteous and cold; he looked like a version of Admiral Rodney
minus the wig. His speech, slow and hesitant like that of all English
people from good families, was held up even further by constant
coughing due to a weak throat. Not very quick on the uptake
because of his scrupulous mind, he possessed utter intellectual
honesty and the will to negotiate with the Soviets in all frankness,
but was baffled by the difficulties and complexity of the task which
had been thrust upon him. Nevertheless his personality was perfectly adapted to what was expected of him: Admiral Drax represented in the highest degree the traditions of England, and in putting him at the head of the mission his Government ensured that,
in so delicate an operation as discussions with their Russian opposite
numbers, the British delegation would always instinctively react,
with the same reflexes which had made the greatness of the
Empire.

Air Vice-Marshal Sir Charles Burnett, KCB, CBE, DSO, head of
the air delegation, was also a traditional figure. Risen from the
ranks, he liked to look back on those days in the Boer War, and he
was the military type made popular in France by Colonel Bramble,
and found also in hunting prints. A high colour, bushy eyebrows, a
good chap, extremely honest and sympathetic, but obstinate—

stonily so—he never agreed to any proposition that was put forward until he understood it thoroughly and this occasionally took some time.

General T.G.G. Haywood, CBE, head of the military delegation, represented the 'technical' element of the mission. Military attaché in Paris for years, speaking perfect French, he had taken part in many conferences both in Paris and Geneva. Extremely diplomatic and able, he possessed all the finer points required in the difficult art of negotiation and he played a considerable role in the discussions.

The head of our delegation, General Doumenc, was our youngest *Général de l'Armée* (but, conforming to the rules at the time, he was still sixty. . . .) Besides his performance at Headquarters during the First World War, to which I have referred, he had made a reputation for himself, exceptional at that time, for bringing a fresh mind to questions of military tactics, particularly motorization and the use of armour. Full of faith in his mission, he fought right to the end to reconcile the irreconcilable, but never succeeded in dispelling the dangers of which his lively intelligence had been well aware from the start.

On board the *City of Exeter* life was very agreeable, punctuated by copious repasts of curry served by Indian stewards in turbans. A deck-tennis tournament between the two delegations was won by the Admiral. But life was very full. Twice a day the delegations came together in what had been the children's playroom and put their various points of view. The ice was very quickly broken, thanks to the great kindness of the hosts of the French mission. But from there to achieving an agreed programme was a big, long step. The principal difficulty sprang from the fact that the British delegation did not appear to have any well-defined, co-ordinated views and on certain points seemed to have ideas as immovable as they were negative. There was no hope of talking to the Russians until this barrier had been broken down.

General Doumenc then tried to put together a text based on the Anglo-Franco-Turkish treaty which had just been signed, from which all detail should be removed and banished to an appendix, since the agreement itself only really dealt with broad principles.

This extremely logical procedure which, as we shall see, was to be inoperable vis-à-vis the Russians, plainly went down well with the English. After four days of courteous but captious discussion a text was unanimously approved. This text, which was never to see the light, makes interesting reading today because it defines better than any explanation the spirit with which the Allied delegates were to approach the negotiations with the Soviets. I will give a summary analysis.

The preamble set out the general method to be followed for the elaboration of the treaty; this was based on a political treaty—yet to be brought about—and 'in view of the present military situation in Europe' it set out to define 'the general dispositions' which were to be completed by an appendix and detailed settlements.

Next, paragraphs one and two set out the general basic principles: fighting to the end, importance of freedom of communications, necessity for the construction of an eastern front 'continuous, solid and durable'.

Two paragraphs on the question of communications and the blockade of Germany, two more paragraphs on aid to Turkey and action in the Balkans, and next came paragraph 7, the essential paragraph, on Poland and Rumania. 'The defence of their national territory is the responsibility of the armed forces of Poland and Rumania. *The three contracting powers are however agreed to come to the aid* of the above mentioned States *as soon as they are requested to do so*, together or separately bringing them all the aid at their disposal and as may be *considered necessary*, particular importance being attached to *air support* and assistance in technical material and the provision of specialists.'

I have underlined the essential passages. That Poland would eventually require support was recognized but the principle was accepted that there should be sent into Polish territory only what the Poles asked for, which most likely would be only aircraft. It was seen that we were far from an accurate reckoning and that this conception was not that of the Russians.

Be that as it may, the approval of this treaty project represented a success for the French delegation, for the text adopted conformed absolutely with the mission with which it was charged and which we examined above. We will soon see how the Soviet reduced this careful preparation to nothing; all that remained to us was to plod on point by point following the instructions we had been given.

During this time the *City of Exeter* was approaching Russia. On the evening of 9 August, deep in the Gulf of Finland, the nordic sky, pale as mother-of-pearl and extraordinarily clear, was reflected in the sea which was as calm as a lake. Kronstadt came into sight, reminding us of the first hours of Franco-Russian alliance, where the Soviet fleet made its existence known by several fast small craft which manoeuvred round the ship.

Then calm returned as we entered a long canal open in the middle of the Gulf, a dredged passage similar to *la Goulette*, which led to the city of Leningrad. Although it was eleven o'clock at night, the sky was still bright and opaline. Leaning over the rail, all the personnel of the mission, in mess kit, as behoved us on an English vessel, enjoyed this magnificent evening and looked across at the unknown shore where the real game was to be played out. Shortly before midnight the *City of Exeter* entered the port, an immense forest of cranes and quays piled with timber, and tied up beside a wooden shed, the sordid maritime station typical of the treatment of visitors to this great country, so isolated from the rest of the world.

On the quay a few Soviet soldiers in green caps and two or three badly dressed bystanders could see on the bridge of the *City of Exeter* twenty-six officers in mess jackets and the Indian crew busy warping the ship in. It would be difficult to find a neater picture to sum up the difference between the two worlds which were now to confront one another.

At this time the USSR was still little known, hidden by opposing propagandas each as untrue as the other. Meeting the real thing was very interesting.

What struck one at once was that one was entering another world, built on the ruins of an older civilization of oriental origin, where a return to the ancient traditions combined with a modernization founded on technics. This duality of tendency foreshadowed a phenomenon which we have seen develop widely in recent years through the former colonies which make up a third of the world. The question is whether this represents the beginning of a future civilization, popular, steeped in folklore, and technic, or if it constitutes just the first reaction against the West of an ill-assimilated proletariat which wants to acquire the advantages and riches of the

West through the use of their technical knowledge, while retaining its own philosophy and civilization.

In Leningrad the fossilized remains of the first westernization of Russia are impressive: the Hermitage, Petropavlovsk, Tsarskoïe-Selo, Peterhof, but as empty of their content as is Versailles in France. Nevertheless this revolution was less iconoclastic than ours: the eagles of the Tsars were still in place, their equestrian statues still galloped across the squares. The USSR had not turned its back on the old Russia. The surprise which this discovery occasioned in us became even greater when we saw the posters exalting the Red Army, the Air Force and the Navy. There was no question that the USSR was in a nationalistic phase much nearer to the atmosphere in Germany than to the debility from which France and Great Britain were suffering at the time.

But this new world offered us one further peculiarity not known in the West with which we were to become, unhappily, only too familiar in the years to follow. This technical world lived with the outward and visible signs of poverty: threadbare clothes of unbelievable ugliness, inferior materials of every kind, even paper of the most inferior quality, queues in front of any shop which had anything to sell, the sadness of the crowds, and the vast cement buildings of uniform grey going up on all sides. The Soviet achievements were spectacular but the general level of life remained terribly low. Nevertheless, such as it was, it represented a notable advance on the annual famines which had gone before and the population, from which the pre-Revolution generations had disappeared, was now made up of old-time workers and mujiks—who had been very unhappy under the previous régime—who thought of nothing except the fact that their lot appeared to improve from day to day.

At the same time one further characteristic cast its shadow on Soviet life: the police, present everywhere and at all times. Not only was every room in the hotels and the Embassy bugged, so that the only safe place to talk was out of doors, but even in the streets people looked away so as to avoid any possible accusation of having anything to do with us. In the high Moscow summer everyone walked in the gardens and it was a curious experience to move among all these people—whether one was in uniform or mufti—as though one were an ectoplasm. Such sense of discipline had not been brought about without the executions, the penal sentences and the concentration camps. In the towns numerous yards encircled by fences and overlooked by watch-towers had been set aside for 'political prisoners', and at our Embassy it was said that every family in the land had one member inside. The result was a stifling atmosphere often described by travellers in the previous century. Communism had done nothing except change the name of the State police and improve their methods.

In sum, the USSR represented merely a translation of the Russian tradition into modern terms, an eastern State which Lenin had started once again on a march towards the West as had Peter the Great two centuries before.

The USSR forged the instruments of this western move with religious enthusiasm. Battered by posters, speeches and radio programmes, the mujiks were aroused towards the creation of a modern economy, which entailed mass production. The first Five Year Plan was a series of battles won: the battle of heavy industry, of transport, iron and corn. The essential was to reach the target, but to attain this millions died of starvation and millions more had been reduced to destitution. Now the directors of this gigantic creation were ready to embark on the next step: the era of well-being. 'Light' industries were to be created, an élite was to be encouraged, elegance and refinement were to be the word. So the heroic, proletarian spirit of the earlier epoch was succeeded by a new feeling born of patriotism and militarism. The international proletariat was no longer the main concern, but rather the Empire of Peter the Great and the frontiers of 1914. In this programme the Red Army did not appear as guardian of the Soviet State but as champion of the Russian Empire. Nor were they stinted for equipment: tanks, aircraft, ack-ack guns—Soviet industry manufactured what was required in thousands and the young Russian Army began to feel its strength. I wrote at the time 'the creation of a great and strong Russia constitutes, with the renaissance of Germany, the capital event in post-war Europe. A fragile colossus no doubt, but one the future stature of which is commensurate with its vast territories and incalculable economic riches which it is now beginning to put to work. If this Russian programme really comes to fruition, it will take a united Europe to balance it.'

Meanwhile Communist Russia noticeably turned back to the

pre-1914 state of things. It was indeed eternal Russia which appeared once again with its over-weighted bureaucracy. The élite today lived in the palaces of yesterday's Boyards. The salary differential made an orgiastic life possible for some, while the people barely subsisted on the product of their labours.

This sense of the perpetuity of Russia struck the French and British delegations when they arrived in Moscow. The reception given to the Allied delegates by Marshal Voroshilov showed, too, that nothing had changed. The delegates went to call upon the Marshal in his office—a modern office in an old administrative building rather like the French Headquarters—and it was agreed that the first session would take place the next day at the Spiridonovka, where the same evening the Marshal would be happy to receive the members of the two delegations.

The Spiridonovka is also called the Fruntze House after the very popular general, the predecessor of Voroshilov, who lived there. When this general seemed dangerous and no one dared to arrest him, he was persuaded that he needed an operation and they killed him under the anaesthetic. This house, once the palace of a wealthy merchant, is used now for the reception of foreign visitors.

A high vestibule leads to the dining-room, a huge room in mock Gothic with a monumental fireplace and an oak roof copied from that in Westminster Hall. A horseshoe table was laid out in the best tradition with fifty covers. All the table-ware bore the arms of the Tsar. The delegates in their finest uniforms (the French had only brought khaki) sat down to table. Marshal Voroshilov and his aides wore impeccable white flannel—Marshal Budyenny, the Soviet Murat, sported a magnificent pair of boots. The banquet lasted some three hours and was throughout remarkable not only for the food and wine but also for the quality of the service. All the same it seemed a pity that the servants were dressed like restaurant waiters when serving a meal of this quality.

After dinner, which vodka had made most cordial, the military cortège moved into the music room, a large white apartment copied from Versailles with a magnificent inlaid parquet floor, but too brightly lit. At a word from the Marshal everyone sat down round the sides and the end of the too-white room forming a semi-circle of uniforms, decorations, cigars and red well-fed faces which would have delighted an anti-military caricaturist. In front, and very moved, a little old man in a dinner jacket dating, like himself, from before the Revolution, announced in the three languages the names of the performers as they appeared. The concert which followed was as remarkable for the talent of the artists as it was for the variety of their clothes: a dinner jacket was finished off with grey slippers or a coloured shirt, one female singer wore a long dress which looked as if it had come from some minor German court in the last century but appeared to be the height of the current fashion, while a woman violinist of exceptional temperament, dressed in a tennis dress with close-cropped hair, represented the last Spartan swan-song of the first Five Year Plan.

That evening, memorable for its quality and for the value of the symbols which it revealed, opened under favourable auspices the negotiations which were to begin the next day. The Soviets seemed very happy to receive the French and British delegations, and the latter had legitimate reason to think that it would be easier to conclude a pact than they had any reason to hope, since broadly the USSR, so different from western Europe, seemed like a sister of the ancient Russian Empire which it had succeeded.

As had been agreed the day before, the first working session took place on the morning of 12 August in the Spiridonovka palace where Marshal Voroshilov had given his banquet. The room set aside for the talks had on its walls a portrait of Stalin and a large battle piece such as we have in the offices of our Headquarters. Soviet protocol limited the number of people who could sit in on the talks to five per delegation.

From the start the difficulties of translation, and the necessity to be near in order to hear what was said, led to everyone sitting democratically round the big table in no clearly defined order. The number of assistants increased regularly at each session, which was necessary so that everything, without shorthand, could be written down in French, English and Russian. This excellent atmosphere of informality was accentuated by the profusion of cigarettes on the table which were smoked by almost everyone, to the great annoyance of Admiral Drax—and his aide, who feared for his master's throat.

This relatively relaxed atmosphere, to the point where one of the assistants could break in to ask for a word to be repeated or to clarify an idea, was purely superficial. Basically the deliberations were extremely tough and conducted by the Soviets in the most careful and often brutal manner.

It is also true that the Soviet delegation, trained to work on com-missions by its govermental duties in the Russian State, was much more experienced than our delegates in the kind of negotiations which we were about to undertake. This came out at the very first meeting at which Marshal Voroshilov posed a number of questions, such as the agenda, procedure, minutes, powers and other details of parliamentary procedure with which the Russians were perfectly familiar and of which we on our side had not even dreamt. Marshal Voroshilov's proposals were therefore adopted without discussion.

All this was pure routine, but already Voroshilov, very much at his ease, emerged as the leader of the discussions. The question of the verification of powers gave him his first positive success.

Marshal Voroshilov rose to his feet and read in solemn tones a document which stated that the Soviet mission 'had the power to sign military agreements for the maintenance of peace and against aggression' and he asked the chiefs of the other missions to state what powers were vested in them. General Doumenc presented his orders signed by President Daladier indicating that he 'had authority to negotiate on all military questions'. This rather vague phrase hap-pily contained the word 'negotiate' which in its broadest sense could be interpreted as carrying much the same weight as the powers vested in Marshal Voroshilov.

Admiral Drax on the other hand, extremely ill at ease and cough-ing a great deal, after some hesitation had to say that he had no written instructions, but that it must be obvious to Marshal Voro-shilov that the British Government would hardly send a mission if it was not empowered to act; nevertheless he had nothing on paper.

Immediately the Marshal took advantage of this to make a point. Visibly displeased, he conferred with General Shapochnikov; then he got to his feet and read a declaration to the effect that he much regretted the fact that the Soviet delegation found itself in the presence of negotiators who had no valid power to sign a military agreement.

He then had to be reassured, and it had to be explained to him that, according to usage, military missions were not in themselves negotiators of treaties but were empowered to recommend to their Governments heads of agreement; nevertheless we were determined to press on as fast as we could and to do as much work as possible. This enabled the Marshal to appear to be doing us a favour by *consenting* to work towards the preparation of an agreement.

I have described this incident, small as it was, in detail because it shows the art with which the negotiations were conducted by the Russians and at the same time the haphazard way in which the preparations had been made on our side. The Soviets knew where they were going and Marshal Voroshilov was a formidable adversary, at least around the conference table. This same session showed from the very start the difficulties we were to encounter throughout the discussions. After the first part was devoted to considering procedure, we went into recess and had a magnificent cold lunch in the big dining-room in which we had enjoyed the banquet the night before; then it was decided to concentrate on the programme for the next session.

Marshal Voroshilov proposed that at the next session each mission should table the plans made by its own Headquarters for safeguarding the common defence of the three countries represented:

> We have a complete outline, down to detailed figures. Have the French and British missions plans and propositions for the defence of our country? We have some proposals to make on this subject; but we hope that the military authorities and the Governments of France and Great Britain have a plan, because we have some delicate matters to discuss and because hitherto political negotiations have not gone well precisely because of the absence of any positive thinking. We need to know from the start the plans which have been made by Great Britain and France with Poland and Turkey, etc., . . . for if we produce our plan, it may be that we will find it is drawn up on a different basis because of our particular situation vis-à-vis an eventual aggressor and because we have no colonies.

The Marshal with an air of apparent straightforwardness had really got us in a corner. No stalling, no diplomatic retreat was possible: we were faced by concrete discussions and with revealing our military secrets which *naturally* we did not want to do until we had some evidence of their good faith.

This direct attack very much upset Admiral Drax, who thought it prudent to introduce at this moment the projected Franco-British agreement which had been drawn up on the voyage, explaining that this project constituted an excellent first step towards our ends; General Doumenc, coming to his aid, agreed, underlining the two basic principles—communications and war on two fronts—by means of which one could forthwith reach a first agreement. But Voroshilov stuck to his guns; 'I would prefer,' he said, 'first to compare our plans, to see whether they differ or not. We must begin by discussing the plans.' It was agreed that the next session should be devoted to a detailed exposition of French intentions and the Marshal insisted that this must go into details with figures of the forces available and means of transport, etc., . . . and not be confined to general abstractions. At the end of this first session it was obvious how great were the difficulties facing us and that only with considerable trouble would the projected agreement drawn up laboriously on the *City of Exeter* ever see the light of day.

With the second session there began the series of expositions by the head of each delegation on the plans drawn up by his country and the forces which would be available to face Germany. These sessions, which it would be most interesting to follow word for word because of the Soviet reactions, their penetrating curiosity and their ability to pose the most embarrassing questions, all followed the same pattern: despite protestations of sincerity, neither side felt any confidence in the other; what was in fact happening was that everyone tried to appear sincere and to give the impression of unveiling secrets, while in fact the details given in the discussions were usually misleading and generally exaggerated.

This comedy of laying military secrets on the table considerably worried both France and Great Britain. It was felt again and again that the Soviet had organized the conference in order to obtain, on the eve of war, an idea of our plans, and then naturally to pass them on to Germany. What they were told in the course of the discussions did not amount to very much. They were of course not taken in at all and obviously the time came when, following their usual direct tactics, they threw the whole thing back in our teeth. But nevertheless during these long days, when the object seemed to be talking for the sake of talking, some words, some answers given to questions put unexpectedly by Marshal Voroshilov, must have given the Soviet useful indications. We will see as we go on how certain verifications served to bear out the opinion which the Russians had themselves formed of our potentialities.

But this comedy was little more than a side issue. The essential target of the Soviet during the negotiations was to present and to gain acceptance for their policy of aggrandisement which they achieved later when they made their pact with Germany. To put forward such a programme at a conference which was supposed to be dealing with defence against aggression was a difficult business and it must be admitted that the Soviet carried it off with great skill. The sessions developed into monotonous and frequently misleading speeches, while all the time, at first insidiously and then with startling brutality, the Soviet pressure was increased to the point at which it led to the breakdown of the talks.

To come back to this second session of 13 August, General Doumenc made a long statement on the French Army, its strength and its plans, of which the least one can say is that truth was a little strained and it is doubtful if our resources could rise to the heights of these estimates. Marshal Voroshilov seemed very interested, but immediately put a number of questions: about the Maginot Line, about the British forces and Belgian participation, and about the screening off of Italy and Spain. The replies which he received, before General Valin and Commandant Willaume gave their statements respectively on the air and naval situations, did not seem to give him much satisfaction. On the contrary, among the points which General Doumenc made, a precept which visibly shook him was the evaluation of the forces which it was considered Germany would have to leave facing France in the event of an attack on Poland. General Doumenc assessed this as at least forty divisions;* one had a distinct impression that this figure was much lower than Marshal Voroshilov had expected, and that thereby the problem of the eastern front became more difficult to resolve than he had imagined.

General Doumenc delivered his statement in such a way as to come round at the end of the session to putting before the Soviet delegation a projected resolution embracing the first paragraphs of the working agreement drawn up on the *City of Exeter*. The Marshal appeared to give this the gravest consideration and announced

* In the event, Germany left only twenty divisions in the West for this purpose.

that he would produce his reply at the next session; he then asked leave to put a question which, he said, seemed to him cardinal to the continuation of the negotiations: 'What action do the General Staffs of France and Great Britain consider the USSR should take in the event of aggression by land and in the air against France and England, or against Poland and Rumania severally or collectively, or against Turkey?' This question, innocent in appearance, tended to bring the debate back to the realities of the hour and also, as we shall see, opened the way for the well-known Russian demands.

The next meeting was for this reason the culminating session of the negotiations. I will describe it in detail.

The Marshal opened by asking for an answer to the question which he had put the previous afternoon, and which was obviously going to be troublesome because bound up in it was the whole question of Russia's relations with her western neighbours.

General Doumenc tried to side-step the difficulty by stating that it was the duty of each country to defend its own territory and that all the great powers could do was to be ready to come to the aid of the armed forces of neighbouring countries and to assure their communications to the rear, if this were asked for, and he pointed out that this was the position of France vis-à-vis Belgium and Switzerland.

Marshal Voroshilov made it plain that this reply gave him little pleasure, particularly because General Doumenc had made the point that Poland and Rumania would, in the event of war, need material and that it was the Red Army which could do most to help them because of its geographical situation.

Marshal Voroshilov got to his feet, rather red in the face, and sharply put the question which was the *raison d'être* of his mission: 'I ask once more, what action do the General Staffs of France and Great Britain consider the USSR should take on land in the event of aggression against France, Poland, etc. . . . Let us not cloud the issue, we are now talking solely of land forces. I will put to you questions which will perhaps clarify my point of view—General, and Admiral: I ask you—will Poland accept the entry of Soviet troops in the Vilna corridor in order to make contact with the enemy; likewise will Poland give our troops access to Galicia;

likewise allow them passage to get to Rumania? For our delegation
these questions are cardinal to our negotiations.'

So the die was cast. On our side it had been agreed from the
beginning that we would not speak about Poland, but here we were
in the middle of it because it was difficult to escape from Marshal
Voroshilov's logic. Admiral Drax might well try rather sadly to
offer his good wishes on Russia's intentions towards Poland;
General Doumenc might well try to gloss over in strategic language the redoubtable Soviet projects. Voroshilov returned to the
charge:

> I want a straight answer. I am not talking about troop
> concentrations. I want to know the view of the French and
> British General Staffs in the event of aggression against
> Poland and Rumania. Is it that Soviet troops may enter Poland
> in order to make contact with the enemy in East Prussia? The
> passage of Soviet troops through Poland and Rumania is a
> first condition; after that is agreed, everything else can be
> discussed. Otherwise, if the Soviet troops are denied the ability
> to move, it is difficult to see how a fundamental agreement
> can be arrived at. Your opinion is that Poland and Rumania
> will ask for our help. I doubt if it would turn out like that.
> They might ask for aid from the USSR or they might not, or
> they might ask for it too late—and in this last situation the
> USSR could do nothing which would be of any help to the
> Allies. A conference of three great powers and their
> representatives at this level has got to make up its mind on
> this. If Rumania and Poland do not ask for aid, or ask for it
> too late, their forces will be destroyed. These troops should
> be used as an additional allied asset; it is in the interest
> neither of England, nor of France, nor of the USSR that they
> should be destroyed. I insist that we must from the start
> discuss the principle of Soviet troops passing through Poland
> and Rumania; this is essential.

After such an attack there was no option but to go into recess,
which was done in considerable turmoil. Admiral Drax, when he
joined his colleagues in the garden, said: 'I think our mission is
finished.' There seemed general agreement that there was little
hope of getting Russian support without coming to agreement on
these perfectly logical basic questions!

It seemed a convenient moment, while the session was in recess,
for General Doumenc to reply to the Marshal's question; this he
did with his usual adroitness, offering congratulations on the

intentions towards the constitution of an eastern front expressed by the USSR. Projects of this kind, he thought, were the soundest means of deterring aggression. He considered it desirable to pass on at once to study the means of realizing these ends, and he invited the Marshal to explain how he saw the possibilities of intervention in all the possible circumstances which had been envisaged. It was a most able manoeuvre: on the one hand it gained time, but above all it helped to bring home to the Soviets the great practical difficulties of their projected immediate entry into Poland.

But Marshal Voroshilov was not the man to allow himself to be caught in a corner like that.

I cannot give such an explanation, because the missions have not replied to the questions which I have put to them: will Soviet troops be allowed through the Polish Corridor towards Vilna or will they not? Will they be permitted to meet the enemy in Galicia, and will Soviet troops be allowed to advance through Rumania if there is an attack in that central zone? I consider that a reply to these questions is of cardinal importance. Without a precise answer, any continuation of these discussions is useless. Once we have an answer to these questions, we will set out our plans and make proposals which we think will fully satisfy the contracting parties.

Thus the danger of breakdown was already hanging over the third day of negotiations. . . . This brutal counter-attack posed a difficult problem for the Franco-British delegation, which they hoped to get round by the following written reply drawn up by General Haywood in an almost warlike atmosphere:

We have already given our personal view most clearly and we have taken note of the summary of the situation given by the Marshal. But it must not be overlooked that both Poland and Rumania are sovereign states and that the authority of which the Marshal speaks can be obtained only from their respective Governments. This therefore becomes a political matter and we suggest that the Soviet Government put the question to the Polish and Rumanian Governments. It is quite certain that this is the simplest and most direct method of procedure. If it is thought particularly desirable, we are prepared to refer to London and Paris to see if our Governments are disposed to put the following question to the Polish and Rumanian Governments:
In the event that the USSR were our ally, would they be prepared to authorize Soviet troops to penetrate the areas of

Vilna, Galicia and Rumanian territory in order to co-operate
in operations against Germany?
It is possible that the German army might march into Poland
tomorrow. If we wish to avoid the loss of precious time, should
we not continue our work on the presumption of an affirmative
answer? In this way our conference could make useful progress.
It would be most interesting for us to know the Marshal's
plans. We have put forward our plans for the West and we
would be in a better position vis-à-vis our own Governments
if we could be aware of the manner in which you intend to use
your forces if the need arises and the authorization is given.

That brought the question out into the clear. The Russians
wanted the authorization first, to which we replied that any authorization was a matter for our Governments, that the necessary steps
should be taken, and in the meanwhile it seemed equitable that the
Soviets should reply to our statement with a similar statement. This
question merited consideration and the Marshal asked for a further
recess in which to consider his reply.

It was nearly an hour before he was ready. No doubt there had
been several telephone calls to the Kremlin and no doubt the matter
had been referred directly to Stalin. Be that as it may, not wishing
to be any less precise than the Franco-British delegation, Marshal
Voroshilov in his turn read out a written declaration which is worth
reproducing *in extenso*:

Reply of the Soviet military mission to the memorandum of
the French and British missions.
1. The Soviet mission has not overlooked nor will overlook
the fact that Poland and Rumania are sovereign states. On the
contrary, as a consequence of this fact, the Soviet mission is
asking the French and British missions to make it clear whether
Soviet forces will be permitted to penetrate Polish and
Rumanian territory towards the Vilna corridor, Galicia and
Rumania in the event of aggression against France and Great
Britain or against Poland and Rumania. This question is the
more legitimate and to the point since France has a military
treaty with Poland and Great Britian has guaranteed the
territorial integrity of both Poland and Rumania.
2. The Soviet mission agrees with the opinions expressed by
the French and British missions that this is a political question.
3. Concerning the declaration by the French and British
missions that the simplest means would be a direct approach
to Poland and Rumania: since the USSR has no military
agreement with Poland or Rumania and since the States

threatened by aggression in Europe appear to be Poland,
Rumania, France and Great Britian, questions relating to the
passage of Soviet troops should be decided by the British and
French Governments in agreement with the Governments of
Poland and Rumania.

4. The Soviet military mission regrets that the French and
British missions are unable to give a precise answer to the
question of the passage of Soviet troops through Polish and
Rumanian territories. The Soviet military mission considers
that, without an answer to this question, all the work entered
upon so far is doomed to failure. For this reason the Soviet
mission cannot recommend its Government to take part in
negotiations which are manifestly condemned to failure.

5. The Soviet mission asks that the obtaining of a reply to
the question from the French and British Governments be
pressed forward with all speed. While awaiting these replies,
the Soviet mission considers it possible to expound its views
on plans against aggression in Europe.

The Soviet reply was extremely frank and, unfortunately for us,
perfectly logical. It was a complete pipe-dream to think of negotiat-
ing with the USSR without resolving, at least on the strategic level,
the question of Russo-Polish collaboration. The Russians made this
abundantly clear to us and did not hide their irritation at discovering
that the military missions had no more practical suggestions to
make than had the diplomatic missions which preceded them. For
the second time the Soviet delegation stressed the probable failure
of the negotiations and, having made its point, was once more in a
position to make us feel that the statement which it would make on
their country's plans and her forces was little more than a favour in
return for our declaration, but that in the long run our delegations
would only be tolerated in Moscow after we had obtained from our
Governments the political agreement envisaged by the Soviet.

This long and extremely dramatic session marked the end of real
negotiations. From that moment the meetings twice daily were
nothing more than a way of filling in time and of trying to pacify the
terrible Voroshilov while awaiting the hypothetical reply to the
telegram which was sent the same day to Paris, of which this is the
text:

The three delegations had two sessions on 13 August and one
long one on 14th.
Soviet delegation expressed desire to bring matters to a

head and asks that general principles accepted by all be put
aside in favour of concrete questions. There has already been
discussion on western front and tomorrow Soviet delegation
will set out military resources and operational plans envisaged
for Russian front. Meanwhile Soviet delegation today put as
condition for achieving military pact assurance that Soviet
Army, in event aggression against Poland and Rumania, will
have right of entry into Vilna corridor, Galicia and Rumanian
territory. Despite this work continues. Our Ambassador
believes and I concur quickest solution to send General Valin
on mission to Warsaw specially accredited by you to Polish
General Staff. We must endeavour obtain from them secret
agreement in principle allowing Franco-British delegations to
treat military aspect of this question without officially
implicating Polish Government.
British mission in entire agreement.
Your instructions requested matter of urgency. Please refer
dispatch from our Ambassador even date. Understood by other two
delegations no statement to be made to Press while *pourparlers*
continue. Hope send you tomorrow details of Rumanian
territory concerned.

Unhappily there was no reply and it became more and more difficult to keep the Marshal quiet. These sessions went on until the day
when the Soviet delegation indicated that it was useless to come
together any further if there was to be no reply to its questions.

Meantime these holding sessions had considerable interest for the
light which they shed on the intentions and the preoccupations of the
Soviet delegation. By far the most interesting was the meeting at
which the Soviet plans against aggression were set out, and this is
worth considering in detail.

General Shapochnikov's statement was a curious mixture of precise facts and vague generalities. Straight away he made it plain
that he had not been taken in by the intentional vagueness with
which the French and British delegations had described their
resources: 'We have listened to General Doumenc's description of
the general disposition of the French forces and we have heard
nothing concrete. The same is true of the operational plan described by General Haywood. Equally we have heard nothing concrete concerning the plan of action drawn up for the united British
and French fleets at sea.' The Soviets imagined that we were with-
holding from them a whole clutch of formidable secrets. I think they
came to realize later that the Anglo-French ideas were in fact no

more concrete than the impression of them which had been given.

In any case, taking a leaf from our book so far as precise figures were concerned, General Chapochnikov then gave us a picture of the Russian forces which cannot have been very confidential since it was reproduced *in extenso* in *L'Humanité* three days later. The USSR, he said, could meet aggression in Europe with 120 infantry divisions, sixteen cavalry divisions and 5,000 fighter aircraft (not counting air co-operation). This redoubtable Army would intervene in a European conflict along the lines of the three following hypotheses:

In the event of aggression against France and Great Britain only, the USSR would commit effective forces equal to 70 per cent of the Franco-British troops deployed on the German front, but demanded the total committal of the Polish forces and the free passage of Soviet troops in the Vilna corridor, Galicia and eventually Rumania, plus an Allied naval operation in the Baltic. Furthermore the Allies would be charged with the task of obtaining from the Baltic States agreement to the temporary occupation of the islands of Aaland, the Baltic Islands and the ports of Hangö, Parnu, Absalu and Libau for the purpose of defending the neutrality and independence of these States against any attack coming from Germany; and finally the severing or interruption of the traffic in basic materials between Germany and Sweden. As far as the Baltic was concerned, the occupation of the islands and ports should be an inter-Allied operation.

In the event of aggression against Poland and Rumania, the USSR would commit effective forces equal to 100 per cent of the Franco-British troops deployed in the West and would ask for the same support as set out in the previous hypothesis. France and Great Britain should immediately declare war on the aggressor, and, further, the Black Sea fleet would seal the mouths of the Danube and block the Bosporus.

Finally in the event that the chief aggressor should use Finland, Estonia and Latvia in directing an attack against Russia, France and Great Britain, as well as Poland, should immediately enter the war and deploy forces equal to 70 per cent of the Soviet Armies engaged on the German front.

It would be difficult to be more positive or more clear. The contrast between this programme, even if a little elementary, and the confused abstractions of the agreement suggested by the French and

British is striking and shows the gulf which separated the two conceptions and the two civilizations.

This gulf was stressed by Marshal Voroshilov with his customary forthrightness when he had to reply to the suggested articles of the military agreement put before him by General Doumenc. These articles were as follows:

Preamble. The present agreement shall apply, consequent upon the stipulations of the treaties which unite the three contracting powers, in the event that one of the situations envisaged by these treaties shall arise.
By reason of the present military situation in Europe, this agreement relates to urgent dispositions which shall be taken in the event of war breaking out in the immediate future.
Article 1. The three contracting parties are agreed on the capital importance of establishing a continuous front, solid and durable, both on the eastern and the western frontiers of Germany.
Article 2. In order to oppose without delay any military action undertaken by the common enemy, the three contracting powers agree to deploy all their forces by land, by sea and in the air against every enemy front on which they can bear effectively and to continue until the German power is defeated. The method of employing these forces shall be decided by the respective High Commands. These decisions shall be co-related as events develop, but the initial common aims are specified by the present agreement.

The following scene, drawn from the detailed record of the 17 August session, shows Marshal Voroshilov's radical opposition to and his judgement upon our old-fashioned way of thinking:

VOROSHILOV (reading): The Soviet military mission has studied with care the three principles set forth by General Doumenc. The three principles of the organization of defence by the three contracting parties are too broad, abstract and immaterial, and commit nobody to anything. I agree with the principles themselves, it would be difficult to do otherwise, but they offer nothing concrete; however they might serve as a basis for some sort of abstract declaration.
We are not gathered here to draw up any general declaration, but to hammer out a concrete military agreement which shall define the number of divisions, guns, aircraft, naval squadrons etc., which shall be committed in collaboration by the three

states. That is my reply.

GENERAL DOUMENC: I must say to the Marshal that he is rather too severe for my principles.

VOROSHILOV: The severity of my reply is in keeping with the severity of the actual situation, both political and military. Two days ago Admiral Drax stated that Germany has already mobilized 2,000,000 men and is ready overnight to launch an attack upon a peaceful power. Even if Admiral Drax's prognostication is not entirely borne out, nevertheless the political tension in Europe has grown no less and is indeed increasing; from this it follows that the military conference of Great Britain and France, if it really wants to make concrete decisions for common action against the aggressor, must stop wasting its time on declarations which have no significance and quickly get down to the actual problems of organization against the aggressor [*sic*].

GENERAL DOUMENC: I want to go along with what Marshal Voroshilov has indicated and I suggest that articles be drafted founded upon the variants set out yesterday by the Chief of Staff.

ADMIRAL DRAX: I am prepared to do the drafting.

VOROSHILOV: I do not think that we have yet got to the point of drafting any document. We have still no decision on the cardinal point regarding the passage of Soviet troops through Polish and Rumanian territory. Only after an affirmative reply to this question can we go on to discuss the plans set out here by the representatives of the three powers. Until then we are doing nothing but exchange ideas which are barely the beginning of a concrete examination of the resources and troops which need to be employed on two fronts against the aggressors.

As can be seen, the discussion came back every time to the one cardinal point which dominated everything. We will see farther on the efforts which were made at the eleventh hour to reconcile the irreconcilable; but before leaving the analysis of these sessions, which we have done somewhat in bits and pieces, it is interesting to mention certain further incidents which seemed to me to have had considerable influence on the Soviet decisions.

The first occurred during General Haywood's statement concerning the British forces. When General Haywood had given the number of divisions which would be put immediately into the field against the aggressor and the further number which could be raised in the first few months of war—figures which were carefully scaled up and which we knew to be three or four times what was in fact practicable—Marshal Voroshilov could not contain his surprise and, fearing that he might not have heard aright, asked for the figures to be repeated. It is certain that he could not understand how, in discussions in which everyone was trying to show himself in the best light, Great Britain could not do better than such a derisory figure. The British delegation made the mistake of not including in their numbers the considerable forces of the Dominions and Colonies, so that in the face of what they were told the Soviet delegation formed an impression as never before of the immense weakness of the British Empire.

The second came during a difficult discussion designed to show the Soviets that it was vital that the *pourparlers* should not be suspended. At this moment Admiral Drax, whose interventions were not always particularly fortunate, after a prolonged fit of coughing eventually came out with an argument which he had put to the French delegation during the crossing and had been begged never to utter; he said; 'Do not forget that Poland, if she is on her own, may be crushed in two weeks.'

Marshal Voroshilov seized on this at once; he stood up, very erect, and made this statement: 'The Soviet delegation takes notice of the statement made by the Admiral to the effect that Poland, if left to fight alone, might well be crushed in two weeks. The Soviet delegation has no comment to make on this subject.' And then he sat down again. There was an impression that he had just received confirmation, in a material way, of Poland's weakness. Given the conditions under which the struggle in the east was likely to take place, this meant that Russia would never be able to come to the help of Poland in time, and thereafter would find herself facing a victorious German Army alone.

These two incidents, to which must be added another concerning the number of divisions which Germany might be capable of deploying in the east, certainly swung the balance Germany's way as much as, if not more than, the bickering over the Vilna corridor and the Baltic States which still remained our major preoccupation.

The situation on the evening of 17 August was agonizing. We were on the verge of a breakdown, with all the grave consequences which this could bring, and we had still had no answer to our telegrams concerning the capital point which Voroshilov had made with such insistence.

As early as the 14th General Doumenc had asked for permission to send to Warsaw his Adjutant, General Valin, who had been Air Attaché in Poland. On the 16th our Government opposed this because of 'the repercussions which might ensue'. In the absence of this solution he organized a sort of semi-official consultation through our Military Attaché in Warsaw, General Musse, whom he suggested might come to Moscow to receive instructions if need be. In the impasse in which we found ourselves, this procedure was much too slow.

On the 17th General Doumenc cabled to Paris: 'The session for the 21st has only been arranged to avoid any public impression that the conversations have been broken off. It is now essential if the discussions are to continue for me to be able to give an affirmative reply to the question which has been put.'

To gain time he decided off his own bat to send me to Warsaw with the following brief:

Captain Beaufre will proceed to Warsaw to give General
Musse all useful information verbally.
He will insist upon the following points:
1. It is of the utmost importance to obtain the agreement of
the Polish General Staff to the principle of this eventual passage
through their territory. The Russians have strictly limited
their request for authorization to the Vilna corridor and Galicia
and on this point we can obtain a formal agreement from them.
The strategic importance of this support is undeniable.
The importance of concluding a military pact is no less so.
2. If this principle is accepted, we must obtain an assurance
that communications will be established across Russian
territory between Poland and ourselves—what are the transit
stations from which these communications should begin in
order best to serve the Polish rear areas?
3. We have said absolutely nothing about the Polish Army,
in accordance with our promise.'

This mission had the important function of making it clear to the Russians that something was being done to get an answer to the famous question, and thus ensure us a respite at least as long as the duration of the journey.

I left Moscow on the evening of the 17th, apparently for Paris.

In my 1900-style *wagon lit* a loudspeaker greeted the train's departure with an air from *Carmen*, very popular in the USSR at that time. Then we ploughed through the monotonous wooded plains of Russia while I meditated on the chain of circumstances which had led to my being entrusted with so important a mission.

At the Russian frontier station my diplomatic passport was stamped immediately, but there were about twenty people from the West who were in trouble and had been waiting several days for an authorization to proceed which seemed problematical. They all clustered round me asking for help or for me to pass on messages. I particularly remember a Belgian workman and a Canadian, completely discouraged by their lengthy and incomprehensible hold-up which turned the station into a sort of purgatory.

Eventually the train moved on without all these wretched people and we reached the frontier. Crossing the Soviet border was something one will not forget: a barbed wire fence running in either direction as far as the eye could see, then a belt cleared of all trees overlooked every kilometre by a watch tower—this was indeed, before Churchill invented the phrase, the Iron Curtain. Armed soldiers of the frontier police in green caps rode in every coach. At the border, closed by a movable barrier above which hung a streamer in red cloth on which was written 'Workers of the World Unite', the train stopped. The barrier was lifted and the train moved forward very slowly while the guards dropped off each coach as it passed through, rifle in hand, to see that no one was hidden underneath or on the roof. The last coach passed, the barrier was closed and the train picked up speed.

As soon as we reached the other side a new world opened. At a level crossing blonde young girls and little children waved. At the first station, a neat and gay-looking building with a pleasant staff, there was a buffet where one could buy anything one wanted. . . .

I arrived in Warsaw on the evening of the 18th and was made to get out at a suburban station in a rather unnecessary show of secrecy.

I was taken straight to the Embassy where round the dinner table were the French Ambassador, M. Léon Noël, the Military Attaché, General Musse, who had just come back from Paris with special instructions, and a few guests. Towards midnight the guests left and a council of war was held to consider the information which I had brought.

When I explained the situation in Moscow, General Musse said that even these tentative conditions were doomed to failure so far as Poland was concerned, because the hatred which existed between the Poles and the Russians was so great that it would be quite useless to attempt to get any agreement on so delicate a question as the occupation of even a part of Polish territory by Russian troops.

For his part, Léon Noël, rather more indirectly, seemed extremely preoccupied with the role he would have to play. He was afraid that his personal position in Warsaw would be compromised. He had arrived in Poland at a time when relations with France had sharply declined and a flirtation with Germany was in full swing. He felt that his actions had contributed towards the restoration of the situation which had come about in the previous March. He considered that the Polish political policy was to try to maintain a balance between the menace of Russia from the east and the threat of Germany in the west; he feared that the revelation of a further menace from Russia would upset the equilibrium and encourage the Poles to turn their eyes once again towards Germany.

General Musse, more straightforward in his arguments and perhaps also more sensitive to Polish influence, feared from the start the bad faith of the Soviets: 'The step which you are asking us to take would end up by favouring a Russian manoeuvre; the Russians have never abandoned the idea of reclaiming the territory which they lost in 1921, and we cannot undertake anything which lends support to such an idea. And then, how do you know that the Russians themselves have not got an understanding with Germany?'

It was difficult to reply to these objections except by trying to relay as exactly as possible the atmosphere of the negotiations in Moscow in order to make it plain how false our position was and to point out that, however much one might distrust the Soviets, their arguments did carry weight. Furthermore the problem did not consist so much of whether Poland would or would not accept the passage of Soviet troops as of finding a basis which would make it possible for the negotiations to continue. If the negotiations broke down, in fact, there was the risk of immediate war against Poland. It appeared that the negotiations, as long as they continued, imposed some element of indecision on Germany and protected our eastern ally far more surely than any military measures could do. We were already nearing the end of August; if we succeeded in holding on for another month the threatened war could not begin in 1939; as to 1940, we would have to wait and see. It therefore appeared essential that the Poles should agree to this manoeuvre; if they refused, they would have to bear the whole responsibility of the misfortunes which might follow; it was essential that this should be made abundantly clear to them.

It was agreed that this further approach should be made on the following day, and that while General Musse saw General Stackiewicz, Chief of the Polish General Staff, M. Léon Noël should see Beck, the Minister for Foreign Affairs. There was nothing to do but wait for the result.

The military situation, as far as one could judge from the information coming in minute by minute to the Polish General Staff Headquarters, seemed extremely grave. For the last fortnight fresh German units had been concentrating all along the border. The command posts of army corps and divisions had been seen and then the advance parties of regiments which day by day were brought up to strength by the arrival of reservists; heavy transport was mostly centred in East Prussia; then the occurrence of serious diplomatic incidents, such as the brush with the Danzig customs officers a few days before which caused the Polish Government to make a most vigorous protest, indicated that the eve of the conflict was upon us.

Warsaw meanwhile was completely normal, a western city, elegant and refined; the very air one breathed was quite different from that of Moscow. By 20 August, that is to say ten days before the outbreak of war, no precautions had yet been taken either against air raids or for the defence of the city. It was profoundly moving to realize that disaster was so soon to fall upon all this charming unconcern.

In actual fact the impression given by the replies from the Poles to our first approaches on the morning of the 19th was evidence of their complete unconcern in the face of the danger which threatened them.

General Stackiewicz was very frank. 'I understand your point of view perfectly,' he said 'but I ask you also to understand ours. We know the Russians better than you do; they are a dishonest people whose word is not to be relied upon by us or anyone else, and it is quite useless to ask us even to contemplate a proposition of this nature. Obviously I realize the general situation and it may be that the advent of war may be accelerated, but even this consideration cannot make us alter our point of view.'

It was a most formal rebuttal.

As for Beck, he was in a thoroughly bad mood because he had been alerted to the approach which Léon Noël was about to make by Lukazievicz, the Polish Ambassador in Paris whom Georges Bonnet had sent for on the previous evening in order to explain the situation. This intervention by Georges Bonnet was particularly unfortunate because Lukazievicz, a Pole of ancient Russian lineage, was very anti-Russian, most wary of them and the least inclined to favour any agreement. The result was that Beck's reply was to take cover behind a decision that he would have to lay the matter before Marshal Rydz-Smigly. The long and short of it was that unless the Marshal had a clearer conception of Poland's interests, we were stymied all along the line.

That evening we had the reply from the oracle. Marshal Rydz-Smigly had spoken and General Stackiewicz conveyed the sense of his words to us: that it was quite impossible for any Polish Government even to consider any proposition which would lead to the occupation of so much as a square inch of Polish territory by Russian troops, whatever the consequences might be. It was less a material question than a sacred principle, a heritage from the political testament of Marshal Pilsudsky: 'With the Germans we risk the loss of our liberty, but with the Russians we lose our soul.' This was a passionate stand far beyond logic, and in consequence any appeal to reason was in vain.

In spite of this we could not sit down under this setback, the more so that even if Poland did have a touchy sense of honour, she was also part of a whole and there should be some pressure which could be brought to bear to make her reconsider her point of view. In the course of a fresh meeting in that charming French Embassy, now destroyed, I asked M. Léon Noël and General Musse to try once more and not to hesitate in presenting the most convincing arguments. We could not remain bound to our treaty of alliance by sentiments based upon the testament of Marshal Pilsudsky. If the

Poles liked to behave like a bunch of Don Quixotes, that was their business, but it seemed proper to point out to them very clearly how precarious their military situation was and to make it plain that no one was talking about airy negotiations but about the very existence of Poland herself. The British evaluation of Polish resistance gave it a fortnight before complete collapse, and it was for this reason that Russian military aid was absolutely vital.

These arguments seemed to impress M. Léon Noël; but on the other hand General Musse and his assistants reacted violently against this appreciation of Polish resistance and said that it was absurd to underestimate to such an extent so good and well equipped an army, the tactical thinking of which had made great strides. This argument shows how easy it is for observers on the ground to form false appreciations, and how a long stay in a country attaches you to it by a thousand and one bonds of sympathy which warp judgement and blunt alertness. It was evident that General Musse was for the Poles against the Russians and prepared to stand up for their ideals. There can be little doubt that in these discussions he was a broken reed because, although he realized their importance, he found himself having to present arguments which he himself believed to be quite wrong.

The next discussion took place on the following day, strengthened by the presence of the British Military Attaché representing the General Staff and the British Ambassador representing the Foreign Office, for in the meantime instructions had been received from London.

The result once again was hardly encouraging. Thanks to the intervention of the British Military Attaché, the Poles had finished by accepting an extremely tenuous formula which may be summed up as follows: 'Since the Polish Government had no wish to be consulted on the question of the passage of Russian troops through Polish territory, it is a matter of which they take no cognizance in order not to be party to any possible manoeuvre on the part of the Soviet; nevertheless they are not opposed to the British and French Governments proceeding with consultations on this subject in Moscow in order to lay before the Polish Government the practical terms of Russian aid in the event of attack by Germany.'

Armed with this meagre result, I returned to Moscow via Riga, where I hoped to find an aircraft, in order to be able to report to the

French delegation before the next session, called for the 21st; but there was no flight that day.

There ends the story of the discussions with the Polish Government, such as they were up to that time. Indications which appeared subsequently shed fresh light on the role which these contacts may have played in the Russian decision.

When I left Moscow General Doumenc had taken precautions to see that the result of the Polish talks remained strictly secret. In order to avoid the use of cipher it was agreed that I would use one of three words in clear indicating a result favourable, unfavourable or doubtful; beyond this no telegram whatever was to be sent. Although this is all the traffic there was between the mission and myself, it was not the same with the Military Attaché and the Ambassador in Poland; these two, giving way to a habit which amounts to something of a professional defect, sent detailed telegrams each day not only to Paris but also to Moscow in which they described exactly the atmosphere of the negotiations and the objections, injurious to the Russians, which the Poles had made.

One can form one's own opinion from the text of the two following telegrams sent by General Musse on his own initiative from Warsaw to Moscow:

Have explained to General Stackiewicz demands of the Russians and necessity for avoiding setback to *pourparlers*. Without disagreeing with any argument Chief of Staff believes neither in good faith of Soviets nor their desire to take part effectively in war. They seek solely political advantage to exploit private aims. In case of war they would march in without effectively opposing Germans. General nevertheless appreciates importance of making decisions and the gravity of refusal. He will refer to Marshal whose decision cannot be foreseen.

Today third interview with Chief of General Staff. Polish resistance insuperable because based on sacrosanct principles. Just as I have dissuaded Captain Beaufre [*sic*], we have reached conclusion approach to Poland impossible of achievement. Delegation at liberty to counter-attack Russians on their premature and vague demands which could only be laid before the countries concerned after detailed study of possible co-operation. Poles convinced of Russian blackmail and inability to carry out suggested offensives.

Other telegrams, even more detailed, were dispatched to Paris.

To anyone who knows anything about the Russian Secret Service it must be obvious than any telegram sent in the normal Military Attaché's code would be immediately deciphered. In almost any embassy in the world the safe is not guarded at night; and a safe unguarded is an open safe.

Be that as it may, everything which happened seemed to indicate that the Russians had cognizance of the telegram of the 19th. Before I had a chance to piece together more or less certainly the diplomatic moves which took place between 10 and 20 August, I got from the Press the actual time—10 p.m. on 19 August—when a meeting of the Politburo was summoned, at which Stalin announced the reversal of the policy of the USSR. This date and time seemed correct to me and correspond exactly to the hour at which the Soviets would have known from General Musse's telegrams that the negotiations with Poland were not going to produce a result and that there was no future in wasting any further time on the Allies. We will see shortly what was the actual sequence of events.

In my train to Riga I was overcome by a feeling of infinite sadness; it was a wonderful summer's day, sunny and hot. The train was full of people talking about their holidays. In the green country-side there were many bathers lying on the river banks and I *knew* that this peaceful picture was soon to give way to a terrible drama, and that this Sunday night might be the last happy one for Poland. I knew that destiny was on the march and no one seemed to be at all concerned.

At Riga our Minister, M. Tripier, drew my attention to an article in the Italian journal *Corriere Diplomatico* which announced a political trend of considerable importance: 'Is there to be a fresh upset in the alliances with Russia?' He showed me the Independence monument, before which two soldiers stood on guard, and took me to meet the Chief of Staff of the Latvian Army, who lived with his daughter in a charming wooden house. I felt as if it were a visit to the condemned cell. . . .

I got back to Moscow on the evening of the 21st. The session

which had been arranged for that day had taken place; each delegation had tried to saddle the other with responsibility for the
suspension of the *pourparlers*.

Voroshilov had opened the session by proposing an adjournment
sine die, until a reply to the famous questions was forthcoming.
Admiral Drax had asked that the conference should reconvene after
a short recess, which gave Voroshilov the opportunity of making a
reply which was very sharply to the point:

The Soviet military mission considers that, since it has no
common frontier with Germany, it cannot give any aid to
France, Great Britain, Poland or Rumania except by having
access to Polish and Rumanian territory, since there is no
other means by which its troops can meet those of the aggressor.
Just as the British and American troops, in the last war,
could not have mounted any military co-operation with the
Armies of France if they had not been given the opportunity of
operating on French soil, so the Soviet forces would be unable
to undertake any co-operation with the armed forces of France
and Great Britain if they were not authorized to enter Polish
and Rumanian territories.
This is a military axiom and is the strong conviction of the
Soviet military mission. The British and French missions to
our astonishment are not in accord on this point with the Soviet
military mission—and this is the basic disagreement.
The Soviet military mission fails to understand how the
Governments and General Staffs of Great Britain and France,
in sending military missions to the USSR with a view to
concluding a military pact, could not have thought to give
them precise and positive instructions concerning a question so
elementary as the free passage and action of Soviet troops
against the forces of the aggressor on the territory of Poland
and Rumania with whom Great Britain and France have both
political and military understandings.
If, however, this axiomatic question presents France and
Great Britain with an arduous problem demanding lengthy
study, there is every reason to doubt the genuineness of their
efforts to reach an effective and serious basis of co-operation
with the USSR.
As far as the long-drawn-out nature of these *pourparlers* as
well as their interruption are concerned, the responsibility lies
squarely with France and Great Britain.

Thus the news which I brought back from Warsaw was already
out of date.

After I had left, a fresh approach had been made by the British Ambassador, who had threatened to suspend the loan to which his country had agreed. The Poles appear then to have given their agreement in principle to the passage of Russian troops through their territory.

There is an element of doubt about this because no precise signal was received confirming it and the only hint reaching Moscow was a somewhat cryptic telegram from the French Government into which could be read that the Government had either reached agreement or felt assured of getting what it wanted.

This is the text of the telegram received in Moscow on 21 August at 10.30 p.m.:

IMMEDIATE ATTENTION GENERAL DOUMENC.
You are authorized sign, in common interest and in agreement with Ambassador, best possible military agreement subject final approval French Government.

DALADIER

Thus the French Government, following its usual custom, made a decision at the eleventh hour instead of facing the problem earlier when it could have achieved some useful purpose. If this telegram had been sent four days earlier it could have changed the whole course of events. But by the evening of the 21st Russia had already made her decision.

That very day we learned that, following prolonged and successful discussions which had begun on the 19th, an economic and commercial agreement between the USSR and Germany had been signed in Berlin. To say the least, the signature of this pact revealed the state of relations between Germany and the Soviet.

Pravda on the 21st ended its leader with this phrase: 'This new economic and commercial agreement between the USSR and Germany, brought about in a most delicate political atmosphere, may serve to alleviate this atmosphere. It could be a great step towards the future extension not only of the economic but also the political relations between the USSR and Germany.'

There was a rumour that Ribbentrop was shortly expected in Moscow.

The last few days were little more than a game of hide-and-seek between the Allies and the Soviets, the former trying to prove that they now had the pact which mattered so much to the Russians, the latter trying to avoid discussions which had now become pointless.

All through the 22nd General Doumenc tried to see Marshal Voroshilov to inform him of the latest situation and to ask him that the suspended meetings be resumed as soon as possible. Finally at 7 p.m. the Marshal intimated that he would be happy to see General Doumenc.

There exists a shorthand record of this meeting, made by the Russians. Actual extracts from the text are better than any analysis:

VOROSHILOV: I would ask General Doumenc to aquaint me with the nature of the document which he has received from his Government, of the existence of which I have been advised by letter. I would also like to know if the British mission has received a reply to the same question.

GENERAL DOUMENC: I have no document, but I have been informed by my Government that the reply to the cardinal point is basically in the affirmative. In other words, my Government has authorized me to sign a military pact which shall stipulate the authorization of the passage of Soviet troops through the areas which you have laid down, that is to say the Vilna corridor, and, if (precise) circumstances make it necessary, through Galicia and Rumania.

VOROSHILOV: That is the communication from the French Government?

DOUMENC: Yes; these are the instructions given to me by the French Government.

VOROSHILOV: And the British Government?

DOUMENC: I do not know if Admiral Drax has received similar instructions from his Government; but I know the Admiral has been advised that the conference can continue.

VOROSHILOV: The British delegation knows about this communication?

DOUMENC: Yes; I have told the Admiral that the French Government's reply has been received. And I am almost certain that the British Government will send the same reply. But since I am primarily responsible for military matters and Admiral Drax is more concerned with naval questions, the reply already received is sufficient to warrant the continuance of the conference.

VOROSHILOV: It is possible that the British mission may be agreeable to General Doumenc pursuing these military matters. Nevertheless it seems to me that the British mission has

played and plays, if not a dominant role, at least an equal one
in all our conversations. That is why in the absence of any
reply from the British Government it will obviously be difficult
to continue the work of the conference.

DOUMENC: I think that the British reply will arrive shortly.

VOROSHILOV: There is one other question which interests
me. I must ask you to excuse me, General, but it is a very
serious question which I feel that I must put to you. You have
not in your reply given any indication of the attitude of the
Polish and Rumanian Governments. Are they aware exactly of
what is going on, or does the reply which you have received
emanate from the French Government without the knowledge
of Poland and Rumania?

DOUMENC: I do not know what conversations have taken
place between Governments; I can only repeat what has been
said to me by my own Government. I would like to take this
opportunity of putting the following question to you: is it, or
is it not, your intention to press on with our conversations
with a view to signing a military pact? I have reached that
point, and time is passing.

VOROSHILOV: That time is passing is indisputable, but it
it is hardly our fault that the representatives of France and
Great Britain have spent so long dallying over these questions.

DOUMENC: I agree. It is possible that from the very
start we encountered difficulties which were natural and did
not depend upon ourselves, but I must say once more to you,
Marshal, that I too am prepared to work fast—indeed, as fast
as possible.

VOROSHILOV: I do not doubt it. In the last few days I
have come to know you, and your sincerity and your genuine
desire to sign a military agreement as fast as possible are
apparent to me.

DOUMENC: Speedily, and with the mutual confidence of
soldiers who face a common enemy.

VOROSHILOV: But eleven days have gone by and all the
work done so far has been merely marking time. I cannot
agree to any further sessions round the conference table until
all official replies have been received. I do not question that
the General has received an affirmative reply from his own
Government. But the attitudes of Poland, Rumania and of
Great Britain are still unknown. That is why further talks can
lead merely to a whole lot of chatter which can only be
politically damaging. I am quite sure that, if the Poles had
given their agreement to the passage of Soviet troops, they
would wish to take part in our discussions. Indeed I am
convinced that they would demand to be present, for I cannot
see their General Staff being willing to remain on the sidelines

while questions which concern them so closely are under
discussion. For this reason, I do not believe they know what is
going on.

DOUMENC: This may be so, but I do not know and I cannot
say.

VOROSHILOV: Let us wait until everything is clear.

DOUMENC: I can wait with pleasure, but I do not wish to
wait to no purpose. I must be frank with you, Marshal. It
has already been announced that 'someone' is due to arrive
and such visits do not fill me with pleasure.

VOROSHILOV: This is quite true, but the responsibility
must be laid at the door of Great Britain and France. The
question of military collaboration has been on the *tapis* for
several years, but nothing has ever come of it. Last year,
when Czechoslovakia went down, we expected a signal from
France and our troops were ready; but nothing happened.

DOUMENC: Our troops were ready too.

VOROSHILOV: But with what object? Here, not only were
our troops ready, but the Government and the people, every
man in the street, was willing to bring help to Czechoslovakia
in accordance with our Treaty obligations.

DOUMENC: If the Marshal had been in France at that
moment he would have seen that everything was ready for war.
After these events in Europe if it was necessary then to
create a peace front, it is just as necessary now. I repeat that
I am at your disposal and ready to work when you wish, how
you wish and in the most positive manner.

VOROSHILOV: If the British and French missions had
arrived with any clear-cut proposals, I am sure that all the
necessary work could have been finished in five or six days
and a military agreement signed.
Let us wait now until the situation is tidied up, that is to
say until the British Government's reply has been received
and the attitude of Poland and Rumania is clear. Then we can
meet again. If this does not come about, there is no point in
meeting because it would serve no useful purpose. It is
necessary that these replies specify without question that
Poland knows what is going on; it is essential that the replies
of the French and British Governments are given in agreement
with the Polish and Rumanian Governments. We do not want
the Poles to turn round and refuse our aid, or that we seem to
seek their acceptance of it. If this main question is resolved,
all the others—provided no political development gets in the
way—can be settled without difficulty. Thus we could quickly
reach an understanding. But I am frightened of one thing. The
French and British representatives have drawn out the political
discussions interminably. For this reason *one cannot exclude the*

possibility that during this time some political development may have taken place. Let us wait. The sooner the reply comes, the sooner we can decide what next to do.

DOUMENC: In the present circumstances time is precious. That is why I agree to examine the headings for a pact proposed by the Marshal and to submit my suggestions for his approval. This will provide an opportunity to correlate in a sufficiently specific way the wishes of the different parties.

VOROSHILOV: We have already put forward preliminary conditions. What we have asked to have cleared up brings us nothing but heavy obligations: committing our troops and fighting a common enemy. Is it possible that we might be forced to beg for the right to engage our common enemy? Until questions of this nature have been settled, there can be no further talks.

DOUMENC: If my Government has replied in the affirmative, they have not, I am sure, done so lightly. If I in turn have stated that my Government said 'yes', we can in my opinion go to work. Now the Marshal is presenting me with the question of fresh political guarantees. I am ready to put these forward, but I fear that they will give the impression that there is no anxiety on our part to conclude this agreement rapidly.

VOROSHILOV: As far as I can see, you have not understood what I said. I have said nothing about fresh guarantees. I have simply said this: *that if nothing political occurs* from now on, we will be able to reach a perfect understanding. As soon as the question is clear and as soon as the reply to our question is given by the Governments of France and Great Britain in agreement with the Polish and Rumanian Governments, we will quickly reach an understanding and all practical problems will be resolved. But this depends, I repeat, on no political events intervening.

I have already said that if the Poles had given an affirmative reply, they would have demanded the right to be present at those discussions. In so far as that is true, it must follow that either they do not know what has been going on or they are not in agreement.

DOUMENC: I can see that the Marshal has no intention, in the next few days, of continuing the work of our conference and I am bound to state that clearly. Nevertheless I still believe that there are good reasons for continuing our work.

VOROSHILOV: On this our delegation has already given its reply: which is that until a clear answer to the questions asked is forthcoming we will go no further.

The Marshal hid any possibility of resuming the discussions behind arguments which were put not entirely in good faith but which showed clearly that he was perfectly well aware of the Polish attitude. On the other hand the allusions to possible political changes were extremely revealing, and confirmed the following short dispatch from the Tass Agency which appeared in the Press on the evening of 22 August:

German-Soviet Relations. 22 August 1939.
Following the conclusion of the Soviet-German economic and commercial agreement, there arises the question of improved political relations between Germany and the USSR. The exchange of views which has taken place between the two Governments has made apparent the desire of both parties to bring about a lessening of the political tension between them, to remove the threat of war and to conclude a non-aggression pact.
Consequently the arrival in Moscow during the next few days of the German Minister for Foreign Affairs, Herr von Ribbentrop, for talks along these lines is envisaged.

The climax was near.

Meanwhile in Paris the Government was getting restless. They no doubt imagined that once an acceptance in principle had been given, signature of an agreement could follow immediately. So on the evening of the 22nd they sent another telegram asking for a reply to theirs of the 21st.

The whole of the 23rd passed in anxiety and consternation. Hour by hour fresh information poured into the French Embassy and every item brought fresh proof that our negotiations had collapsed.

The German delegation, which consisted of some thirty officials, arrived at the Moscow airport which was decorated in the Nazi colours. It was received cordially and officially by Potemkin, national anthems were played, etc. . . . Ribbentrop was housed in a small palace, formerly the Austrian Embassy, a few yards from General Doumenc's quarters, and which had been specially prepared. (It is interesting to note that work on the palace began on the 18th or 19th which shows that the Russian decision may well have been taken earlier than I have said above.)

Scarcely had he arrived than Ribbentrop was received, at 3.30 p.m., at the Kremlin for the first interview, and saw Stalin. That was all that we knew so far, but it boded no good. Then in the evening came a rumour that the pact was already signed. We were far away from the backing and filling of the Anglo-Franco-Russian negotiations!

However, bearing in mind the exceptional importance of the matter in hand, there was no desire to admit defeat; perhaps the Germans would refuse to comply with the Russian exigencies, perhaps the whole thing was nothing more than last-minute blackmail designed to make us give up all reservations regarding Russia's territorial aims. In any case the French delegation was determined to pursue every possibility of discussion.

In addition there arrived in Moscow on the evening of the 23rd a long telegram not only directing us not to leave but also to put before the Russians a series of arguments based on the deteriorating situation in Europe. The text read as follows:

[The French Government] cannot contemplate recall [of the military mission] which would admit definite rupture of discussions which German propaganda anticipates and announces and we must keep going until the USSR Government indicates that it refuses any form of co-operation with democratic powers. M. Molotov as well as Marshal Voroshilov has yesterday once again indicated willingness for political resistance to aggression. Development of German military preparations indicates military action against Poland as probable eventuality in near future.
Militarily we are taking all useful precautions; anti-aircraft defences deployed and all leave cancelled; all troops on north and south-east frontiers stood to; other important measures under consideration with view general mobilization.
Present negotiations Moscow risk being overtaken by events and eventualities which led to their beginning will no doubt occur before conclusion can be reached. Russians must now be asked if prepared to stand firm on their understanding with us against aggression and conclude as matter of urgency military pact on minimum immediately practical basis for military, naval and air action and supplies of material.
Assistance reduced to these limited elements would constitute moral aid far above actual technical value. Even if falling short in the event, this affirmation of Russian solidarity will hearten others and in consequence stiffen resistance to German aggression plans. Should be indicated also to Russians that we clearly realize anxiety to hasten [. . .] military participation as complete as ours in land operations. Polish

objections up to now [. . .] foresee conditions but
circumstances will doubtless immediately modify this attitude.
But absence of co-operation on pretext that one element is
temporarily in default assumes without moral or technical
justification a responsibility which it is incumbent [on you]
to make abundantly clear [to your] opposite number.

GAMELIN

But once again it was too late. On the morning of the 24th the
Soviet Press was covered with banner heads and photographs of
Stalin, Ribbentrop and Molotov together, followed by the text of
the treaty signed the previous evening.

This text was seized upon avidly in the hope that we might find
some loophole, some evidence of Russian manoeuvring which might
give us a chance. Unhappily the treaty allowed of no illusion. It is
sufficient to quote article 4, which sounded the death-knell of our
mission: 'Each of the two contracting parties undertakes not to join
in any group whatsoever of Powers directed directly or indirectly
against the other.'

Still, once more one would attempt the impossible. London's
instructions to Admiral Drax were to remain in Moscow until the
Russians flatly indicated that pursuing the discussions was useless.
The only hope was the possibility of some political deception which
might give us a little room in which to manoeuvre. We were
slightly encouraged in this by a dispatch from the Tass Agency, and
hence quasi-official, saying that the German-Soviet pact had no
purpose beyond the reinforcement of peace and hence did not modify
in any way the traditional policy of the USSR. It was therefore possible to see—with a pinch of optimism, it is true—the signature of
this pact as the realization of a direct manoeuvre by the Soviet
Government to stabilize the situation in eastern Europe.

Whatever the situation, it was essential to get to the bottom of
it and that meant seeing the representatives of the Soviet Government.

But these gentry had become strictly unseeable. On the 24th
attempts were made all day to get in touch with either Voroshilov
or Molotov without success, until the evening when a telephone call
in Russian was received at the Embassy asking for General

Doumenc to go to see Marshal Voroshilov. Because of the lateness
of the hour and in order to get the French and British missions
together it was decided not to reply to this invitation until the
following morning. This last interview took place at 1 p.m. on the
25th. Colonel Firebrace, British Military Attaché in Moscow, made
the following summary of the proceedings:

> After greeting the Marshal, the Admiral spoke as follows:
> 'We regret not being able to come to see you last night at
> such short notice.
> We would now like to ask you, in view of the change in the
> political situation announced yesterday, whether it is your
> view that the Soviet Government will wish the military
> missions to continue their discussions.'
> The Marshal answered by expressing his regret that he had
> not been able to reply sooner to our letter, but he had been
> duck shooting. He said that to his regret, in view of the
> changed political situation, the continuation of the discussions
> would be pointless.
> The Admiral said that we would report this decision to our
> Governments and await instructions, and that we would keep
> the Marshal informed of our movements. The Admiral went
> on to say that he hoped the Soviet Union in the new political
> circumstances would continue to work for the cause of peace.
> The Marshal replied that this was the traditional policy of
> the Soviet Union and there was no reason to doubt that they
> would continue their efforts for the maintenance of peace as
> heretofore. He then remarked that he found himself in a most
> unusual position, but this was all the fault of our Governments.
> The Admiral then rose to take his leave of the Marshal. As
> he was saying good-bye, the Marshal spontaneously added:
> 'During the whole of our talks the Press and the people of
> Poland have continually repeated that they did not want Soviet
> aid and, furthermore, from Rumania there has been no reply
> whatever. Do we have to conquer Poland in order to offer help
> to the Polish people? This position is utterly insupportable
> for us.'

Today, looking back, Marshal Voroshilov's remarks seem
entirely well founded and it would be quite understandable that he
felt a certain resentment because, to anyone who had any perception,
it was apparent that at the outset he had every wish to bring the
negotiations to a successful conclusion.

What I have set out above was written (mostly since 1940) before I subsequently became aware of a fascinating file of documents which allow one to see exactly what did go on between Germany and the Soviet Union in 1939 and which largely bears out my own thoughts. It comes from the secret German archives seized by the Americans at the end of the war.*

In these irrefutable documents the progress of events can be clearly followed.

The whole affair begins with a 'come on' which Stalin put like a meaningful wink towards Germany in his report to the XVIIIth Congress of the Party on 10 March 1939: while speaking of the 'three imperialist nations' (Germany, Italy and Japan) which threatened possible war in the future, he stated that the USSR wished for nothing but peace and 'would not pull anyone else's chestnuts out of the fire'.

This discreet hint did not pass unnoticed in Berlin and led the way to a prolonged but cautious flirtation by both sides. After rather tentative approaches, Germany decided on *30 May* to open commercial negotiations. But the first contacts were unsatisfactory and on *29 June* Hitler put a stop to the negotiations.

Then, once the invasion of Poland had been decided upon, it became evident that some understanding with the USSR was essential. On *29 July* Ribbentrop decided to make contact again in order to 'find out what Molotov wanted', and directed Schulenburg, the German Ambassador at Moscow, to note that Russian interests in Poland and the Baltic States should be respected.

On *4 August*, the very day that we left for Moscow, Schulenburg reported that 'Molotov had been unusually frank', that the question of the Baltic States had been lightly touched upon but the Polish problem had been gone into thoroughly. Schulenburg concluded his telegram by saying rather pessimistically: 'My over-all impression is that the Soviet Government is at present determined to sign with England and France if they fulfil all Soviet wishes.'

On *10 August* the Soviet Ambassador in Berlin, Astakhov, raised the subject of Soviet interests in Poland but it was not until the *14th* that the irons were really put into the fire: Astakhov stated that the Soviets were interested in a discussion of the individual groups of

* Raymond James Sontag and James Stuart Beddik, (Editors), *Nazi Soviet Relations* 1939–41 (U.S. Dept. of State, 1948).

questions that had heretofore been taken up. Astakhov designated as such questions, among others, besides the pending economic negotiations, questions of the press, cultural collaboration, the Polish question, the matter of the old German-Soviet political agreements. Such a discussion, however, could be undertaken only, *by degrees* or, as we have expressed it, by stages. The Soviet Government proposed Moscow as the place for these discussions.

It was on this very day that Voroshilov presented to us the 'cardinal question' of Poland.

The Soviet approach opened the way for German action: Ribbentrop telegraphed the same day to Schulenburg directing him to propose to Molotov, and if possible to Stalin himself, a pact of non-aggression. On *16 August* Molotov accepted in principle but asked in return for a joint guarantee over the Baltic States. Ribbentrop accepted at once and said that he had recommended Hitler to sign. He then asked if he could come to Moscow at the end of that week. The reaction of Molotov on the *17th* (the day we felt that we were on the verge of a breakdown and I left for Warsaw) was more cautious: 'The Soviet Government has taken cognizance of the statement of the German Government . . . concerning its desire for a real improvement in the political relations between Germany and the USSR.' German policy hitherto had been hostile and 'had compelled the USSR to participate in the organization of a defensive front of a group of states against such an aggression.

If, however, the German Government now undertakes a change from the old policy in the direction of a sincere improvement in political relations with the USSR, the Soviet Government can look upon such a change and is in its own part prepared to alter its policy in the direction of an appreciable improvement in relations with Germany.

. . . The principle of a peaceful existence of various political systems side by side represents a long established principle of the foreign policy of the USSR . . . [and could lead to] serious and practical steps in that direction.'

The first step would be a financial and commercial agreement, the second, soon after, a non-aggression pact and the reaffirmation of the 1926 Treaty of neutrality.

'A journey by the Reich Foreign Minister, however, required thorough preparation.'

On the *18th* (I was in Warsaw) Ribbentrop telegraphed that a meeting in Moscow should take place without delay because 'this is the only method of obtaining quick results and to take into consideration Russian interests in the event of war.' The commercial Treaty was now agreed, and he went on to to put forward the following text for the next step:

Article 1. The German Reich and the USSR will in no event resort to war or any other use of force with respect to each other.
Article 2. This agreement shall enter into force immediately upon signature and shall be valid and undenounceable thereafter for a term of twenty-five years.
I am also in a position to sign a special protocol regulating the interests of both parties in question of foreign policy of one kind or another; for instance, the settlement of spheres of interest in the Baltic area, the problem of the Baltic States, etc. . . .
In this connection you must keep in mind the decisive fact that an early outbreak of open German-Polish conflict is probable and that we therefore have the greatest interest in having my visit to Moscow take place immediately.

19 August was the day of Soviet decision.

Schulenburg telegraphed: 'The Soviet Government agrees to the Reich Foreign Minister's coming to Moscow one week after proclamation of the signing of the economic agreement. Molotov stated that if the conclusion of the economic agreement is proclaimed tomorrow, the Reich Foreign Minister might arrive in Moscow on August 26 or 27.' He added that the Soviet proposed a different text for the non-aggression pact but that they did not want to rush it.

Then the Germans played a trump card to accelerate the rhythm of the discussions. On *20 August* Hitler sent a personal message to Stalin saying that he was delighted with the progress of the negotiations, that he accepted the Soviet text but there was need for a supplementary protocol which must be negotiated face to face, and that because of the tension with Poland there was no time to lose. He asked for an immediate answer.

Stalin replied on the *21st*: 'I thank you for the letter. I hope that the German-Soviet non-aggression pact will mark a decided turn for the better in the political relations between our countries.

'The people of our countries need peaceful relations with each other. The assent of the German Government to the conclusion of the non-aggression pact provides the foundation for eliminating the political tension and for the establishment of peace and collaboration between our countries.'

Ribbentrop's visit was fixed for the 23rd. Thus, in contrast with our long-drawn-out negotiations, the turn-about had been accomplished in a few days (the 14th to the 23rd) and the decisive action took four days!

There exists a memorandum of the conversation between Ribbentrop and Stalin. It ranged over a wide field: Japan, Italy, Turkey. Apropos of Great Britain Stalin said: 'The military mission in Moscow, which had never told the Soviet Government what it really wanted', which well shows that our hesitant attitude was not appreciated. 'The British Army is weak,' confirming what I noted at the time when the British described their resources. But 'Stalin further expressed the opinion that England, despite its weakness, would wage war craftily and stubbornly.'

As to France 'Stalin expressed the opinion that France, nevertheless, had an Army worthy of consideration', to which Ribbentrop replied that France would certainly be conquered. . . .

At the dinner which followed numerous toasts were exchanged. The one proposed by Molotov was particularly interesting: 'Molotov raised his glass to Stalin and said that it was he, by his speech in the previous March which had been fully appreciated in Germany, who had paved the way for this reversal in political relations.'

The cynicism and brutality of this concrete example of 'Realpolitik'* has almost an air of hallucination about it. But it can be seen that the drama latent in the understanding between Germany and Russia really only led to agreement at the last moment. A better advised policy on our part might have completely changed the course of events.

But the gods did not wish it.

Leaving Moscow that same evening, seen off by the same officials who had met them, the British and French missions could not help but realize the enormous mistake which had been made by engaging

* See the text of the secret German-Soviet protocol signed at Moscow on 23 August 1939 in Appendix II, page 144.

in negotiations without having solved in their own minds the principal difficulties. Certainly the fault did not lie with the missions themselves who knew that they had done everything they could; it lay with their Governments and even more perhaps with the sort of paralysis so far as any decision or thought were concerned which had been characteristic of the policy of the western democracies since 1924.

The route back was not the same as that taken on the way out for the news was bad and Paris sent us a telegram directing us not to come via Poland and Germany, nor the Baltic for the same reason. We therefore went through Finland, Sweden and Norway whence the British fleet could if necessary cover our passage in the open sea.

Although we all felt the need for speed, the journey, arranged by the Soviet authorities, entailed spending the whole of the 26th in Leningrad where, as on our arrival, the missions had cars and Intourist guides placed at their disposal and were able to visit Peterhof, like a Russian Versailles, on the southern shore of the Gulf of Finland. There we saw the charming little pavilion in the Dutch style built of wood by Peter the Great to remind him of the country where he had first come in contact with civilization. Beside it stands the palace, built in the Italian style, as usual rather over-ornamented but still grand, and connected with the sea by cascades and a canal. The whole is a most noble ensemble but less moving than Pouchkine (Krasnoïe-Selo) because less redolent of the atmosphere of Catherine the Great and the last Tsar; but it forms nevertheless a sort of cradle of the great empire brought together and colonized by Peter the Great, that emigrant of genius who shows himself at Peterhof to have been a sort of over-grown half-civilized child, amusing himself with practical jokes in doubtful taste, like the chair which squirted water, or retiring to the wooden house for drinking bouts which are by no means a lost tradition in Russia today.

In the park huge propaganda posters gave the military missions an opportunity of seeing how political themes, which are drummed into the people, can rapidly change. One of the posters depicted the enemies of Russia, naturally impaled by a Red Guard; one of them was the classic capitalist in a top hat, and another was an ugly Nazi brute. It is probable that the latter would be replaced in short order by an image of the western plutocracies.

At about five in the afternoon the missions left Leningrad for Finland. After an hour's journey we came to the business of crossing the frontier.

The impression made upon us was just as great as that which I had felt a few days earlier, especially as we had to wait for over an hour for orders to come from no one knew where but which were apparently essential—specifically to allow a one-time French Deputy and Minister, M. Hymans, to join our special train and leave Soviet territory.

At the first station in Finland, Terijoki, there was such a feeling of liberty that the members of the missions one and all heaved a sigh of relief, which was so heart-felt that Admiral Drax even executed a little dance on the platform! Despite the seriousness of the moment and the preoccupations which weighed heavily upon us all, the feeling of freedom and unanimous pleasure turned the stops at each station into a sort of small party, as if, after a long nightmare, each one of us had woken up again in a familiar and happy world.

Alas, when we got to Helsinki the next day the news was bad. Germany had mobilized the passenger planes used on the Scandinavian airlines which they ran jointly with Sweden. This news showed that there was not a moment to lose. After a quick visit to the city and its surroundings, it was thought best to cross the Gulf of Bothnia that night and to charter aircraft for the purpose.

From then onwards events moved at a more and more rapid pace. Scarcely had we arrived in Stockholm when the Military Attaché told us that rail communications between Germany and her neighbours had been cut. The military missions immediately took seats in all the available aircraft leaving forthwith, one from Stockholm to London, the other from Malmö to Amsterdam and Paris. The next morning at Amsterdam we learned that Holland was mobilizing and at Paris, when we all got back on the 29th, that the situation was as bad as could be imagined: the reserves had been called up; general mobilization had not yet been declared, but was imminent. All hope of keeping the peace seemed lost.

For all the members of the two missions fresh tasks were about to begin.

Appendix I

It is interesting to compare the instructions given to the French military mission with the opinion on the Moscow negotiations expressed the same day by the German Ambassador at Paris in a telegram to the Wilhelmstrasse. This telegram was published in a German White Book and bears the stamp of authenticity. It shows how well informed Germany diplomacy was, and how much more clear and simple their appreciation was than our own.

TELEGRAM

Paris 28 July 1939

Subject of Moscow negotiations I learn the following from well-informed circles:

1. If at this moment Great Britain and France prepared to enter into military conversations before reaching political understanding and further pursuing the idea of military conversations with particular ardour it is due to the following considerations:

a. Great Britain and France desirous at any price of avoiding any adjournment or rupture of negotiations because they believe so long as these negotiations continue Germany will make no move at Danzig. Political negotiations have practically reached conclusion with agreement on all points *except for definition of indirect attack and means of furnishing aid.* So many different points of view on military possibilities on this last point that no further progress can be made without simultaneous military discussions.

b. In sending two fully representative military missions to Moscow, it is thought possible to influence favourably the general atmosphere while political treaty is being entered into at same time.

c. By eventual military understanding, politicians hope exert pressure to surmount final difficulties even though unable to disguise fact that *military conversations encountering from Russian side, not only problems of Baltic States, but also difficult problem of military aid entering Poland and Rumania.*

2. Conclusion of Anglo-Japanese convention said used by British in Moscow negotiations in this sense: Great Britain paid high price Tien-tsin negotiations in recognizing Japanese interests in China and standing aside duration of conflict. Great Britain obliged because must have free hand in Europe so long as no treaty achieved Moscow. If negotiations break down Great Britain's position in eastern Asia very difficult and Russia in long run more exposed to Japanese pressure.

3. Correlated with Moscow negotiations question of maintenance of Russo-German Treaty of 1926 said to be on the

tapis from Franco-British side. Question examined of whether to ask Russia denounce Treaty or let it lapse but said that question skirted in order not to render negotiations even more difficult.

Appendix II

SECRET PROTOCOL BETWEEN USSR AND GERMANY

1. In the event of a territorial and political rearrangement in the areas belonging to the Baltic States (Finland, Estonia, Latvia, Lithuania), the northern boundary of Lithuania shall represent the boundary of the spheres of influence of Germany and the USSR. In this connection the interest of Lithuania in the Vilna area is recognized by each party.
2. In the event of a territorial and political rearrangement of the areas belonging to the Polish state the spheres of influence of Germany and the USSR shall be bounded approximately by the line of the rivers Narew, Vistula and San.
The question of whether the interests of both parties make desirable the maintenance of an independent Polish state and how such a state should be bounded can only be definitely determined in the course of further political developments.
3. With regard to south-eastern Europe attention is called by the Soviet side to its interest in Bessarabia. The German side declares its complete political disinterestedness in these areas.

Chapter 7
The Phoney War

*

THE RETURN FROM Russia had given us our first impressions of war. At Malmö I made sure that the Swedish airline plane on which I was leaving for Amsterdam did not touch down at Hamburg, where I was afraid of being interned. But over the North Sea a German fighter buzzed us. Were we to be forced down? To my great relief he contented himself with just having a close look at us.

At Amsterdam we found ourselves in the thick of mobilization. The airfield was packed with young reservists, wearing the most astonishing tall shakos. In the city the thousands of cyclists sported every conceivable combination of uniform and civilian dress.

In Paris mobilization was already well under way. It represented, after the previous alerts, a more complete repetition of what had already been tried out. No enthusiasm, no protests: merely a calm resignation to the inevitable, coloured for us by the very varying thoughts of what might have been.

I found Army Headquarters at the War Office completely transformed. Most of my friends had departed to set up the General Headquarters. My mission to Russia meant that I had missed out on this. I remained posted to the offices in the boulevard Saint-Germain which had filled up with reservists slightly bewildered by their new duties. In the temporary disorder I chose a small but agreeable office for myself, found a comfortable armchair for my visitors, and a personal secretary, which at the time represented the height of luxury. After several days of flap, work settled down. This was war; there were no more Sundays—nor Saturdays either. We wore uniform all the time, with a gas-mask slung over the shoulder. Soon these were issued to civilians, which gave a rather ridiculous quasi-military look to the streets of Paris. After dark the lights went out; there was nothing but a dim blue. France was to live in this twilight for six years.

Amidst all this new routine we heard the terrible news of the crushing of Poland and her partition once again between Germany and the USSR. Under the hammer-blows of the German armour the slender Polish forces, not even up to strength since their mobilization was not completed, collapsed, and the German columns then went on to vast turning movements. Cut up and encircled, the Polish Army lasted no more than the two weeks which Ironside had predicted. All this was terrible but unhappily foreseen. No one doubted the heroism of the Poles—which was shown again and again throughout the war—but, despite the reports coming in to us, one questioned the military value of their preparations. There was for example talk of lancers charging German armour. In any case how could thirty under-strength divisions cover more than four hundred miles of frontier? The example of Poland did not seem to apply to ourselves with our greater density of troops reinforced by the Maginot Line. In spite of the study which I had made at Marrakesh of the possibility of armoured thrusts, I too fell into this erroneous way of thinking, which shows just how much one's judgement can be affected by one's surroundings.

The news of the Soviet invasion, a stab in the back if ever there was one, made us wonder how we could ever have contemplated allying ourselves with such people. The general view was that the negotiations in Moscow had been nothing more than a farce. Knowing rather more about it, I found my thoughts dwelling on the complete disregard shown by the Polish leaders for the danger threatening their country, even though I felt the greatest sympathy for this unfortunate country the fate of which I had foreseen ever since that terrible Sunday in Warsaw when I took the train back to Riga. Beck and Rydz-Smigly eluded their fate by fleeing to Rumania, but I could not find it in myself to feel sorry for them!

Meanwhile what was happening on our front? Contrary to all logic—since logic indicated that we should have attacked to take the pressure off Poland—nothing was happening, or at any rate very little. Our great Army had been mobilized and concentrated on the frontier along the Maginot Line. Now we could see the extraordinary influence of these fortifications: if we advanced, we lost the benefit of their protection; and to attack, one must advance.

Gamelin, true to type, decided to do nothing more than make a

gesture: he ordered an 'offensive reconnaissance' in the direction of
Saarbrücken (shades of 1870!). One Army Corps advanced to contact
and found nothing but masses of mines. This was a new element
with which in due course we were to become only too familiar, but
was surprising at the time. As at the beginning of all wars, the
remedies were rudimentary: infantrymen set them off by hitting
them with a stick or herds of cattle were driven on to them . . . .
Finally the operation, directed in a very half-hearted and desultory
way, bogged down in the minefields under artillery fire after advancing no more than a few miles. The Germans did not react.
Gamelin decided to pull back. So much for our help to Poland.

After this apology for an attack, our front became static. Activi-
ties were limited to patrols and the occasional *coup de main* in which
we usually came off worst because our men, enervated by this static
life, found themselves face to face with young and fanatical Germans
on their toes who were rushed up from the rear in motorized transport to counter any move. There were a few artillery duels; no aerial
combat whatever. Along the length of the Rhine (the opposite bank
of which we were forbidden to shell), the Germans hung out their
washing, harangued our troops through loudspeakers and, with
impunity, under our noses sent a stream of trains bearing coal from
the Ruhr to Italy. . . . One day I was told to escort the Prince of
Cambodia, who was doing a tour with the Army Corps of General
Frère. The impression which I brought back from Lorraine was
incredible: the Army was rotting from inaction.

This was quite absurd. Why were we acting like this? Or, more
properly, why were we not acting?

The explanation for this extraordinary situation known as the
'phoney war' is not simple because it brings together a number of
surprising factors.

The first of these factors is the shackles of historical circumstance.
We must go back once more because it is impossible to understand
the events of September 1939 without reference to Munich. Up to
Munich French policy was dominated by paralysis: successive
Governments were almost entirely preoccupied with financial difficulties round which everything else revolved. Internally France was
divided into two equibalanced sides; externally we were on the

slippery slope of abandon which we accepted with fatalism and the irresponsibility of a son who ruins himself in the belief that he will never exhaust the family fortune. People were constantly saying that 'something must be done' to find a concrete solution to the problems which faced us in Europe; but what? As soon as anything was put forward, everything reacted against it—finance, ideology, alliances. As we saw immediately after the elections of 6 February 1936 France, bedevilled by devaluation and the Spanish affair, was unanimous on one thing only: maintaining the *status quo*. As some- one remarked intelligently of Daladier, 'the country keeps a medio- crity in power for fear of anything worse'. Bourgeois, introverted and quite satisfied with her lot, France refused to adapt herself and hoped to avoid all the political storms which were brewing by burying her head in the sand.

Munich destroyed all that. It was a rude awakening: not only were we an inch away from war, that abomination abhorred by all, but everyone realized that the renaissance of Germany imposed a simple choice: either the complete abandonment of all that Ver- sailles stood for, or an open struggle in the near future. Implicitly we had all hoped that things would sort themselves out, but here we were on the very brink.

It was a difficult choice. Militarily we were not ready to confront Germany with an Army done on the cheap and an Air Force with no resources. Morally the situation was even worse: for twenty years peace had been the watchword and the national energy had dwindled accordingly. But on the other hand it was obvious that in letting our Czechoslovak ally go by the board we would not only lose one of our trump cards but also hazard every other card in the hand which Foch had so painstakingly put together in central and eastern Europe—with the result that thereafter we would be powerless to oppose Hitler's designs. Logically the answer was to go to war, but conditions did not seem favourable; and most people conscientiously felt that anything would be preferable, and perhaps some last- minute solution might yet be found.

It was this last thought, entirely sentimental, which was carried into the council chambers of Munich. Chamberlain, without believ- ing it, convinced himself that Germany had no more than limited and acceptable intentions. Daladier—overwhelmed by the dilemma and haunted by the thought of the responsibilities imposed upon him—suddenly flung away all reason and 'fell back into peace with an instinctive gesture of hope and weakness', while realizing exactly the enormity of the mistake which he was making. He returned to Paris completely defeated, but the triumphal reception accorded to him made him realize that his mediocre reaction fitted the views of the majority.

Then, like the re-opening of an old affair, there was a period of optimism and wilful blindness. Why not let Germany push on eastwards? Let us cultivate our garden, which is so great and so beautiful. That was indeed a task which we could cope with. And in this state of euphoria, gently encouraged by the propaganda of Abetz and the visit of Ribbentrop, we liked to think that we could continue to live our agreeable life and that nothing would threaten us. All right, the anti-fascists and a few patriots of the old school were making noises about the scandalous and cowardly state of affairs and, rather more worrying, the extreme right which admired Hitlerism was talking openly of our associating ourselves with the German movement and taking a leaf from their book. But why worry? The tearing up of the Treaty of Versailles was not a bad thing, really; no one can for ever maintain the status of victor, and was it not by now generally recognized that the whole treaty was nothing more than a tissue of ethnic and political absurdities?

Unhappily in March 1939 Hitler and Mussolini took off their masks: only yesterday they had promised verbally and in writing that they would go no further, but still they went on; 'Pan-Germanism' had been spoken of, but now they were annexing the Czechs and Albanians. There was no more room for illusion. Compliance or opposition—there was a clear choice. Public opinion at last realized what was going on.

There were few in favour of compliance. They were those who for the last year had promoted active pro-fascist propaganda, joined by the supporters of peace at any price. Then there was a small number of Germanophiles, who came to the surface after the defeat; they were mostly those who since 1936 had turned against the *Front Populaire* and who made anti-Communism the criterion of everything they did. As happens in all great internal crises they put party before country. They rallied to the idea of war after the 'Bolshevik betrayal' of the

Ribbentrop-Molotov pact, and gravitated back towards Germany when she started her European crusade against Russia. In 1939 they had little influence.

For opposing Germany there was a great majority: anti-fascists and pacifists believing in Geneva who hoped for the downfall of the Nazi régime for the reasons opposite to our Hitlerians; soldiers and patriots alarmed at the increase of the odds against us; and, above all, the great mass of ordinary people in whom the old national instinct, so profoundly deadened, was roused once more by the traditional German menace. We were the enemies of Germany.

But it was not possible to change overnight from illusion to reality, nor from idleness to courage. France was almost unanimously in favour of a resolute resistance but, apart from some who foresaw the future and a few others in high office who were later branded as 'warmongers', there was still a widely felt hope that war might be avoided, for this was rightly regarded with horror and as contrary to nature. The end was desired, but not the means by which history dictated that it must be achieved. Munich was much discussed: now that the emotions aroused by the event had settled down, there seemed a large element of bluff in Hitler's game—what would he have done if we had not given way? His military forces were not yet ready, the German economy was vulnerable, the Nazi régime still meeting opposition. There was nothing in it for him to start a war which, if it were prolonged, was bound to prove fatal. Then people turned their minds to our Army which had been forgotten and run down over twenty years; they were astonished to discover that it was still almost intact despite disaffection and the inroads of politics. This happy surprise, ill merited, cloaked the weaknesses and the senility. At cinemas shots of the Maginot Line were shown and *Trois de Saint-Cyr*, a rather mediocre film, was very popular; in these grave times it gave the feeling that peace depended upon our strength. This strength seemed to be great: we had 'the finest Army in the world' based upon the most modern defensive system in existence; its leaders were interviewed and, confident in their doctrine, assured their questioners that any German attack would be smashed at the frontier. Since Hitler could not defeat us, why should he want war with us? To stop him it was necessary to persuade him that if he continued in his present ways he would be forced to fight a war which he could not win and which would eventually bring toppling down the fragile structure which he had built up over the last few years. Thence the idea arose that bluff must be met with bluff, the threat of war by a threat of war: by taking a stand of energetic opposition we were sure to win the peace.

To these arguments, which looked reasonable enough, were added others which were less so; the country was tired of these crises and annual or bi-annual mobilization which disrupted daily life and impeded progress. People wanted to finish with it once and for all, and at least do something. In the midst of the nightmare of the last few years they had lost faith in 'the renewal of peace' which had swept over them in 1936 and produced a pacific attitude. In a nutshell the general feeling was, as Jouvenel put it so well, for 'a leap into the unknown through disillusion with what was all too well known'.

Wherever one turned in the summer of 1939 one found a marked reaction against the spirit of Munich. It was felt that there could be no more of it, that no more bluff could be tolerated, and that Germany with her constant threats was becoming a bore. There was no general desire for war, but there was an almost unanimous support for what was called 'France's No.'

This slant of public opinion certainly had an effect on government decisions. But against this background which constituted the climate of the country as the summer wore on there began to shape the calculations and the actions of the statesmen, torn by conflicting sentiments.

At the time of Munich, and even more thereafter, there was an accounting, a good deal of arithmetic. In the rue Saint-Dominique it was appreciated that the loss of Czechoslovakia had seriously weakened us: the alliance of forces which previously had given us a numerical advantage in divisions had now dwindled to parity. If we allowed even one more of our partners to be overwhelmed we would lose our last chance of facing the Axis with sufficient means.

The same calculations were made in London: officially the resisters, Eden and Duff Cooper who had left the Government, were beaten, but in fact the Government was now completely resigned to the idea of resistance. The main preoccupation was an attempt to rebuild in the east a group of powers capable of standing up to the next German thrust and to form a second front if it should prove necessary: Chamberlain guaranteed Poland and Rumania, and opened negotiations with the USSR. There were also doubts about the firmness of France's attitude in another crisis and it was hoped to bind us more firmly to a policy of resistance by a common treaty with Russia like that which we had just signed with Turkey. It was hoped to check Germany without recourse to arms, but from this time forward it was decided to wage war if all else failed. All in all the British Government was thinking along the same lines as our military leaders.

In Paris, at the Quai d'Orsay, the hardening of the British policy was regarded as a French victory. For years we had been facing Germany alone and this was why we had always had to give way. Now that 'Mr Britling sees it through' we would have the strength to oppose the German manoeuvres. It was easy to feel that we had been taken for a ride at Munich but that it must never happen again. While the British were worrying about whether they would get France to the point if the necessity arose, we on our side were avidly watching their every movement in this reborn Entente Cordiale, and an attempt was made to give it more deep-felt value by an exchange of visits between the King and President Lebrun.

It was in this much firmer atmosphere that the next phase of the German offensive began to show itself. In March our Ambassador at Berlin sent news that Hitler had made up his mind 'to dispose of the Polish question once and for all' in the coming autumn, and that he was reckoning on Anglo-French complaisance. In fact the manoeuvre developed day by day exactly on the lines of the previous year's crisis and the pace quickened.

The Allied reaction centred on eastern Europe. The policy of guarantees which had been launched somewhat airily in March and April now had to translate itself into a firm front of which the binding strength could only be the USSR. The negotiations dragged on in a manner inexplicable to an impatient public. The truth was, as we have seen, that the Soviets presented a programme of intervention in the Baltic States, Poland and Rumania which risked engendering serious difficulties with those countries which were unable to disguise their distaste for the idea. Optimistically there was hope of getting Russian aid without giving a positive solution to the problems raised by the Russians, that is to say without settling in advance the conditions for their action on the territories of their future allies. This inability to adjust our eastern policy to the exigencies of the time removed all efficacy from the negotiations, so long-drawn-out in the hope of impressing Germany and pushing back the aggression against Poland into 1940.

In effect we were not yet ready. The backlog of weakness which was revealed at the time of Munich imposed the necessity for a serious military recovery; while the British had to start practically from scratch, we were in much the same position in the air, and so far as our ground forces were concerned in 1938 we had to face serious deficiencies. The effort was made but the results were inadequate: much more was needed before we would be ready to wage war.

This shortfall had a political side to it: the resistance of various parties had to be overcome in order to get workers to put their backs into war production instead of continuing their endless strikes. Daladier felt that he could not resolve the thousand problems which surrounded him without full powers—which in due course he obtained easily—to speed up the change-over. The reason for this near-paralysis lay, as I have said earlier, in the great weakness of the administrative machine which was capable neither of serious reform nor quick results. In the late spring of 1939 France was trying, bit by bit, to the hundred-year-old tempo of Monsieur Le Bureau, to build up a force which everyone knew would be put to the test before the leaves of autumn were on the ground.

Furthermore military opinion both in Paris and in London was convinced that any delay was to our advantage. This calculation was completely ill founded, as 1940 showed, but at the time it dominated our every move, from Russia to the Rhine. From this time on it was agreed that, if the Germans forced us to take up arms, we would not attack in order 'to wait until we were stronger'.

This decision, in itself very debatable, opened the way for opposing tendencies to converge in such a way that the September crisis became a whirlpool of misunderstandings. If Germany attacked

Poland, should we mobilize or not, should we go to war or not? Instead of a clear answer, our policy of waiting prevented us from getting to the heart of the matter: because we were not going to attack, the bridges with Germany should not be destroyed and we could play the rest by ear.

This point of view satisfied the Munichites: when Poland was attacked, we would reply with a feint, fairly strong but something like the traditional security stand-to; this gesture would not stop Germany, but at least we would give the *impression* of honouring our commitments and would put up a show to satisfy our foreign friends and above all the patriot and anti-fascist parties in our own country. De Monzie followed this line of thought, and perhaps also Bonnet.

The idea of an apparently energetic feint also appealed to the Quai d'Orsay. 'Hold on,' wrote Coulondre from Berlin, 'if you hold on Hitler will founder.' Nothing would be lost if, as in 1938, there were Italian mediation under another name. If war broke out one could always disengage 'afterwards'. This thought was at the back of the minds of Daladier and Bonnet. Apparent firmness seemed a good risk: by mobilization Daladier hoped to get wider powers and also the moral spur which our people needed; the Army could demonstrate the efficiency of our military system and Parliament could face our financial difficulties later.

On the other hand a solution by force would satisfy those who believed that a second Munich would be very much to France's detriment, to the anti-Nazi crusaders, and also to Great Britain which feared that we would once more renegue at the psychological moment.

Curiously enough this manoeuvre played Germany's game to perfection. Since April Hitler had counted upon it: his Polish plans foresaw that from the French side there would be a gesture of solidarity going as far as a declaration of war but that 'they would do nothing' and that 'they would use the whole winter in trying to contain the conflict by diplomatic means'. His words were known in Paris and it may be that he had means of ensuring that they were known. The result was an extraordinary feeling of security: for the initiated war was not 'a leap into the unknown' but a sort of giant charade acted out by mutual consent from which nothing serious could emerge if we played our part right. We must take note of this conception which during the winter of 1939–40 had the effect of anaesthetising willpower. It is perhaps no exaggeration to think that Hitler played up to it, since so many Frenchmen, and by no means small fry at that, swallowed this terrible bait.

Oblivious of this combination of ideas, deeply felt however absurd, public opinion appeared as a curious mixture of determination and resignation, of pacifism or indifference and of patriotism. The good sense of the man in the street felt that war was coming and was indeed inevitable, but there was no enthusiasm for 'shouldering a knapsack' as the current phrase was. The general feeling was flabby; the first call-up of reservists was received with dignity but complete lack of enthusiasm. 'No sense of thrill,' de Monzie noted. And then against this gloomy, stolid background there appeared various agitations which were not without their consequences: Céline and Darquier de Pellepoix tried to raise a feeling of anti-Semitism in France; Doriot, Déat and others, now long forgotten, attempted openly to promote pro-German propaganda. The latter made some impression with Déat's equivocal phrase: 'Why die for Danzig?' When they reacted instinctively the masses in France were sound, but when they started to 'think' doubts came into their minds, born from the old pacifism of the First War veterans and nourished by the political atmosphere of the previous few years and the Hitlerian slogans. In this confusion there was no great enthusiasm for the struggle but merely a hope that the worst might be avoided. It was summed up in one striking phrase, 'the nation went to war looking over its shoulder, its eyes seeking for peace.'

I have tried to describe the atmosphere through which I lived in Paris and which I do not report from hearsay. There is no point in setting out the facts step by step, they are on the record: the Russian defection, the Polish insouciance, the Fabian prudence of Bonnet, the hesitations and perpetual see-saw of Daladier, the telephone calls to Berlin and London—and finally the two declarations of war several hours apart.

What must be remembered from all this is that the main decision —although less important than has been made out since the war was in fact fatal to Germany—was not so much a choice as an attempt to avoid making a choice between contradicting tendencies. The

Government was divided, the people were not united and to a great extent strangely amorphous. Duty and honour could be clearly seen but energy was lacking. Thus one fell back on a policy of waiting, a bastard movement which satisfied everyone without committing us to the future—at least that was the idea. On 31 August the Council of Ministers showed to perfection this character of compromise which we succeeded in giving to a definitive decision which normally is a straightforward declaration of war.

It is because of this spirit of compromise that we entered the war without pride, one might say almost shamefacedly; that the debate in the Chamber was conducted as if it were a vote on some minor Act, that those who believed the war to be just and necessary could not express their enthusiasm, while those who were against it did not dare to express their views. Everyone felt that there was this precarious balance but everyone hoped to avoid going over the edge. Giraudoux, who now found himself charged with the task of replying to Goebbels, had summed it up several years before in his play, the title of which was *La Guerre de Troie n'aura pas lieu*. This negative view summed up the irony of the situation in the face of fate and was a criticism of the pacifist attitude at the time. If Giraudoux had written his play in 1939 he would have set it in the midst of the Trojan war and could have called it *La Guerre de Troie aura-t-elle lieu?*

Thus we moved on—as I put it in an article in the '*Revue des Deux Mondes*'—from the 'warlike peace' to the 'peaceful war'. It was an unusual situation. What we know now of the events which followed leads us to pass a severe judgement on those responsible for this policy. I think that those who carried this responsibility must be given credit for the fact that they had every reason to be fearful of a major conflict, since no good could come of it. Their mistake was not in temporizing, but in temporizing ineffectively without taking real steps to stop Hitler in his frantic and unthinking march to the abyss.

It is not without interest to examine the basis of our thinking in order to understand the various aspects of what had gone before.

We have looked at the purely political aspect of what happened, but this would be unbalanced if we did not take into consideration the military side of the compromise: it is precisely because the strategic conceptions of the Allies aligned themselves to some extent with the hesitation of the statesmen that such equivocation became possible. But any equivocation carries within itself fatal germs and we shall see that it was these germs which eventually led to the ruin of Franco-British military co-operation.

In fact, contrary to what was felt immediately after the defeat, we had a military plan which was quite logical but ill-founded. This resulted in a remarkable convergence between the French and the British conceptions—conceptions which, in spite of such different points of departure, finished up with a common object.

I have already tried to describe in a preceding chapter the broad outline of French doctrine. It can be summed up in the following points: offensive action had become extremely difficult and demanded enormous resources, and thus a defensive front seemed to have everything to recommend it; it would buy time in which to mobilize industry on a war footing and provide the sinews for the second year's struggle. As I have said, the idea was to recreate the conditions of 1918—and wait.

The British mentality in 1939 has never received any official consideration, but it, and the ideas underlying it, have been examined in great detail by my friend Captain Liddell Hart, the great military critic who has produced important original thinking on our problems. As soon as the First War ended he left the Army and applied his mind to the problem of how to avoid a repetition of the frontal slaughters of 1918. His first studies led him to express views highly critical of the events which took place between 1914 and 1918 which not only cut across the views of the British military authorities but also irritated the ruling Army clique in France: he had the effrontery to criticize Joffre and Foch, which was unforgivable. But he could have taught us many things, not least the benefit of that critical military sense which we needed so much.

After ten years of research he formulated a doctrine which he put forward as the traditional British doctrine: 'A romantic habit has led us to hide, and has even hidden from us, our essentially businesslike tradition in the conduct of war. . . . Our historic practice . . . was based on economic pressure exercised through sea-power. This

naval body had two arms; one financial, which embraced the sub-
sidizing and military provisioning of allies; the other military,
which embraced sea-borne expeditions against the enemy's vulnerable extremities. By our practice we safeguarded ourselves where
we were weakest, and exerted our strength where the enemy was
weakest.'

In these circumstances he believed in military forces limited in
size but possessing great mobility through the use of armour: 'The
Armies of 1914–18 were like huge fungoid plants, firm-rooted and
nourished through long stems. An armoured force has the power to
be a deadly vapour which "bloweth where it listeth"; an influence,
invulnerable less through its armour than through its power to move
away. Thus it would be intangible, and all the more demoraliz-
ing.'

These remarkable words met with no very great reception in
Great Britain and were refuted in French military journals. But on
the other hand they enjoyed prodigious success in Germany; that
is why I stop at this phase of Liddell Hart's thinking. He was in
touch with General von Blomberg, then Minister for the Reichswehr, and he had definite influence on the resurgent German doctrine. The prestige which he enjoyed on the other side of the Rhine
is borne out by the fact, reported in the Press, that his writings
formed part of the travelling library which Hitler took with him
wherever he went, side by side with Clausewitz and the letters of
Napoleon. He was another example of the old adage that 'a prophet
is not without honour save in his own country'.

It fell to Liddell Hart to appear as a prophet in Great Britain on
the eve of the war. It is true he had not completely overcome
the prejudice against him in military circles, but he had succeeded in
convincing the civilian Ministers, Duff Cooper and Hore-Belisha,
with whom he worked before Munich. It was he who inspired the
reorganization of the British Army and his last book before the war,
The Defence of Britain, which appeared in July 1939, was the foundation of British thinking. But here came out the cruel irony of fate:
the Liddell Hart of 1939 had moved on from the Liddell Hart of
1935 and his new ideas were now more concerned with the means
and object of defence against an aggression which he saw clearly was
at hand.

I think that it is interesting to quote these new conceptions at length because of the highly important role which they played in the conduct of the war.

The wars in Spain and China have provided a test of post-Great War developments in armament. They have shown the difficulty of overcoming the resistance even of ill-organized armies which suffer from a very marked material inferiority—and the increased difficulty as compared with the past. They afford no encouragement to the idea that 'victory' is practicable in another great war where the Armies of great powers, differing little in armament and potential scale, would be pitted against each other. *The dream of victory in modern war has nothing beyond mere speculation to sustain it.* And it is faced by the hard fact of the long-proved superiority of the modern tactical defensive.

Our greater object will be to ensure, in face of an aggressor, the continuance of liberal civilization—those larger ideals which we epitomize when we speak of 'England'. To attain that object, however, *need not imply on our part a war à outrance.* . . . Our object is fulfilled if we can convince the enemy that he cannot conquer. . . . So why prepare to waste our strength in the vain attempt? Surely it would be wiser to confine our military aim to what is possible—*convincing any opponent that he cannot defeat us.*

These reflections lead to speculation on the future of war. *The assumption—that war inevitably means a fight to a finish—has an illusory foundation.*

Strength to meet any threat at sea or in the air is a *necessity* for us; that cannot be said, strictly, of any land force beyond the minimum requirements for the defence of our oversea territories. *It would be folly to develop any effort on land* which could weaken our sea-power or air power.

Then Liddell Hart turned to the French Army:

The French have pinned their faith to the strength and solidity of the Army. This offered good ground on which to base trust, even though a large part of its equipment is far from up to date. Contrary to traditional notions of the French Army it is . . . solid rather than brilliant in performance; but its training has a thoroughness which that of the newly expanded German Army can hardly expect to attain as yet—and its steps are very sure. Its prospects, also, are improved by the fact that French policy, having no aggressive designs, is more suited to modern military conditions *wherein the offensive starts with a heavy handicap.* The necessity of giving her all possible support in the air, and at the quickest possible

moment, is unmistakable. Help in safeguarding her at sea is likewise indicated. The point that is more open to question is the need for, and the measure of, a land contribution. . . .
Once the French Army had mobilized, that field force, in which infantry predominate, would add but a trifle to their strength. Its value to them might be much less than *the risk to us of being drawn, by degrees, into a fresh mass-effort on land* that would offer less prospect of result and more of exhaustion than even in the last war.
The same reasons which cast doubt on the practicability of a German attack against the French frontier apply still more strongly to a French move in the opposite direction. . . . It is an unfortunate aspect of the present situation that, if Poland were attacked, the French could not give direct help in reinforcing her defence; thus, although now defensively minded in contrast to 1914, they might feel impelled to take the offensive by the sense of 'What else can we do?' Once they were committed to an unhopeful effort of this nature, and our forces were drawn into it, an increasing extension of our land commitment is not difficult to foresee.*

There clearly expressed are all the ideas which dominated the first part of the war: no will to victory, a defensive attitude with automatic limitation of action, the blockade, lack of enthusiasm for military effort—above all on the Continent (from the British point of view)—and a fixed belief in the uselessness of a fight to the end. The theory is clearly and starkly set out with its fallacious interpretation of the Spanish war (as ours was), its illusions over the value of the defensive (as ours were), and its dangerous misapprehensions over the possible development of the war. Furthermore there was no more talk, as there had been earlier, of mobility and a revolution of strategy through the use of armour.

I have dwelt at some length on these British conceptions because they sum up better than anything else the spirit in which the war was undertaken on the Allied side, and also because they show that we were not alone in the erroneous thinking of which our General Staff has been accused. Liddell Hart is one of the great military thinkers of his age and certainly cannot be accused of mentally falling into line nor of misunderstanding the use of armour; nevertheless he too was to a degree led away and his thinking changed in the years preceding the war until he reached a formula, as we have seen, which tallied with our own.

* General Beaufre's italics.

At the War Office I now had a lot to do: I was charged with the task of forming seven new divisions, to be made up of foreign volunteers such as Poles and colonial personnel, by the winter.

This was the application of Daladier's main idea: strengthening of the military effort while 'saving French blood'. This phrase, which he set out in a directive, was based upon a conscious lack of enthusiasm which found its beginnings in the slaughter of 1914–18. It was deep-seated in the minds of the veterans of the Great War who were now in command. The generals were haunted by the idea of avoiding useless losses and conducting the 'limited' operations which had kept our Armies going once the front had stabilized in 1914. It was this attitude of mind as much as the political attitude which provides the reason for our complete lack of action on the Lorraine front. At a higher level it led the Government to 'save French blood' by withdrawing reservists to the rear and replacing them with an equal number of foreigners recruited in our territory or *indigènes* brought over from our colonies. It was in pursuance of this principle that Mandel demanded the constitution of an enormous coloured army, which could not be realized through the absence both of ships and equipment; the first attempts in this direction merely succeeded in disorganizing several first-class white divisions.

This idea also moved Daladier to reduce our military effort by urging the British to increase theirs. He evidently had not read the passage from Liddell Hart which I have quoted above, or he would have realized in advance that this could merely serve to restrict our power. In any case, he decided that an increasing proportion of our production of arms and armour should be reserved for our Allies in order to accelerate the mobilization of more British divisions. I do not know how much was in fact delivered, but the British Expeditionary Force which should have been raised to thirty divisions by the end of a year of war in fact numbered only ten in May 1940.

Even more than by these conceptions, which one must say were a little naïve even if well intentioned, our military effort was very seriously curtailed by the needs of the economy. Our mobilization had been too strictly military because only the Army had made any serious provisions against a state of war.

It became immediately apparent that we would have to go into reverse and organize partial demobilization in the interests of production. Here the general theory of warfare made itself felt: because if we were not intending to wage war, at least not before 1941 or 1942, our huge Army was manifestly a useless luxury. This idea was generally accepted except at General Headquarters—certainly not in the spring of 1940—and required a fresh look at the Army. Dautry had already gone on record that he could not manufacture a sufficiency of warlike stores unless several hundred thousand men were returned to him; then agriculture asked not only for men, but for whole units, and horses; then the politicians put in their bids; why not release the fathers of four or more children, sons of widows, ex-Service men, etc. . . . All through the winter the struggle went on between General Headquarters, trying to husband its resources on the one hand, and a thousand interested parties on the other, each more voracious than the other. As a result in May 1940 the effective strength of the Army was lower than it had been in 1917.

But during this time the rate of production remained terribly low. One day there is a big book to be written on the drama of armaments. The process is complex: administrative responsibilities, politics and industry are inextricably mixed and make a solution difficult. The figures are there, and are overwhelming: we produced sixty aircraft in the month of September 1939 and sixty in May 1940—a complete absence of progress. As for armament on land, the situation was worse: Dautry when he set up his Ministry tore up the plans laïd down by the Ministry of War as being insufficient. He thought big, very big, but the change-about produced catastrophic results: production in October 1939 sank far below that of the previous month; after that the graph started to climb slowly, but so slowly that in many respects it was still lower in May 1940 than it had been even in October 1939. Defeat overtook us with hundreds of new factories not yet in production, which caused one of my colleagues in the armament section to remark (with obvious exaggeration) that 'Dautry is a traitor!'

We gained nothing from this policy of useless delay. It certainly deprived the Army of its sense of its own importance and almost everyone thought only of getting out. Moreover the Army of the Interior without sufficient resources, diluted with reservists or ageing officers who were not up to their job, presented a spectacle which reflected harshly on the efficiency of the military organization built up during years of peace.

This situation was certainly made worse by the weakness of Gamelin who temporized over everything. One day General Colson, head of the Staff Offices of the Army of the Interior, sent me to see him urgently at Vincennes in order to obtain his authorization to get a new factory going. He received me in the fortified blockhouse—now destroyed—which served him as living quarters and office: a vaulted monastic cell. I told him the reason for my reporting to him. He thanked me. I then asked him what his decision was. He seemed surprised and rather irritated: 'How do you expect me to make a decision? I must take advice. . . . ' And when I stressed the urgency of the matter, my impression was that my insistence rather frightened him. He was still the same placid and timorous man whom I had accompanied to Vimy. I had to go back without any decision. The officers around him—at least certain of them—did what they could to combat this indecision. Captains Le Puloch and de Crouy Chanel (one was to become Chief of the General Staff and the other an ambassador) laid before him a memorandum which began: 'Failing to take a decision influences future events just as surely as taking one. . . .' Naturally this simple piece of good sense had no effect. If Gamelin had been a different man, he might perhaps have had something of Joffre's intransigence in insisting upon his own way; but he was quite incapable of it. Hence the most important interests of the Army were not upheld either before or during the war. These factors contributed as much as any theories to the feeling of depression and the uselessness of any effort.

In January Gamelin delivered a lightning blow—not against the Germans, needless to say—but by reorganizing General Headquarters from top to bottom. Hitherto Headquarters and its head, a Major-General, constituted the chain of command between the Commander-in-Chief (Gamelin) and the Commander of the northeast front (Georges). It was a bastard but economic solution which made Georges deputy in the north-east to the Commander-in-Chief. Georges, who had been my chief in Algeria, enjoyed a great reputation for his keen intelligence and his solid character. For good reasons he was the successor designate to Gamelin. He had been seriously wounded when King Alexander of Yugoslavia was assassinated in Marseilles, wounds which, as we shall see, took their toll when the fighting really began. But Georges had allowed himself to be regarded as a candidate to supersede Gamelin. In consequence the two of them were not on good terms, and Gamelin was anxious to keep his rival at a distance. He decided therefore to give Georges his own headquarters on the north-east front and to form half-way between Vincennes and La-Ferté-sous-Jouarre (where Georges was) a headquarters for control of all fronts and answerable directly and solely to himself. The previous 'Major-General',* Bineau, was replaced by Doumenc, under whom I had served in Moscow, and who now sent for me. Overnight I left Paris for 'the field', that is to say the Château de Montry where Doumenc was establishing himself.

Montry was one of the houses belonging to the Rothschilds: a large building of the 1880s, in which we had our offices, set in a handsome park. We were billeted in houses in the vicinity, on the banks of the Marne. Life was austere and monastic. At his table Doumenc had the general officers of Headquarters, his personal adjutants, Captain Schmuckel, Captain de Reinkesen, his ADC, and myself. We seemed like children in the presence of our elders who had indeed nearly all passed sixty and of whom the least that could be said was that they were lacking a sense of humour. To offset this austerity, I at least found myself at the centre of things and in a position from which I would be able to see everything that was going on.

We were welcomed by Lieutenant-Colonel Revers, personal assistant to the preceding 'Major-General'. The instructions which he gave us disappointed me by their simplicity. Without question the important things were merely implied and we would have to find these out for ourselves.

The work which Schmuckel and I had to do was wearing: in addition to the mail addressed to the General we received copies of all documents issued at Headquarters. We had to read everything and make up our minds what we ought to put before the General as being of interest. As one of us always accompanied the General

* In the French Army in war the 'Major-General' is the Chief of Staff of the Commander-in-Chief.

wherever he went, the other had to fight his way through this continual avalanche of paper in which was inextricably mixed up pure
routine with matters of urgency and importance. But at least we
saw everything.

My investigations led me towards the battle plans and the disposition of our forces. The latter was astonishing because more
than half our divisions were in the eastern part of the front, while it
was generally thought that the thrust must come through Belgium.
It was explained to me that the eastern Army Group had been
steadily built up because it was in contact and furthermore that it
did not seem a bad idea to 'break in' a considerable number of
divisions on this front. When I said that the front was so quiet that
not much 'breaking in' was actually happening, Doumenc told me
I didn't know anything about it, so I held my peace.

But what were the plans? I was hoping to find some long-term
thinking, but all I found was short-term considerations based on the
hypothesis that Germany must sooner or later attack in the
West.

We had the Maginot Line, a shield which faced Germany but
which could be outflanked either to the north or to the south—more
likely the north, because in the south Switzerland was a serious
obstacle. To the north there was a reasonable expectation of
military collaboration by the Belgian and possibly also the Dutch
forces—which between them mustered thirty-two divisions, equal
to nearly a third of the French Army; but the difficulty was to shake
these countries out of their neutrality.

We were torn between the desire to assure a solid front in
Belgium to cover the North Sea ports and the fear of driving our
neighbours into the arms of Germany. The logical thing would have
been to resolve this dilemma to our advantage while the Germans
were busy with Poland, but no one dared because of political
difficulties: Belgium had been completely neutral for several years
and *wished* to keep out of the conflict; Holland *believed* she could
remain neutral as she had in 1914; both countries took advantage
of the blockade to trade with Germany. As our ideas about the war
were not then very concrete, we hit on the following solution.
During the winter various alarms would lead us to believe that a
German invasion of Belgium was imminent; when this happened
we would reconsider our position vis-à-vis Belgium; but as opinions

would be divided, we would end up by doing nothing and leave the initiative to Germany.

Thence two courses would be open to us: one, to await the German onslaught within our own prepared positions in the north, the other to march into Belgium at the same time. The former seemed to find favour with Gamelin and was the more prudent from the point of view of our Army, but there were two major drawbacks: we would leave the North Sea coast to the Germans without firing a shot, and we would abandon the Belgian and Dutch armies to their fate. It was feared that if this decision became known to our neighbours they would be inclined to give free passage to the Germans, if not even to come in on their side. These considerations, which should have brought about preventive action, led to a decision in favour of the second solution.

The plans drawn up during the winter for our entry into Belgium presupposed several hypotheses. The general idea was to penetrate Belgium behind a screen of Belgian troops and form a new defensive line before the Germans arrived. The essential, underlined heavily by Gamelin, was to avoid a 'battle of encounter', which is exactly what when the time came we got into. The depth of our penetration into the country would depend on the speed or the tardiness of our advance in relation to the enemy's movements. If the Germans beat us to it, we would take up a position along the Escaut and on our own frontier beyond Maubeuge. If both sides advanced simultaneously our line would be established: Antwerp—the Dyle—the Meuse (this is what actually happened); finally, if the Germans were very slow we would push on to the Albert Canal where the Belgian Army would delay the enemy while we deployed. Finally these positions were to be prepared for us by the Belgians, whom we asked very obliquely but who, without actually refusing, did nothing. Our relations with the Belgian General Staff were not very easy because of the fears which they felt of endangering their neutrality. Our information about the Belgian Army was pretty vague and everything had to be jacked up at the last moment.

It was hoped to fight a defensive battle in Belgium and then mount a counter-attack from the line on which we had contained the enemy. In order to make outflanking movements possible—remembering the counter-attacks on the flanks of the pockets in 1918—a concave line was favoured, giving maximum coverage of the North

Sea coast in the west and linking up with the Maginot Line in the east. As the Ardennes had left very unpleasant memories in the minds of those who had fought there in 1914, this area was designated as 'non-strategic' and one foresaw nothing but advantage accruing from the Germans' getting mixed up there. For these reasons our deployment was intended to refuse our centre while containing the enemy whose plan postulated a central thrust. It is not illogical to suppose that the Germans knew what we had in mind.

Be that as it may, the conceptions of our defence in the north, in the principal and decisive theatre, led to our adopting a solution which contained the most unknown factors, even though it offered the best chance and was the nearest for our own forces. We saw no opportunity of uniting our troops with the Belgians at a moment when the Germans would not be in a position to prevent us from doing so.

I felt the same misgivings about these plans as I had ten years before when faced by the insufficiency of our military thought. I found it all terribly limited and not very reassuring. But I must add truthfully that I did not think that we would be beaten. I was at once uneasy yet optimistic, sad to see our Army not at its peak as I had hoped, but confident in the future of France and the virtues of our people. For years I had seen nothing but negative omens and now I wanted to believe in something positive. The enormous French war machine, of which I saw every detail, seemed to me to be too heavy and out-of-date, but it still represented a redoubtable force. If I mention this state of my mind, which may be surprising, it is to underline the fact that my foresight had been progressively stifled by the surroundings in which I had found myself. I must add that at that moment of time I did not imagine that our high command, when put to the test, could be quite so mediocre. The history of 1914 had taught us that defeat on the frontiers can be absorbed, because there can always come another miracle of the Marne. I knew too that Colonel de Gaulle had expressed himself pessimistically about the opening actions, but optimistic of the eventual outcome. I do not think that he ever imagined that things could go as they eventually did: his conduct in June 1940, as we shall see, indicated that he too believed in the possibility of another Marne. The only pessimist I met, and he more paradoxical than really convinced, was Major Dromard, the future Chief Engineer of de Lattre's Army, who said in jest: 'We will be beaten next time just because we won last time.'

But all this concerned the resumption of hostilities which still seemed a long way away. Meantime hope was centred on the efficacy of the blockade. We received from Paris tables on the cobalt and manganese situation, in which we read of some startling rates of exchange. At our table a courteous old admiral who was a specialist in Soviet gold affairs made various predictions which I have never forgotten. Once a week we had delightful gramophone recitals given by General Halbwachs, who brought a collection of Dvořák records from his home.

Now our 'peaceful war' was beginning to move.

In January the German aircraft which landed in Belgium by mistake and had aboard the plans for an imminent attack had caused an alert. We know now that this was quite fortuitous and caused the Germans to alter completely their operational plan. At the time one did not know whether it was a trick or not. Movements towards the Belgian border took place, then everything settled down again.

Far away the Soviet aggression against Poland led on to the Russo-Finnish war. The Russians applied precisely the programme which Shapochnikov had outlined to us: they wished to isolate Finland (and the Gulf of Finland) from the west by occupying Hangôe. The Finns did not give in without a fight, as Lithuania, Estonia and Latvia had. As they had explained to us during our short stay in Helsinki, they waged a mobile war based on skiers and used their vast forests in which the heavy Soviet columns suffered a series of heavy reverses.

As the war dragged on, a larger and larger part of public opinion was disturbed by our inertia and there was a movement in Parliament for a change of method. The courageous resistance of Finland against Russian aggression and its contrast with our passive attitude constituted a message and a lesson. The anti-Russian feelings which our public opinion held, its hatred of Bolshevism, sympathy for a small brave people and reaction against our constipated policy all raised a passionate enthusiasm for Finland much like that which had been felt for Poland a century earlier.

Then there came a wave of sentiment which was to sweep away Daladier and should have removed Gamelin as well. Public opinion wanted to support Finland and voiced the following reasons: since one supposed the USSR to be aligned with Germany (which was seen later to be wrong), her set-back in Finland made her appear as a colossus with feet of clay; the downfall of Russia would be a triumph for the anti-Communist ideology to which the Government had turned at the end of August, and also the ruin of Germany's associate over the partition of Poland and a complete closing of the blockade. Why not try to get in first? In fact this thinking against Russia which should better have been applied to Italy lacked realism; this can be explained by ignorance of the enemy, and political feelings which were hostile to the Russian régime but sympathetic to the Italian régime.

But what kind of adventure were we trying to get mixed up in? Under pressure of public opinion, all sorts of extravagant plans were hatched: Baku was to be bombed by aircraft based on Syria; a Caucasian Legion was to be raised, although no one had any idea where it could be used, particularly since Turkey, whose policy towards Russia had been very conservative since the days of Mustafa Kemal, had no intention of coming in on our side—rather the reverse. Four French and British divisions were to be sent to Finland; the equipping of them had already begun. This aid was derisory to the Finns and could do little to help them; on the contrary, we would gaily be taking on 100 to 150 Russian divisions and would seriously risk alienating Turkey and the Balkans. It was real lunacy.

The British, who better understood the nature of the Russian problem, regarded the whole thing with caution and followed us with reluctance; but the pay-off came from the Scandinavians who refused to allow our expeditionary forces to cross their territory. It is curious today to think that the eventual defeat of Germany may have descended from this decision which at the time caused such distress in France. Be that as it may, all these fine plans once more came to nothing. But from this futile agitation came the serious affair of Norway, which was soon to be upon us.

In reality our great strategic problem at the time was Italy, pivot of the German coalition.

She represented not only a force of seventy divisions but a potential threat to Tunisia and Suez, and her threatening shadow paralysed our action in the Balkans where we could have brought nearly ninety divisions to face the twenty-five which Hungary and Bulgaria could muster. Of questionable military value and lacking internal stability, Italy appeared on all counts to be the weak link against which we should have concentrated our blows: Italy defeated or forced into unequivocal neutrality would leave the Mediterranean with no strings attached and we could have formed a firm base for a flanking action against Germany in 1941. Good sense demanded preventive action against Italy. For this operation we could call upon ten crack French divisions and three British, all in North Africa, and we could concentrate on the Alps some thirty divisions which could be withdrawn from Lorraine where we were not doing anything useful and anyway outnumbered the enemy by three to one.

A move of this nature did not lack supporters: their views were examined at a high level, but nothing was done because such a decision required a firmness which was quite foreign to the nature of our leaders and the confused motives which had led us into the war. Gamelin, as Trochu seventy years before him, preferred to wait. Georges, impressed by exercises at Headquarters which had revealed the difficulty of conducting operations in the Alps and fearful of any weakening of the north-east front for which he was responsible, was against it.

However, the basic reason was that there was still a vain hope of detaching Italy from Germany politically. The precedent of 1914, ably used by Italian Macchiavellism, seemed to suggest the possibility of a turn about, and it was feared that a resolute attitude would compromise this possibility. Badoglio had said confidentially: 'I will never make war against France and as long as I am here you need have no fear'. Balbo had given similar assurances. Ciano, more cagey, was content to let it be known that the official policy was not irrevocable.

These illusions were strengthened by the uneasiness felt in Italy at the Soviet-German *rapprochement*. Beyond all reality, we vaguely hoped to profit from some sort of anti-bolshevik solidarity.

Furthermore at the same time the extreme left was talking about the possibility of an Italian revolution which would tear the country away from Axis influence. In the midst of all this, Monzie, who as well as Minister of Public Works was spokesman on Italian affairs in the Cabinet, brought all his influence to bear in favour of our Latin neighbour.

The result was that we were forced to avoid the slightest gesture which might offend the Italians and this in turn kept twenty divisions tied up in France and Africa to face them. The Italians were not only exempt from the blockade, but our troops had to sit and watch the galling spectacle of coal trains making their way south from the Ruhr on the far bank of the Rhine. In order not to displease them we gave up any idea of initiative in the Balkans and likewise a declaration against Spanish designs on the Straits of Gibraltar. All the reward we got was a stab in the back on 10 June 1940.

We still had our minds to some extent on the Balkans—not unreasonably since, as we have seen, we could have brought into the field there nearly ninety divisions. This conception of a powerful force bore little resemblance to what eventually happened: the formation of General Weygand's phantom Army.

Immediately after the Franco-Anglo-Turkish agreement it was decided to constitute in Syria an expeditionary force which could show the Tricolour along the Turkish border in Thrace and the Union Jack in Egypt. This token gesture was not to exceed a strength of one division.

The idea of sending Weygand to this theatre of operations was not based on the strength of the force to be involved, but it was hoped that his personal prestige would assure unity of command; and there was also a thought that it might not be a bad thing to have a possible contender for supreme command away from the centre of things. As soon as he arrived there Weygand made it known that the means at his disposal were quite inadequate for the bringing of any useful assistance to the badly equipped Allied Armies which he was supposed to amalgamate. But in spite of his pressing demands he succeeded in obtaining only two further divisions in nine months. So the 'Weygand Army' about which the most fantastic rumours circulated was in fact nothing more than a shadow.

When it came to considering the possible use of this force, it was at once apparent that the position of Syria was a difficult one: the lack of shipping, which was felt so bitterly at the time of the Norwegian campaign, did not permit the permanent retention of sea transport in the eastern Mediterranean. It would therefore be necessary to allow at least a month to move even three divisions to Salonika. As to the Turkish railway system, that could not handle more than one division a month. The solution arrived at, therefore, was to send no reinforcements to the Middle East at all but to plan for the landing of a major force brought together from France and Africa if the necessity arose.

At the same time these thoughts of action in the Balkans, already undermined by hopes of a change in the political atmosphere vis-à-vis Italy, were further complicated by a difference of opinion with the British. Due to contribute the two or three divisions stationed in Egypt and Palestine, they did not favour the idea of a landing in Salonika; they preferred the idea of isolating Turkey by a thrust against Bulgaria through Thrace without prematurely raising a problem in Greece, for which to them the time did not seem to be ripe. Conference followed conference; the inter-Allied war committees exchanged endless questionnaires and nothing was done. After nine months the idea of a Balkan campaign was just as vague as it had been on the first day. Of his 'Army' Weygand was the only member who took part in the war and his three divisions were eventually put in the bag . . . by the British, after they—alone and too late—tried the Salonika operation to link up with Yugoslavia which Weygand had advocated without success.

All these vast schemes, full of wishful thinking but getting no further—which was no doubt just as well—filtered through to the big hall at Montry where the 3° Bureau had set up its maps. With bewilderment I tried to follow the evolution of these plans, which were to fall into the hands of the Germans at La Charité* and caused Hitler to remark that our affairs were run 'either by lunatics or

* During the French retreat, the Germans captured at La Charité (on the Loire) a train in which these archives were being transported.

imbeciles'. Only the second adjective is applicable, and the men I
knew were far from being imbeciles. But it was the will of Jupiter
to destroy them. . . .

A particularly hard winter gave way eventually and there were
buds on the trees. Perhaps the spring would bring the war back to
life. The north-east front was still hibernating, its only recompense
being good billets and plenty of leave.

But during all this I recall one Cassandra. M. Taittinger, who
after a tour of the Armies as a Member of Parliament, wrote a
remarkably prophetic letter to General Gamelin. He had been struck
by the weakness of our defences in the Sedan area and in drawing
the general's attention to this shortcoming he used a striking
phrase: 'These are sinister battlefields for our arms'. The letter was
so strongly worded that Gamelin, little as he believed it, felt that
he must do something. A visit was laid on for him—a major undertaking as if he were head of State—and when he returned he told us
in his quiet voice that all these alarms were quite unnecessary,
but nevertheless he had decided to strengthen the Givet area—with
one battalion! It was really like Bazaine aiming one gun at St
Privat.*

I also remember a meeting presided over by Gamelin at which,
stroking his hands in a characteristic gesture, he said that he
thought he would use the old 1918 Renault tanks dug in as pill-
boxes. . . .

But suddenly reality overtook us and we became aware of a new
way of waging war. In forty-eight hours Germany overran Denmark and landed in Norway. How had it come about?

When we were studying the problem of transporting our divisions to Finland, the Allied Headquarters had centred its attention
on Narvik and its railway leading to Lulea on the Gulf of Bothnia:
this was the only possible route. The British, more practical than
ourselves and more blockade-minded, realized the importance to
German industry of Swedish iron ore which in winter could be
transported only through Narvik and Norwegian territorial
waters; for this reason they wanted to get their hands on Narvik.

* During the battle of St Privat in 1870 Marshal Bazaine gave no orders and
is reported to have himself aimed a gun instead of commanding the battle.

Perhaps this desire to cut off the flow of production from the Swedish mines influenced their reluctant acquiescence in the Finnish adventure. But since that had come to nothing and the forces earmarked for it were still available, why not attempt a *coup de main?*

This idea, sound in itself, led as usual to endless coming and going. Summit meeting followed summit meeting; it was agreed that the British would run the operation, which was to be limited in scope and should take place on 25 April. But, no doubt through Churchill's impatience, it was decided to begin it, as a quarter of a century before in the Dardanelles, with naval action which could serve no purpose except to alert the Germans and, above all, give them an excuse for intervening.

The Germans therefore moved first, on 7 April, and cut the ground from under our feet with a lightning blow which for the first time in the war was destined to bring British and French troops face to face with their enemy. The surprise was complete from every point of view. Overnight we came to know what a terrible opponent we faced: this was war unlike anything which we had known before. The German fleet broke the British blockade and, casting its net wide, landed on that immense coast a series of small detachments which paved the way for a *coup d'état* carried out by paratroops and followed by light motorized columns penetrating deep into the still snow-covered country.

Our reaction was by no means on the same scale. The decision to intervene was taken on the 8th but it was four days before transport had been assembled at Brest in which to ship our first division. Meanwhile the British were hesitating between securing Narvik and joining hands with the Norwegian troops in the interior. The idea of a thrust through Trondheim was abandoned in favour of action at Narvik. It was not until the 15th, eight days after the campaign had begun, that our troops disembarked at Namsos and Andalesness.

But our terrible inferiority immediately became apparent: Stukas hindered the unloading of heavy stores and burnt about our heads the wooden buildings which were the only cover against the snow. What was needed was aircraft, and anti-aircraft defence. What was needed above all was boldness and mobility.

Instead of that, there was the usual timidity to which our long

period on the defensive had accustomed us: at the news that a
German battalion had turned the flank of a few British troops fifty
miles from Namsos our division formed a position, sent a signal for
help and did nothing until it was re-embarked. The situation
deteriorated hourly; the British, adventuring into the centre of the
country, were thrown back. On the 22nd a fresh council of war was
held in London at which Gamelin expressed his dissatisfaction with
the way in which the British were conducting the campaign: every
politician was an amateur strategist and had not the British Commander-in-Chief promised his 'plan of campaign' for tomorrow, a
fortnight after operations had begun? On the 27th the council met
again in an atmosphere as bitter as it was confused. On the 30th the
various German columns joined hands and it was all too late.

On 2 May the Franco-British detachments at Namsos and
Andalesness were taken off again and the rout was complete. Only
Narvik remained, but here our attack, in which one French division
was to participate, was slow to develop. We know that one month
later it was to enjoy some success—an heroic but tardy effort, but
one which boded ill for the drama which was soon to overtake
France.

The short Norwegian campaign was a sort of dummy run in
which the two sides tried out their own methods of fighting. Our
inferiority was terrifying. We lacked imagination, character and
organization: responsibility was shared between two Allies, each of
which in turn was divided into land, air and naval commands, the
whole thing lumbered with an utterly useless committee of politicians. Furthermore our fatal weaknesses were shown up in a glaring
light: no modern equipment, no ack-ack, no decisive bombing
policy, no drive in the troops—except the very best—and no
incisive command. At its first test our military system showed itself
to be out-of-date. This unpleasant fact was borne home to thinking
people who were resigned to it. Hitler was the man who had
judged the situation to perfection: he had hesitated to begin his
offensive against France, but now he had proof that he would risk
nothing if he did so because he was the stronger. The Norwegian
campaign gave him the proof he needed. He made his irrevocable
decision: *blitzkrieg* would destroy France.

Thus right across Europe our strategic concept had led us into passivity, a confusion of ideas, an inability to make a decision and, above all, a fear of taking the slightest risk. Thus one by one we let all the trump cards which we had held slip out of our hands, and unwittingly created a situation ripe for Hitler's attack.

In order to understand the price which we paid for our inertia, it is necessary to return once more to the balance of power which existed at the outbreak of war and the possibilities of coalition which existed at that time.

We broke out (if that is the right phrase) over the ruins of the Versailles Treaty which had made it possible for us to think in terms of *over 400 divisions* to be mobilized against a Germany surrounded and practically disarmed. After Munich, as we have seen, Germany had rallied to her side Italy, Hungary and Bulgaria which produced a total of 200 divisions, while we, with Great Britain, could muster no more than 100 divisions; but we could still count on what remained of the Little Entente and the Balkans—say 130 divisions— and could hope for help from Russia to the tune of 100 divisions; so, with a possibility of 300 divisions, the balance was still in our favour. It is certainly this consideration that determined our intransigence in the face of fresh German threats in 1939 and led to our trying to constitute an Eastern bloc based on the USSR.

The reversal of Russia's policy had grave consequences for us: Germany and her satellites could still only muster 200 divisions, but our score came down to a reluctant Little Entente and even more reluctant Balkans which totted up to about 130 divisions. The two sides, mustering all their potential, were more or less equal. It was for this reason that we knew that we could afford to lose no more.

When Germany attacked Poland, the combined forces of France, Great Britain and Poland together mustered 140 divisions, which gave us a slight numerical superiority over the enemy and, if the struggle were prolonged, it looked as if the balance would remain much the same. Logically, statistically we were right to undertake the struggle at this moment. But of course in two weeks forty Polish divisions went out of the window; it was hoped that a greater effort from Britain would make up this loss.

But, and this is the essential point, it was necessary that, during the period of waiting which the slowness of our industrial mobilization imposed, the balance of our 'possible' maximum forces should not be whittled down by the defection or destruction of our eventual Allies. Our effort on the Lorraine front should therefore have been a contribution to the overall European strategy on what was bound to become in the end the quintessential front.

But when it came to the pinch it is easy to see how our policy of waiting led us to the edge of the abyss.

In our own country we had been unable to choose between peace and war and as a result our industrial effort was far below potential. Instead of making up in the first nine months for the enormous lag in our preparations, we were still in the planning stages of production and our material deficiencies were still considerable.

Beyond our frontiers, we had allowed Poland to be overrun without striking a blow. Paralysed by the thought of risk and inability to make any decision, we wallowed in hypotheses without resolving to our advantage any of the problems which lay before us. Spain and Italy continued to be a thorn in our flesh and we did nothing to come to grips with the situations which they imposed— neither in North Africa, Europe, Suez or Gibraltar—while at the same time none of our potential Allies, and in particular Turkey, was bound closely enough to us.

On the other side Germany, whose prestige was mounting daily, had eliminated the danger of an eastern front, had overrun Denmark and Norway, had dealt apparently satisfactorily with the Baltic problem and had opened a line of approach to Great Britain and the Atlantic.

Time, which we thought was working for us, was in fact entirely on the enemy's side. The young German Army, which was not yet ready for a major test at arms, needed time in which to weld together those units which had not yet seen service and above all to form cadres for expansion; time also was needed in which to reorganize the units which had been through the Polish campaign. The nine months during which we did so little, and during which the German factories were on full production, were used by the enemy to manufacture modern equipment while we were making do with the old stuff which we already had. Basically it was a problem of armaments: by acquiring Czechoslovakia they found themselves in possession of weapons for forty divisions, by overrunning Poland the material for another twenty or thirty divisions fell into their hands—which together represents an increase of 50 per cent over that which they had before. In the face of such enormous pillage and the precautions taken under the Göring plan, what good was our blockade doing?

In the face of these results nothing remained to us but the prolongation of certain dangerous illusions. We had lost our possible coalition and failed to build up our own strength; we had allowed our prestige in Europe to plummet; we had missed every chance offered to us, and, now that the enemy's preparations for war were complete, we found ourselves alone with the British, with no solid military understanding with our Belgian neighbours, no proper arrangements on land with our British partners, with an old-fashioned Army—overblown and bureaucratic—an unproven high command, and above all suspect morale and a public spirit which had no conception of the gravity of the situation. The conditions for defeat were all there—and it was our own fault.

All Hitler had to do was to strike.

Chapter 8
The Downfall seen from GHQ
*

ON THE MORNING of 10 May I was woken by the sound of bombs, as was most of the French Army. Now we were emerging from the long period of torpor and daydreams which I have to tried to describe. Now the war of waiting was over; now the battle was about to begin after twenty years of preparation. Destiny on that lovely May morning had come to confront us with the pitiless proof of hard facts. I think that few of the actors in this immense tragedy were unaware of how vital was this moment, so full of imponderables.

Even today when I try to describe the extraordinary events which followed, a flood of mixed images and feelings pours through my mind. Nightmare is a word not strong enough to describe the memory which remains so bitterly clear. This few weeks' campaign, which led to a defeat so total and so sudden, was from first to last an endless surprise exposing our inability to cope with the enemy's torrential advance or find any answer to it. Like a bad dream, the enemy's forces were everywhere, striking at will with diabolical freedom, while our feet remained rooted to the ground and we seemed constrained by a thousand invisible bonds which slowed down all our movements. But scarcely had such movements got under way than they were rendered useless by the collapse of the dispositions which it was hoped would limit the disaster. With a desperate effort a fresh deployment would be organized, but once more the machine could not answer to what was required of it, nothing could be done in the time available and the defeat grew and grew at an alarming pace. The men who were witnessing and living through this drama beneath a cloudless sky did so with stupor and dejection, but could not bring themselves to believe that this was real, that France was dying and that something would not happen to save us at the last moment. But nothing did come and destiny inexorably crushed us more and more every moment. The helpless ship was making water through every seam, could no longer answer the helm, and the terrifying waves were battering her old worm-eaten hull.

I want to describe this terrible atmosphere in which I was not living with the fighting troops, but in an absurd succession of châteaux, in order to explain the reasons. Details of the battles come better from the historians than from me because they have more complete documentation; impressions of the fighting and of the defeat belong to eyewitnesses. My object is only to show why we were beaten and how the military instrument of which we have seen the build-up was commanded in the searching test of battle. This terrible lesson will not have been useless if we can draw from it a lesson for the future.

The attack launched on 10 May was not a complete surprise. In the preceding days we had received numerous hints, largely from Belgium, without being able to find out if they were well founded. But during the night of 9/10 May news began to build up: the sound of columns moving on the frontier of Germany and Belgium, then the invasion of Luxemburg. The order to stand to was sent out during the evening of the 9th. After a short night the sound of bombs early the following morning was merely a confirmation.

Doumenc sent me at once to Vincennes to report to General Gamelin. I arrived at 6.30 a.m. at the moment when the order had just been given for the huge machine to go into operation: the advance into Belgium. Gamelin was striding up and down the corridor in his fort, humming, with a pleased and martial air which I had never seen before. It has been said since that he expected defeat, but I could see no evidence of it at the time.

The decision which had just been taken was vital: on what line should we stand and meet the German onslaught?

As we have seen, there were three variants, each according to whatever moment we began our movement to meet the enemy: if we were ahead we would go through to the Albert Canal; if we were late we would stand upon the Escaut; if the timing of the two sides was similar the line would be along the Dyle and Scheldt, with the left flank on Antwerp. In the circumstances Gamelin, true to form, settled for the Dyle. He said later that he had never been in favour of advancing into Belgium at all but he had been forced to do so for political reasons. That may be so, but on the morning of 10 May he seemed to me to be perfectly confident in the outcome

of the manœuvre, which he had conceived and now put into operation. It was, as Gamelin wrote, 'the battle foreseen since September', one might say always foreseen. Our dispositions were worked
out in the greatest detail for exactly this situation; there was no
surprise on that score.

The Armies moved to a detailed march table and less than an
hour later were greeted amid general enthusiasm in Belgium. But
bad news was already pouring in. Suddenly in Holland the situation
was critical. Parachutists and a fifth column were causing trouble at
The Hague. On the 11th a German detachment seized the bridge
at Moërdyck, thus cutting off Holland from all possible help. This
did not affect our plans because we had given up any idea of defending Holland, but we saw at once that we were facing an adversary
who waged a kind of war for which we were ill prepared. What was
even more serious was what was happening on the front of the
Belgians, because it was they who were to hold the Albert Canal
long enough for us to establish our positions on the Dyle. But all
along the line they were pulling back at an alarming pace, sometimes without being attacked, and our columns were meeting
numerous fugitives on bicycles. By the 11th they were already
talking of abandoning the Albert Canal. Would we have time to
form our own front before the arrival of the enemy?

There was one worrying moment: on the left of the British Army,
Giraud's Army was moving too fast, while in the centre Blanchard's
Army was behind schedule. On the 12th our Armies arrived on the
agreed line where they made the unpleasant discovery that the
anti-tank defences which the Belgians should have built did not
exist. The threat facing the Belgian front seemed to indicate that
the main German thrust would come in the Liège–Brussels area.
We expected to fight next day on the traditional battlefield of
Waterloo–Charleroi. The preliminaries were over, action was about
to begin.

Very early on the morning of the 13th I put up on General
Doumenc's map board the information which had come in during
the night. The air reconnaissance reports were the clearest: it was
evident that the main German thrust was not coming in Belgium
but on the Luxemburg–Mézières axis. I marked this axis with a

large chinagraph arrow and everyone came in to look. At General Georges' headquarters, where they had reached the same conclusion at the same time, Colonel Baril, head of Intelligence, said 'we've got that German plan' and went off to look for it. But we had six or seven different plans and no way of knowing which was the right one.

The direction of the German effort corresponded with one of the possible eventualities which had been foreseen. It seemed particularly favourable to us: it was thought to be a good thing for the enemy to enter this difficult terrain which formed a sort of trap between the Meuse and the Maginot Line from which he could not get out. So sure were we of the defensive value of our position that the angle at Sedan was occupied only by the two divisions of reservists which had so worried Taittinger.

This was going to simplify our operations in Belgium which had already produced a crop of extravagant rumours: as always in the early days of war, accounts, blown up by the imagination, produced some startling novelties—everywhere swarms of parachutists, saboteurs and spies, sometimes dummies and sometimes purely imaginary. One liaison officer told us of Germans dressed up as nuns and of ridiculous scenes of espionage. More serious was the report that the German tanks were firing 'balls of fire' which turned out merely to be tracer ammunition but raised the thought of some possible new weapon.

The day passed in a flood of information, much of it in great detail because we were linked with the Headquarters of the Armies by telephone and they thought it best to tell us everything. This information we centralized and transferred to ticker-tape which I nicknamed the 'fiction flood'. Every hour a dispatch rider took the fiction flood to Gamelin at Vincennes, for at that time we had no teletypes. Several of the motorcyclists were killed in traffic accidents while carrying out these inglorious missions. . . .

Late that night when I had only just got to sleep I was awakened by a telephone call from General Georges: 'Ask General Doumenc to come here at once.' An hour later we arrived at the Château des Bondons, at La-Ferté-sous-Jouarre, where General Georges and his staff had their command post. In the château, which was rather more a big villa set in a park on a hill, the large salon had been made the map room. Around a long trestle table the staff officers answered the telephone and made notes.

When we arrived at about three o'clock in the morning all was dark except in this room which was barely half-lit. At the telephone Major Navereau was repeating in a low voice the information coming in. Everyone else was silent. General Roton, Chief of Staff, was stretched out in an armchair. The atmosphere was that of a family in which there had just been a death. Georges got up quickly and came to Doumenc. He was terribly pale. 'Our front has been broken at Sedan! There has been a collapse. . . .' He flung himself into a chair and burst into tears.

He was the first man I had seen weep in this campaign. Alas, there were to be others. It made a terrible impression on me.

Doumenc, taken aback by this greeting, reacted immediately. 'General, this is war and in war things like this are bound to happen!' Then Georges, still pale, explained: following a terrible bombardment from the air the two inferior divisions had taken to their heels. Ten Corps signalled that the position was penetrated and that German tanks had arrived in Bulson at about midnight. Here there was another flood of tears. Everyone else remained silent, shattered by what had happened.

'Well, General,' said Doumenc, 'all wars have their routs. Let us look at the map and see what can be done.' He spoke firmly in these darkened surroundings and it made me feel better.

Before the map Doumenc sketched out a plan: the mouth of the gap must be stopped, 'sewn up' as they said in 1918. We had at our disposal three armoured divisions (the whole of our reserve of tanks). One, 1st DCR, was in Belgium about to detrain in the Charleroi area for the battle of the Dyle; it would be redirected and attack from north to south. Another, 3rd DCR, was immediately south of Sedan and would attack northwards. 2nd DCR which was on its way to the Dyle should be detrained in the Vervins area and counter-attack from the west to east. These three divisions, mustering 600 tanks, would engage the pocket concentrically and drive the Germans back across the Meuse. Any troops in the area of Sedan must attack in the morning as a matter of urgency. But broadly speaking the situation could be considered as restored.

Georges agreed with all these proposals and the orders were given. For myself, I relit the lamps and woke up the cook to make some coffee. The nightmare was over—we went back to Montry.

This scene, which perhaps sealed the fate of the whole campaign, appears in perspective when one has all the facts which we know today.

On the evening of the 13th the Germans attacked at Sedan and got infantry across the Meuse. In spite of heavy fire, our troops defended themselves. At the time when we were making our decisions the stop line of our position had not been broached at any point. But during the night there took place one of those events which show the finger of fate. XI Corps Artillery got a message—erroneous—that the front was broken. The Commander of the Corps artillery gave the message to Georges; but there is no doubt that he was in an abnormal state of mind because the Commander killed himself the next day. Georges himself telephoned to all his Group commanders and ordered them to destroy their guns and get out. Thus in the rear areas behind the two divisions which were still engaged there developed complete panic. A French tank unit which was moving to Bulson during the night was mistaken by the fugitives for German armour. This rumour was passed on to Army and GHQ. It was this combination of false information, coming at a time when the whole of the German armour was still east of the Meuse, that led to our witnessing the collapse of confidence of the Commander-in-Chief in the north-east.

This collapse sprang from several causes. First there was the health of General Georges; he had never recovered from the terrible wounds which he received at the time of King Alexander's and M. Barthou's assassination in Marseilles. This man, respected by the entire army and whom I had seen brilliant and resolute, no longer had the nerve to face up to the great uncertainties of battle. It could be said that the Hungarian Oustachi, armed I believe by the Italians, who assassinated King Alexander, destroyed not only the stability of the Balkans but also, by wounding Georges, prepared the way to some extent for the fall of France. Fate!

There was also the great virtue of surprise: the Germans, if they fought as we did, could not have had the time to bring forward sufficient troops for an attack in strength. The breaching of our front seemed diabolical, then credible. It was like the pale apparition of inexorable destiny. We began to feel that we could not break the terrible spell which had given the Germans their continual run of successes against Poland, Norway, Holland and Belgium. Would

we be equally impotent? All our doctrine was founded on faith in
the value of defence, and now, at the first blow our position
organized over nine months broke into little pieces. This revelation
struck chill.

Furthermore for three days the constant influx of information of
all sorts made everyone breathless. Those who had to cope with
this plethora of ill-assorted messages were overwhelmed and got
little sleep. For three days all the news had been bad. Faith can be
worn away like a stone with water. When catastrophic news came
in, the atmosphere was ready: no one doubted its truth.

Thus on the evening of 13 May the French Army was still
almost intact. But the morale of the high command was damaged
and was never to recover.

Doumenc went back anxious but confident. One of us was to go
permanently to represent him at General Georges' Headquarters at
the Château des Bondons to which all the latest information of the
battle would be coming direct. The atmosphere there was worrying
and it was agreed that Schmuckel and I should take turn and turn
about.

On the morning of the 14th we were waiting for news of the
counter-attack by the 3rd Armoured Division which was to be
delivered against Sedan. Then the nightmare began again. The
counter-attack had been put back to 1600 hours and no one knew
why. During this time we learnt that General Corap's Army, which
was supposed to hold the Meuse from Givet to Namur, was being
roughly handled all along the line. The counter-attack on Sedan
was postponed again. Hours went by and one could feel the situation deteriorating minute by minute. The Germans had now crossed
the Meuse on a wide front and before their advance Corap's Army
seemed to break up with the greatest of ease. What had happened
was quite simple: Corap's Army had a difficult movement to per-
form because of the small number of roads available. They ap-
proached the Meuse at the time laid down, but only with their
advance elements which tried to hold a wide front with inadequate
means, and they further made the mistake of taking up positions on
the hills overlooking the river and not on the bank itself. Thence
these weak elements watched the Germans throwing their bridges

across the river without being able to do anything about it. The appearance of armour and bombers did the rest. The advance guard withdrew and spread disorder among the main body which was still coming forward. The morale of the whole was broken before they had even been committed to battle. But the breach which the night before had seemed simply the result of one annoying incident had now assumed such proportions that there was no longer any denying the catastrophe. The French Armies had received a blow struck right into their centre. This was the 14th, merely the fourth day of fighting.

The reaction is always the same: piece things together and counter-attack. Energetic measures were taken on the 15th: General Corap, speaking on the telephone to General Georges, seemed to have lost his nerve and was accordingly relieved of his command. Also relieved was the commander of the 3rd Armoured Division: his counter-attack had been awaited for thirty-six hours, and still he had not moved. Facing the breakthrough was installed the solid General Touchon with fresh resources, while to the north General Giraud, our most dashing leader, was appointed in place of Corap. The order was to hold on and wait for the decisive action of the three armoured divisions.

Alas, ill fortune stepped in. Of the three armoured divisions there was no information. As far as one could see they had either done nothing, or whatever they had done was useless, for the German advance continued inexorably. The real history of our armoured divisions is brief and lamentable. 1st Armoured Division, coming from Charleroi, found itself in an unequal contest and was overtaken through running out of petrol: the personnel and the divisional commander were lost. 3rd Armoured, the one at Sedan, had been allotted by General Huntziger to Army Corps, which in turn had spread it out in penny packets among the divisions. Instead of a mass of armour there was a smattering of tanks with no offensive power, which could only be brought into action bit by bit as a result of a great deal of motoring. 2nd Armoured, which was to come from Vervins, was surprised by the German advance in the course of detraining at ten railheads spread over more than thirty-five miles in depth. Its elements were engaged haphazard as the occasion arose, almost tank by tank, trying to hold a bridge or cover a column. The powerful counter-attack was dead before it was born. . . . Also despite Giraud and Touchon the armies were breaking up. Touchon barely got away from a small village after the German armour had passed through. Giraud was in the bag. The fugitives were blazing off in all directions as far as 150 miles to the rear. The Germans reached Vervins on the 15th. There was nothing between them and Paris and no reserves available. From that day the battle appeared to be irremediably lost.

On the 16th the situation worsened. The German armour reached Laon; if they kept up the pace they would be in Paris in two days. This time it really did seem to be all over. In Paris the Government was worried about possible revolution; the *Garde Mobile* was being strengthened and troops were mustered for defence. But what could be done against this torrent of magic tanks?

On the 17th there was a dramatic change: the Panzers left the direct route to Paris and moved westwards. Paul Reynaud compared this with the mistake made by von Klück on the eve of the Marne. Were we to be saved by another miracle?

But the pessimism of the day before overcame us again on the 18th. We would try to stop the Germans by an encircling movement based on the Aisne and our position at Maubeuge, while a counter-attack would be delivered from the south by a new armoured division which had been put under the command of Colonel de Gaulle.

But by the 19th Amiens was already threatened and it fell the following day. This made the situation of our Armies fighting valiantly in Belgium very dangerous. We could not fail to react to this attempt to cut off our Armies in the north from the balance of the French forces. General Doumenc, who was the link between Gamelin and Georges, considered that the moment had come for Gamelin's direct intervention. 'I'm going to fetch him,' Doumenc said to me.

So we came to another historic scene. I was on duty at Bondons when he arrived with Doumenc. As soon as he was in the big salon he set forth his new directives in measured tones, beginning, curiously, by saying: 'Without wishing to interfere in the conduct of the battle. . . .' He recommended the withdrawal of the northern Armies, the Belgians and British included, south of the Somme. This decision was somewhat late but essential.

Then, with Gamelin still calm and apparently indifferent, we sat down to lunch. This meal left me with a horrible memory. The cook, like all of us in despair at the defeat, had put all his frustrated patriotism into the preparation of a veritable wedding breakfast. With Georges pale and beaten and his senior officers practically dead with fatigue and worry, the lunch had more the atmosphere of funeral baked meats. But, sitting in the centre, Gamelin, who knew even then that he had lost the confidence of the Government (Paul Reynaud was in power and Weygand had already been appointed) felt it necessary to put on an act, to talk of this, that and the other and make jokes; it all sounded terribly false. Then came the sweet: an enormous confection covered with spun sugar. It was grotesque and pathetic. I felt like weeping or hoping that the ceiling would fall on us. . . . Gamelin ate heartily, drank his coffee and left, as imperturbable as ever; the guard turned out on the steps of the château and regimental trumpets sounded.

I was never to see him again.

Once he had gone, we went back to our drama. Had the Armies of the north time to withdraw? Attention was concentrated on the armoured spearhead of the German Army which was penetrating deeper and deeper towards the sea with the relentlessness of a train. Telephone messages coming in told us of its progress. . . . Orders were given for various cutting-off operations, for stands 'to the death'; nothing happened; nothing could slow up the advance. We knew exactly the strength of their advance guard; it consisted of a few dozen tanks with lorry-borne infantry and motor-cyclists; an officer had seen them and counted them. Warning had been given of their arrival but in spite of this all resistance evaporated. At Amiens the population and the local troops baled out at the simple news that the Germans were in the offing. Two guns and a hundred determined men could have held them up for half a day, but nowhere was there any real action. It was realized in all this that the problem was more moral than material. But how could people get a grip of themselves in the midst of this general chaos? Civilians fled, headed by their own officials, and the determination of the troops was undermined. Paris was saved for the moment, but our Armies of the north were practically cut off from the rest.

The attempted containment which had saved us four times in

1918 had completely failed because of the speed of the German armour and the nervous condition of our troops under continual bombardment from the air. This attempt had caused us to deploy our strongest reserves to no purpose and meant that we had left till too late the withdrawal of the enormous forces we had in Belgium. By the 19th the French Army had no more reserves except what it could draw from the still considerable Army of Lorraine, while the armoured strength of General von Kleist had driven through its centre and cut it in two halves which were never to come together again.

It was in the midst of this catastrophic situation on the 19th that General Weygand was called upon to replace Gamelin. Never was a change more overwhelming. At once he assumed the mantle of command with a boldness, passion and determination which contrasted strikingly with the pale, frigid calm of his predecessor.

He had arrived the night before and was able to acquaint himself with the magnitude of the disaster. We saw him arrive at Montry with his military aide, the tall Commandant Gasser, his ADC Lieutenant de Leusse and his Paris liaison officer Captain Lemaigre Dubreuil. Abandoning the fortifications at Vincennes which were haunted too much by the ghost of Gamelin, he set up at Montry with his general staff, thus showing that he intended to conduct operations very closely himself. We were a long way from the formula of 'not wishing to interfere in the conduct of the battle'!

As there was really no room at Montry for further offices, he simply took over those occupied by General Doumenc and his immediate staff. Those officers in turn had to move into the accommodation occupied by Schmuckel and myself. He ate at our table, from which, if I remember right, several generals less concerned with active operations were banished to make room. I lived very close to him during this time.

Small and slim, he seemed extremely young although he was actually over seventy. Elegant, well turned out, straightforward, amiable, but often abrupt and easily crushing, he generated immense energy and at the same time possessed astonishing physical flexibility. On the first day, having had the situation explained to him at great length and realizing the necessity to relax for a while, he left his office, called Gasser, went down the stairs four at a time, jumped the front steps and went for a hundred-yard run across the lawn! We were, as they say, breathless. . . . Instead of an ectoplasm, we had a man!

The Government had counted on his appointment to give the country and the Army a psychological shock: it did. The shock was immense and reawakened enthusiasm for the fight. But Weygand did more: he assumed complete responsibility for the battle, refused to consider defeat, and hoped even at the last moment to retrieve the situation while instilling into the Army the burning sense of purpose which consumed him. The morning he took over the whole tone of orders changed. The high command became a dynamo of energy. Was the miracle after all to come about?

Our Armies had been broken in the centre, but the considerable armoured forces which had pushed through our troops and were advancing towards Abbeville seemed at hazard because they were unsupported and were several days' march ahead of the main body of the German troops which had still barely crossed the Meuse. As Churchill said in a letter which he addressed to Weygand: 'the beast has stuck his head out of his shell'; the neck constituted a few divisions strung out with very long flanks. Could we not draw back the two halves of our severed Armies and cut through this weakly held neck, thus encircling the enemy's armoured forces which were attempting to roll up our left flank?

It was this scissors movement which was in the air when Weygand arrived and which he seized upon at once. On the 20th he gave his verbal orders. He telephoned General Billotte and told him that he had got to fight 'like a beast' and drive his way to the south. To make sure that his orders were clearly understood, he flew to see Billotte on the 21st, despite the danger of enemy fighters. It was a dramatic journey and we were very worried, but the meeting took place. He gave his orders verbally and as soon as he got back on the night 21/22 May confirmed them in writing in his general order No. 1.

His words were straightforward: they were concerned with 're-establishing contact with the major part of the French forces'. . . . 'The Germans will be contained, then beaten by counter-attacks.'

The forces in the north will therefore mount an 'offensive movement to the south' . . . an action 'to be completed by the occupation
or if necessary the retaking of the crossings of the Somme' by the
group which we were bringing together in the area south of Amiens.
'Enemy elements between the frontier and the Somme have stuck
their necks out and must be destroyed . . .' 'The German Panzer
Divisions will be held in the narrow area into which they have so
boldly thrust themselves. They will not be allowed to get out.'
The style gave the measure of the man.

Also on this day, the 22nd, there was a gleam of hope. The Army
Group of the north had mounted its movement southwards and had
retaken Arras and Cambrai. The German forces continued to push
on to the west and the gap behind them narrowed: it was less than
forty miles, which could be closed in one day's fighting if the two
arms of the pincer worked in unison. Were we saved?

Alas, fate still had no mercy. At the Army Group of the north,
General Billotte was killed in a road accident after leaving the
conference which he had had with General Weygand. Thus at one
blow were lost the drive which the Commander-in-Chief had
imparted and a general of great character for whom the only
replacement was a man whose morale had been shaken by the
twelve days' ordeal in Belgium. Furthermore this man had shown
an authority vis-à-vis his British and Belgian Allies the absence of
which was to be cruelly felt. This fatality deprived us of the one
man capable of bringing off the difficult manœuvre on which so
much depended. From that day on our Armies in the north, whose
defence was heroic to the end, were at sixes and sevens and incapable of imposing their will on the enemy.

It is easy now, away from the heat of battle, to outline a course of
action which could have led to success. But men are but human.
They were submitted to a terrible strain; they had gone through
two weeks of ceaseless fighting all the way back from the Dyle and
only with the greatest effort had succeeded in holding the enemy.
Harassed repeatedly from the air, kept continually keyed up by the
multitudinous activites of fifth columnists and parachute troops,
drowned in a flood of refugees, demoralized by an influx of Belgian
fugitives, their nerve was stretched to breaking-point. They were

outflanked on their right, cut off from the main forces in France and menaced from the rear by the Panzer Divisions which were coming up from Boulogne; and now they were asked to attack, with mixed columns made up of decimated units. It was beyond human capacity.

Furthermore, in this extremity of danger, everyone reacted according to his own national interests. The Belgians, who only a fortnight ago had hoped to remain neutral, felt that they had played their part and lost. The British, who had precious few land forces other than those in France, were now concerned with saving what they could for the defence of their own island. It is possible to take a poor view of these reactions and to consider them as contrary to military honour and inter-Allied discipline. On the other hand I find these reactions quite normal, and fully anticipated by the enemy. We should have foreseen that they would be the first consequences of our defeat and the direct result of the absence of a commander on the spot capable of imposing a unified intention. Furthermore we were in a somewhat delicate position: having assumed the overall command, we could not avoid the responsibility for this unprecedented disaster into which we had dragged our Allies; our prestige was naturally deeply tainted, which to some extent justified everyone reserving to himself liberty of action. At this time it seemed easy to saddle the Belgians with the responsibility for this moral disaster. This was a mistake. Later, much was made out of certain disagreements which arose with the British command, which very early began to act independently. This was another mistake. Our Allies were never really integrated with us, it is true, and this shortcoming played a considerable part in the failure of the manœuvre which we were trying to push through. But one must be honest with oneself: our command failed where Foch in 1914 had succeeded with the same partners and in circumstances every bit as serious. Therefore our command on the spot did not have the necessary faith and prestige. It is difficult to criticize: the situation was terrible, one of the most terrible known to history; but a lack of obedience is the fault of the leader and, our situation being what it was, we are in no position to criticize the shortcomings of subordinates.

What exactly happened? This is for the historians to say. On the 22nd the movement ordered by Weygand on the 20th began to get under way. On the 23rd it made a little progress. Weygand, sensing the irresolution caused by the death of Billotte, sent an urgent order on the morning of the 24th: 'I confirm your instructions . . . co-ordinate firmly the Allies' movements and give them formal orders. Success depends upon the continuation of your advance south-wards . . . I count on the ferocious resolution of every man'.

But this resolution was lacking at the Headquarters of the Armies of the north. We had confirmation of this from the visit of Colonel Fauvelle who explained the situation to us. For several days there had no longer been any feeling of hope that the situation could be put to rights. This attack to the south seemed to them a useless effort. Morale was gone. It was in this atmosphere that it was learnt on the 24th, before the receipt of Weygand's order which I have just quoted, that during the night the British had fallen back to the Haute Deule canal and had given up Arras, for from this moment they felt that they would have to evacuate and were acting accordingly. This latest blow finally destroyed the last vestiges of will-power. The difficult movement which was only being attempted half-heartedly was obviously no longer on. GHQ was informed at once with a request for fresh orders.

Weygand got the news in the morning. His dilemma was a terrible one. During the four days of his command he had put all his faith in this attack to the south. Tirelessly, with fierce energy, he had tried to communicate his will to his subordinates, to drive them into action, to give them faith in eventual victory. But now the chief elements in his plan were deaf to his appeal and had stopped trying. To give in to their objections was to accept defeat. But how could he insist upon his order to attack without seeing the situation for himself and if necessary being able to appoint a new commander? One would like to know what passed through his mind that day when he saw the end of his first hopes. Anyway it was during the afternoon that he gave up his primary intention and came around to General Blanchard's way of thinking: 'You inform me of the withdrawal decided upon and carried out by the British during the night . . . if this withdrawal renders impossible the movement which I have ordered, you will take steps *to create a bridgehead covering Dunkirk.* . . . ' It was a loose, almost timid phrase. *If* the commander of the Armies on the north considered the move-ment impossible, he was to fall back on Dunkirk. From this moment, 1600 hours on the 24th, ninety hours after Weygand assumed command, the movement was dead and any hope of restoring the situation was gone.

This drama is in itself enough to explain the breakdown of Weygand's efforts, but at the same time other events threw a harsh light on the powerlessness of the French forces to find any answer to the German offensive by appropriate manoeuvres. The defection of the Armies in the north was to some extent to be expected: their ability to fight was seriously impaired by the terrible battle which they had been through and finally paralysed by disunity between the Allies. But the situation was by no means the same in the Somme area south of the penetration. In this area we had steadily built up a Group composed of units, intact and in good heart, drawn from our right. This Group consisted of Touchon's Army on the Aisne and that of Frère on the Somme; it was to be completed by the deployment of Altmeyer's Army around the lower Somme on the 24th; the whole were under Third Army Group commanded by General Besson.

Let us for a moment take a look at this Army Group. On 5 June it comprised forty divisions, of which over twenty were west of the Oise, and represented a force superior in strength to the four Franco-British Armies which had advanced into Belgium and were now surrounded in the Dunkirk area. By 22 May General Touchon's Sixth Army had two-thirds of its strength deployed to cover the direct route to Paris. On its left was General Frère's Seventh Army, made up of no more than six or seven divisions, of which part was on the move to deny the routes southwards from Péronne and Amiens; it further received two armoured divisions somewhat below strength but still able to muster about two hundred tanks. Between Abbeville and the sea was General Altmeyer's Group which was not yet given Army status; it was made up of a British division, some cavalry and a British armoured division. Thus our forces between the Oise and the Channel coast made up in itself a powerful Army, but little enough when one realizes that it had to cover a hundred miles without knowing which way the enemy's armour—with its advance elements at Saint-Valéry-sur-Somme and Montreuil-sur-Mer and its main body between Amiens and Doullens —was likely to turn.

From the 21st the task of the Seventh Army was 'to extend its cover from Peronne to Amiens and Abbeville, thus masking all the roads leading to Paris from Ham to Abbeville', and further 'to be prepared as rapidly as possible to mount an operation on the Péronne–Bapaume axis against the flank or rear of the German column moving to the north-west'. When it was learned that the enemy had thrust southwards and formed several bridgeheads across the Somme, the operation order for the 22nd made it clear that the converging movement which we earlier considered 'will be completed by the occupation and *if necessary the recapture* of the Somme crossings.' On the 23rd it became clear that the main body of the Panzer Divisions was pressing on towards Boulogne and that before us we had little more than a thin screen. The masking operation therefore became of secondary importance: according to Weygand's orders 'the supreme object is to press on to effect a junction between the First Army Group in the north and the Third Army Group in the south' . . . 'In the box formed by the sea on the west, by the Somme on the south, to the south-west by the converging forces of Generals Frère and Blanchard and to the east by the Belgians, the main body of the Panzer Divisions will be ground down'. This idea was given added force in a further order: 'The General Commanding in Chief lays it down that: 1. *The movement to effect the junction of the First and Third Army Groups will be pursued* in order to close all routes of possible German armoured withdrawal . . . in the general direction of Albert–Bapaume; 2. this operation will be completed by masking operations, particularly on the Somme'. Thus the Seventh Army's task was primarily to be offensive.

On the 24th when Weygand, as we have seen, was forced to give up the idea of effecting this vital junction, he still maintained the offensive mission of the Seventh Army in order to clear the south bank of the Somme and so ensure the use of the river as a barrier: 'It is essential that all intact bridges across the Somme be seized and bridgeheads on the northern bank be established'. On the 26th, when he was laying down the general lines of the defensive battle which he now found forced upon him, he was still preoccupied with the River Somme: 'At the risk of repetition, the Commander-in-Chief cannot underline too strongly the prime importance attaching to this objective . . . of dominating the lower reaches of the Somme. *In consequence nothing must be spared in order to clear the enemy from the south bank of the river and to deny him any further crossing. . . .'*

The idea of an offensive north of the river seemed to him necessary in order to relieve the heavy pressure on Dunkirk. On the same day he sent a signal to the Army Group North saying '*. . . Third Army Group will continue its operations to clear the Somme* and will do everything within its powers on the Authie'. On the 27th he again called for 'resolute and aggressive action on the Somme' and on the 29th he wrote again that 'it is essential to fling the enemy back north of the river'. The intention of the Commander was clear and his orders unambiguous.

What in fact was the enemy's strength facing our left wing? On this subject we had precise information because, contrary to what some people may think, the 2ᵉ Bureau did a very good job. On the 22nd there was between Péronne and the sea one motorized division, the 2nd, but further north there were several Panzer Divisions. By the 24th there were only two motorized divisions very much extended and behind them nothing more than an armoured division and one more motorized division. By the 27th two infantry divisions had made their appearance in the Péronne — Amiens area, but the Panzer Divisions and the motorized division which had seemed to be in reserve had pushed on and were engaged south of Calais. There was therefore in front of us nothing more than a screen without depth which on the 28th could be strengthened solely by bringing one armoured division back from Dunkirk. On this front, so long as the Army Group North kept up its heroic resistance and did not permit the disengagement of those German forces which were trying to prevent its evacuation, our own superiority was undoubted because we had four complete divisions already on the spot on the 28th which could be built up to fifteen by 4 June. The elements of success had been brought together.

However, once again there was a set-back. In spite of such urgent orders from the high command, Third Army Group did nothing except undertake three minor and unsuccessful operations: on the 25th a first attack on Amiens was mounted on too wide a front by a single division, which was driven back behind its start-line; on the 27th a fresh push was made against Amiens, Picquigny and Abbeville without any positive results. On the 29th a more serious attack was mounted against Abbeville with General de Gaulle's

armoured division; it drove in the German outposts but foundered
on their screen of ack-ack guns employed in an anti-tank role.
Finally on 4 June stronger forces were committed: twenty artillery
groups and over 100 tanks. Once more the target was Abbeville
and the success was no greater than that of its predecessor. Thus,
when on the following day the German offensive was unleashed
from their bridgeheads, there was nothing which we could do to
contain it. Everything swept over us as though we had not even
been aware of the danger.

I have dwelt for some time on this phase of the battle because it
seems to me to give the real clue to the value of our Army. At
Sedan there had been the element of surprise and the fact that we
had local inferiority. In Belgium we had been driven back by an
enemy who gave an impression of being superior and who used
unaccustomed methods of fighting; but on the Somme we were
facing an enemy who was on the defensive and weaker than ourselves. There could be no doubt about the firm intention of the
high command. Speed, massed strength and drive were needed.
What we saw instead was units committed piecemeal, making
contact over too wide a front, and primarily concerned with self-
defence. The attacks came to nothing because they were badly
mounted in insufficient strength after delays which were quite un-
acceptable in view of the speed at which our enemy was moving.
The first attack was mounted five days after General Weygand's
verbal instructions and three days after his written orders; the
second needed seven days' preparation, the third no less than nine.
As to the final action, a whole fortnight passed before it could be
got off the ground. . . . We must not forget the vital urgency of
these attacks, the role they played in the overall plan and the fact
that our troops were fresh. Their steadiness under fire in the sub-
sequent defensive battle showed that they possessed the right spirit.
The men themselves cannot be blamed but the verdict must go
against the French Army itself.

History's judgement must be passed upon those few days: the
French Army was nothing more than a vast inefficient tool, incapable of quick reaction or adaptation, quite incapable of taking
the offensive or of any mobility. We were reaping the logical

consequences of twenty years of ill-conceived doctrine aggravated by the nine months of somnolence which made up for us the first period of the war. In other words in May 1940 we showed ourselves to be just as cumbersome and just as immature as we were during the first skirmishes in Lorraine in 1939. Much discussion has gone on over the reason for our defeat. There has been much talk of shortcomings in equipment, morale and command. Certainly all these factors played their part and helped in our downfall, but the end was inevitable because, faced by an able and swift-moving adversary, our Army could not find any answer even when it enjoyed numerical superiority. The machine was old and rusty. A repetition of the Marne was impossible, however great the qualities of the commander.

This knowledge bore down bitterly upon our minds from the first days of June in 1940.

In these nightmare days, interest was centred on Dunkirk. The news was terrible; there was indescribable chaos on the beaches. The British were evacuating their troops in priority under constant bombardment from the air. For some inexplicable reason the German armoured divisions did not attack (we knew after the war that it was the decision of Hitler to spare Great Britain in the hope of a compromise peace), but the situation was more and more critical. Like everyone else we followed the drama by telephone. At the end I spoke for the last time via England with Admiral Abrial, commanding the fortress at Dunkirk. Weygand came into my office and seized the telephone, could not hear well, and seized the second receiver, kneeling among lines on the floor; 'Abrial, you've got to hold on . . . hold on'. We were cut off. He remained prostrate for a moment, then got up sharply; I admired this old man who carried on his frail shoulders the crushing weight of a lost campaign.

At the end of May the situation was grave but we had succeeded in re-forming a front from the Channel to Switzerland. The northern half of our forces, more than sixty Allied divisions, was surrounded and thrown into the sea. The 300,000 men who were saved (only

100,000 of them French) were nothing more than a mob without arms who took no further part in the battle. We were left with no more than sixty divisions and barely a few hundred tanks scattered along a hastily constructed front from the Channel to the Swiss border. Only in the east we leaned upon the Maginot Line which was intact. What was our strategy now to be?

The choice was a difficult one. One wonders, and one will go on wondering more and more, if it would not have been better to stage a fighting withdrawal, playing for time and watching for a fresh chance to stand. This theory seems attractive and will find more supporters as the realities of the actual moment sink into the past. But there were several determining reasons which militated against this heroic solution. The main one, in my opinion, was the inability to manœuvre which our troops had just displayed on the Somme. With so inefficient a weapon, was it wise voluntarily to give ground in the hope that the enemy would eventually make a mistake, of which we would not be able to take advantage anyway? Furthermore any withdrawal would undoubtedly cost us Paris and the Maginot Line, two moral factors of prime importance. No one at the time could visualize such sacrifice without one more fight.

Our commanders, haunted by memories of March 1918, thought that they could survive the German penetration once again. What they felt should be done was to tighten up their forces and cover Paris. One might say: 'Haven't they yet learnt that static defence is valueless against tanks?' Yes and no. We had watched with stupefaction the collapse of our Armies on the Meuse, but this failure was attributed to the moral surprise and bad anti-tank defence. But there was still an idea that now, after the first baptism of fire, the defence against armour would recover the efficiency it had shown in peacetime exercises. It was not a question of revolution but of simple adaptation. One immediate reaction was to try to reorganize the defence into strong-points made up of infantry and artillery. It was what was called then the 'quadrillage',* a discontinuous tactical disposition of a greater depth than the one used previously, and by which General Weygand felt that he might check the Panzer divisions, if everyone followed the formula and really fought 'like beasts'. For twenty years we had relied

---

* This method of defence was used by the British in the Western Desert and there referred to as the 'box' system (Trs.).

upon the value of defence; it was impossible to change our outlook overnight.

In any case—and here I am on delicate ground—I do not believe that by this time our high command had any further hope of success; the constant series of rebuffs which they had suffered, the constant surprises, the disappointments which followed every attempt to rally, had broken the spirit of our leaders; if defeat was not already accepted as inevitable, it was certainly regarded as just around the corner. This mental outlook which had become obvious in some quarters from 14 May had spread despite the dynamic action of General Weygand. Weygand himself, a doctor called in at the last moment to heal a man dying of an incurable disease, had done his best; but fundamentally he must have felt that he had little chance of success. On 29 May in fact he made it known to the Government that 'a moment may well come when France, however willing, may find it impossible to continue military operations in defence of her homeland'. This mental reservation which he was expressing was common throughout Headquarters and this fate was generally considered to be inescapable. But before that everything had to be done to check the enemy. We felt ourselves beaten but no one would admit it until our defeat was absolute. It seemed that thus the honour of our arms would be saved.

I have tried to give some idea of the atmosphere in which the next phase of the battle was prepared during the breathing-space which the agony of Dunkirk allowed us. It is difficult to describe such complex and dramatic feelings, when no one uttered more than a part of what was in his mind and documents were prepared with systematic optimism. Furthermore the reactions of individuals were widely different. The general view was that defeat was probable but that we must try everything, and perhaps another defensive battle would bring success. In this supreme trial, we held to the only manœuvre of which our Army was capable, to which all our reflexes were conditioned: to stand our ground 'without any question of withdrawal from the positions which we now occupy', as General Weygand ordered with his usual clarity and energy on 26 May.

This important decision was to attempt, in worse conditions because our forces were reduced by half, to win the battle which we had already lost between the 10th and 15th. The confidence of the command at certain levels was very limited. No one dared refuse to obey or even to speak of it, but there was a reluctance to stake all on this single card, from which sprang a marked tendency to prepare a succession of positions for withdrawal which further weakened our troops who were already thin on the ground.

The result was an ambivalence between conception and execution which is interesting, because it shows the real character of this last battle—at once resolute yet bedevilled by afterthoughts, a last stand tainted with thoughts of the morrow.

Weygand's thinking, as I have said, was set out on the 26th in terms which admit of no misunderstanding: 'The battle on which the fate of our country depends will be fought *without any question of withdrawal* from the positions which we now occupy'. In spite of this, on the 29th an order issued by General Georges defined a position to the rear of a line between Beauvais—Creil and the Aisne and envisaged, 'in the event that a deep penetration . . . renders this straightening of the line impossible', a re-forming from the lower Seine across the routes to Paris. On the 30th a fresh order made it plain that the organization of these three lines would become incumbent upon the Armies, except on the Oise.

Thus on the 31st General Weygand found it necessary to lay it on the line again:

Certain dispositions taken up by Third Army Group make
me feel that my orders have not been correctly understood. . . .
The general feeling of Third Army Group's orders is not
implacable static resistance but of a delaying action in depth. . . .
The deployment which has been undertaken . . . and the siting
of fighting divisions far back and their organization in a
defensive zone as much as thirty miles behind the line of
battle at a time when our left flank in the lower Somme is
inadequately supported in depth shows clearly the divergence
of views. This must be put right forthwith. We are engaged
in a defensive battle on the Somme. Every effort must be made
to find ourselves as strong as possible in that area not only
to resist the enemy but to provide a spring-board for possible
counter-attack. . . . The need for a position further to the rear
cannot in the long run be overlooked, but everything in its
own time . . . the large units employed should not distract us from

the demands of the main front. I order therefore that you take all steps necessary to restore the position forthwith. Let us not risk losing the battle of the Somme in the hope of winning the battle of Paris.'

In spite of this the position was not completely restored. The compromise which emerged was to put into the line divisions which until now had been held in reserve, but to replace them in the rear with troops who were coming in later. By 5 June between the sea and the Oise there were eleven divisions in contact, but in the rear there were six infantry divisions and six more of armour or cavalry, the latter very experienced but short of material. This staggering of resources, absolutely contrary to General Weygand's intentions, might be considered justified with counter-attack in mind, but in fact, as time was to show, it was a mental preparation for further retreat. Thus once more Weygand was unable to get his orders carried out.

Meanwhile great hopes were placed in the change in our defensive tactics: the adoption of the 'all-round defence' (the 'quadrillage') based on woods or villages, strengthened with field-pieces in an anti-tank role, tactics which Doumenc had recommended and Weygand had adopted with enthusiasm. This was the state of affairs on 5 June when, according to Hitler's grandiloquent announcement 'the greatest offensive of modern times' was launched. I got the news very early on the telephone and immediately told Weygand and Doumenc. The information coming in was encouraging. Our troops, whose morale had risen and who believed that there were substantial reserves behind them, fought magnificently. Almost everywhere the strong-points held, even when surrounded, and the German attack lost its impetus.

These almost unexpected results brought a gleam of hope. Would the 'quadrillage' tactics and the determination which had come back to us succeed in breaking the terrible spell which for more than a month had been cast over our Army? Nevertheless our positions were in danger in several places. We needed to throw in our reserves to counter-attack. It had always been Weygand's idea that our greatest effort should be concentrated on the Somme. It was this which was uppermost in his mind when on the night of 5/6 June he realized that the directions given by Third Army Group were in 'direct contradiction' of his formal orders. Early on the morning of the 6th Weygand ordered me to summon to a council of war in his office General Georges, General Doumenc and General Besson —commanding Third Army Group—and I wondered if Besson was not on the verge of being relieved of his command.

When they came out from Weygand's office I hurried up to Doumenc and asked him what decisions had been taken; to my great surprise he replied, 'Besson spoke up for himself very well'.

'What,' I said, 'it's to be delaying action manoeuvre?' Doumenc nodded.

I was staggered. How could this be? For ten days General Weygand had been laying down and holding to a plan in which he believed. This plan so far had stood up with remarkable success because nowhere had our positions been driven in, yet here he was giving up all he believed without any contrary proof! It was a catastrophe because the strong-points, if they withdrew, would have to abandon their major equipment and would completely lose confidence in their ability to hold on. This was opening the way to a rout which could only grow faster and faster.

Once more this brings home sharply how difficult it is for a commander to impose his way of thinking. Once he has made his decision known, everything conspires against him; on top of the doubts which must exist in his own mind are piled the information coming in of the course of the operation and the objections of his subordinates. Napoleon said 'It is difficult to realize the strength of will which is needed to fight a battle.' Weygand's strength of will was undeniable yet twice, on 24 May and 6 June, he found himself forced to abandon his first intentions.

This new concept did not become apparent on the 6th except in one phrase in the order he issued congratulating the troops on their magnificent resistance: 'After the movements now being carried out *which will replace* our forces now locked in action with the enemy. . . .' But in effect it led to our keeping our reserves where they were and ruled out any counter-attack in strength, and from the 7th orders were given within the Armies to pull back, entailing the abandonment of all heavy equipment within the strong-points. The battle 'with no thought of withdrawal' had lasted forty-eight hours.

My remaining memories of this ill-fated period are no more than incidents, flashes each more depressing than the last.

On the 7th I went with Doumenc to the Command Post of the Seventh Army near Forges-les-Eaux. On the way, through a countryside already devoid of its inhabitants, we watched with a kind of fascinated horror a German fighter literally murder one of our cumbersome fighter-bombers, which fluttered slowly down in flames. When we reached the command post other enemy aircraft were flying over it and the officers were out in the streets shooting at them with small arms in a sort of frustrated rage. The Germans had broken through in the Rouen–Soissons area. On the 8th the order was given by Third Army Group to withdraw to the Seine and the so-called Paris line.

At General Georges's command post, at Bondons, the atmosphere had become unbearable. At the switchboard, which was receiving bad news at monotonous one-minute intervals, there was no longer any reaction: one officer would acknowledge messages in a quiet, soft voice, another with an almost hysterical giggle—'Ah, yes, your left has been driven in; oh, I see, they're in behind you. I'll make a note of it!' Everyone else in the room, prostrate and silent, was sitting about in armchairs.

In the morning when I was marking up the wall map I was watched by the Major-General Ops., a firm and proud instructor when I had been at Saint-Cyr; he wept openly, his face screwed up like a baby's. In this horrible atmosphere I tried to keep a hold on myself, forcing myself to keep calm and do my job as efficiently as I could.

Alas, on the 9th the enemy offensive spread eastwards into the Rethel area against the front of Fourth Army Group, brought together to hold the gap formed by the flat country of Champagne, and made rapid progress. By the following day the front was completely broken; the Germans exploited their success with deep thrusts and had already reached the Seine between Rouen and the Oise, fanning out south of Soissons and isolating our right wing by a drive from Rethel towards the Seine. Our entire defensive disposition west of the Maginot Line was dislocated and we had no more reserves. This time all hope was gone, the game was up, and nothing could save us.

We would have to leave Montry, as the Government was leaving Paris. The first move visualized was a short one, to the Loire: we would go to Briare and the Government to Tours (shades of 1871). Our monstrous GHQ could hardly be described as mobile. It was not a movement in the military sense but a household removal.

Weygand took us with him to Paris where he was to have a last meeting with the Government. He sent them a note: 'The events of the last two days' fighting make it incumbent on me to inform M. le Président du Conseil that the collapse of our lines of defence must be expected at any moment' [It had already occurred]. 'If this should come about, our troops will continue to fight until their means and their strength are exhausted, but their complete dissolution can only be a matter of time'. This grave communication was unfortunately an understatement and did not bring out the full tragedy of the situation. The reservations in the mind of the Commander-in-Chief are understandable, but they nevertheless contributed to keeping alive baseless illusions in the minds of the Government.

During this time, off the record we were bringing ourselves to talk about bringing the débâcle to an end before the whole country was overrun. The word 'armistice' was first used, if I remember right, at Vincennes, in Gamelin's erstwhile command post. We had just learned that Italy proposed to enter the war. While we were having lunch in the officers' mess the crackling radio picked up an Italian broadcast—a speech, cheers from the crowd and *giovinezza*. This gesture of 'political realism' was the last straw. Were we to go on and on to total disaster? There was at that time—and I write as a witness—no thought of suing Germany for peace, but only of stopping the fighting, the literal meaning of the word 'armistice'.

Subsequently there has been a great deal of despondent talk about the birth of this armistice which I have never understood. I do not want to get involved here in this argument, conclusions on which will belong to history when all the facts are available. I will confine myself, as I have tried to do up till now, to describing the atmosphere in which we found ourselves and the state of mind which resulted. The idea of some long prepared 'treason' springs from a sordid imagination and has no basis in fact, as these pages have shown. The argument which was to develop in the next few days between Weygand and Reynaud on the relative merits of an armistice and of capitulation, seems to me equally pointless. Whatever way one looks at it, we had tried and we had lost. Without admitting complete defeat, it was essential to disengage and wait for better times. To argue the toss in the midst of defeat made no sense; the only thing which mattered was to find a way of disengaging.

Weygand came back from his meeting with the Government in a highly nervous state. Paris was already very empty. Everywhere archives were being burnt and a pall of thick black smoke from the oil storage tanks of Havre, which were being destroyed, put the first grey sky over the city in a spring which had been endlessly beautiful.

The march table allowed for our leaving Paris in a special train which was drawn up in Vincennes station. The idea of a special train was a good one because the roads were hopelessly congested, but I feared that we might be strafed from the air. But nothing happened and we carried our misery away in sumptuous drawing-room cars.

At Briare the command post was set up in the Château du Muguet, a stuffy house at the bottom of a damp valley. Communications were unreliable, but good enough for us to follow the progress of the Germans' inexorable advance. Often the best way of finding out if a town had been taken was to ring up the Post Office where the switchboard operators, who devotedly stuck to their posts, would say if the Germans had arrived or not.

The Château du Muguet is associated in my mind with two important memories: the first concerns General de Gaulle who for several days had been Under Secretary of State for War. One of my main tasks was to keep him informed of the progress of operations. Unfortunately the news which I had to telephone to him was absolutely horrifying and the General, who, like all of us, was suffering bitterly, listened to my recitals as if I were personally responsible. I remember one day when I reported that our Armies had been cut to ribbons by the German penetration, he said to me severely, 'You have no right to say that'. Perhaps not, but. . . .

It was about this time that there was born the idea of the 'Breton Redoubt', of which General de Gaulle has in his Memoirs denied paternity—yet one cannot help thinking that it must have had some connection with his desire to ignore defeat and to do something 'come what might'. Naturally the Breton Redoubt was stillborn. Soon after we were asked to work out a plan for transporting all the recruits under instruction to North Africa. We had neither the ships nor the organization to carry out an operation (involving 300,000 men) so important, so difficult and of doubtful value. In fact in the general mental disarray the majority sank into fatalism or despair and those who retained any feeling of hope were few and far between. In the midst of a thousand difficulties de Gaulle was to build his reputation on a proud refusal to recognize the sad realities of the present, but this refusal made no sense until it could be based upon and allied to the British determination to continue the fight. In France in 1940 the will for war, which had never been particularly strong, was completely shattered.

My second memory is of the last meeting of the Supreme Franco-British Council which was held at the Château du Muguet. All the heads of the coalition were there: on the British side Churchill, Eden, Alan Brooke and Spears; on the French side Reynaud, Pétain, Weygand, Darlan, Vuillemin and Doumenc, Baudouin and de Gaulle. The conference was to take place after dinner and the General's ADC had spent a long time on the table plan.

Before dinner, in the drawing-room, Paul Reynaud, utterly exhausted and a bundle of nerves, walked up and down, twitching in a way which I have never seen since. Pétain was Olympian. Darlan solid and cunning. Eden seemed to me rather fragile and a little '*fin de race*'. Churchill, dynamic as always, held court solidly settled in an armchair. I remember a moment when Spears went across to him and said that he would like to introduce de Gaulle to him and then went off to bring the General across—'General de Gaulle whom I have mentioned to you.' In his Memoirs the General speaks of a previous interview with Churchill. They had already met. But I must bear witness to the fact that the first real contact between them was on this evening. Their conversation was very lively and when we rose to go in to dinner Churchill said in his own particular brand of French: 'I have had a very interesting conversation with General de Gaulle and I would like to keep him next to me'. The table plan, worked out with so much care, was in ruins . . . but on these ruins were built the first foundations of the Liberation.

After the meal was over the conference took place in the dining-room. The subjects for discussion were numerous. Our immediate problem was to get more help from the United Kingdom, particularly in the air. Churchill offered *one* division, and made some play out of future help from America. He did what he could, but very loyally he made it plain that he was not prepared to disperse the RAF which was and had to be an essential instrument in the defence of the British Isles.

The description which Weygand gave him of the general picture underlined the gravity of the whole situation. On the front facing the Alps our troops were victoriously resisting without difficulty, but on the German frontier the situation was rapidly deteriorating. Our forces to the north and north-west of Paris, apart from those concentrated round Havre, were pulling out as best they could, abandoning most of their material as they went. Their collapse, which had already begun, could only accelerate. But their line of retreat was still open. On the other hand the German offensive which had broken through in Champagne was turning towards the Jura and was about to devolve upon our Army Group East, still holding the Maginot Line; this would represent the same threat of encirclement which we had already experienced around Abbeville. Time was pressing if we were not to lose our last intact Army Group.

The battle in the north had cost us thirty-five divisions, the battle of the Somme had either destroyed or broken up twenty to twenty-five more divisions. We now had left to us no more than some forty divisions for the whole western front. There was only one answer which had been decided upon that morning and accepted by the Government: this was a general withdrawal, and the first step was back to a line drawn from Caen, the Loire, the Côte d'Or, to the Jura.

Churchill tried to combat these disastrous indications by recalling the precedent of 25 March 1918, but Pétain interpolated that in 1918 he had needed forty divisions simply to close the gap: that is to say as much as the maximum remaining forces now available of the French Army. We were lost because we had no further reserves. Then Churchill, very serious, said that he understood that France might well have to give up the fight, but, if that should come about, he wished to make it plain that Great Britain would relentlessly pursue the struggle to its very end.

The conference ended without any further definite decisions: it was agreed that France would hold on for a few more days as she slipped down to the depths. The British, thanks to their island fastness, would not give up. But was there any reason why the Germans should not be able to effect a landing? Churchill neither accepted nor formally objected to the idea of French capitulation, which from our side had still not been put to him as an unavoidable eventuality. The real detailed discussion between the military command and the Government was to begin the next day at Cangé, near Tours.

Churchill went to bed—late. A bottle of brandy had been put on his bedside table and it was found to be empty in the morning, after he had appeared in a red dressing-gown at the top of the staircase shouting for his valet because the bath-water was not hot enough.

On our side, our worries over the fate of our Army Group East after the breakthrough in Champagne, together with the disintegration of our front from the Channel to the Marne, forced two decisions upon us on the 12th: a general order to withdraw, and the abandonment of the Maginot Line. Almost simultaneously Paris was declared an open city in order to avoid its destruction. General Dentz was sent in to acknowledge the Germans on their arrival.

For all of us the battle was over.

From that day on General Headquarters abandoned its Olympian role and came down to the level of every Frenchman: in other words they were just refugees on the road.

We bummed along with less and less dignity from Briare to Vichy, where the British mission left us; then on to Mont-Dore, where General Réquin reproached me bitterly, in the absence of anyone else, for having been slow in telling him to pull his Army Group out; then from Mont-Dore to Montauban where the armistice caused us to pause for a moment.

After we left Briare I was able to make a quick detour to my parents at Saint-Thibault to tell them that there was no point in trying to escape and they should stay where they were—advice which did them little good, since an evacuation order was served on them the next day by a hysterical colonel.

A strange feeling came over me at this stage: the war was now spreading into the land of my childhood. It seemed incredible to me that this peaceful valley of the Loire, in which I had so often canoed and bathed, could become a theatre of war. I had never imagined this could happen, but here it was. When we pulled out of Briare in a long line of trucks and crossed the Loire we saw bombers destroying Gien seven miles north of us. Along the road ahead of us an Italian fighter was shooting up the refugees.

This procession of cars heading South has been often described. It was at once tragic and comic, a sort of sad funfair on the move made up of disbanded soldiers, girls, frightened families, rich cars piled high with miscellaneous baggage, perambulators filled with pots and pans pushed by two old people. Numberless individual dramas lived out within the incomprehensible drama of France herself, a great deal of resignation, occasional flashes of humour. In this great migration the Frenchman showed once more his extraordinary aptitude for improvisation.

Life in the midst of this mob made only too plain the complete disorganization of the Army and of France. During our short stops our role was now confined to discussions with the civil and military authorities as to whether there was still anywhere to fight or whether still to press on down the road. Each seemed equally absurd. Here, at Vierzon, a tank officer who wanted to defend the outskirts of the town was killed by the population to save their homes from destruction; there, at Clermont-Ferrand, the troops were confined to barracks for an orderly surrender when the Germans arrived, while the General went off on his own. We tried to make the civil authorities, who too often were giving way to the general panic, stay at their posts.

It was during one of these stops that I heard the message from Marshal Pétain announcing the request for an armistice. This, while perhaps reassuring for the multitude of civilian refugees, sounded the deathknell of any organized military resistance. Nevertheless this impossible situation continued for a further eight days, creating total material and moral confusion.

During another stop I heard one of the first messages sent out by General de Gaulle. To give here my deepest and most sincere thoughts, the fact is that we could not take it in because we were still too stunned by the defeat—which we did not accept morally but from the total effect of which we had no idea how to escape. The resistance being built up in London had our sympathy but at the time it seemed an easy way out and the least urgent of the matters in hand. The most vital task seemed somehow to drag the country out of the terrifying shambles into which defeat had plunged it. This rescue operation was a thankless and difficult business but it seemed our clear duty at the time.

Weygand had left us and gone on to Bordeaux to fight the battle often described already for the cessation of hostilities. We knew nothing about all this and in consequence the armistice took us by surprise when we were in Montauban.

From the Atlantic Ocean to the Alps our forces were in a state of complete disruption. Only two points held on. On the one hand the six divisions of the Army of the Alps, with the Germans in their rear, held off thirty Italian divisions. This at least shows that our preparations for war were not so completely useless as some like to think and that our defeat sprang not so much from absolute spine-lessness as from the great superiority of the new way of fighting exploited by the Germans.

On the other hand, to the north-east the great forts of the Maginot Line held on and refused to surrender unless a direct order was brought to them by French officers, which is in accord-ance with military ethics. Officers were sent to them with these orders and, by some sort of irony of fate, those selected for the task were all ex-members of Gamelin's staff.

Epilogue

*

THE COLLAPSE OF THE French Army is the most important event of the twentieth century. Our downfall upset the balance which had been built up and maintained through the ages. Europe, the mother of modern civilization, found itself deprived of its western counter-balance. The destruction of Germany which was to come left in place of the traditional Europe only a zone of weakness, while the USA and the USSR, now overwhelming powers, disputed between themselves the dominance of the world which Europe had lost, and which led inevitably to the fashion for decolonization.

All this grew out of the thinking of our military leaders and the courage of our soldiers. If they had been more effective the face of the world today would be different.

Thus, before the Bar of history, we have a terrible responsibility.

I have tried to describe, in all its complexity, the chain of causes which led to our downfall. Contrary to various biased theses which have been put forward, it is apparent that everyone was in some degree party to what happened. That is the way it goes in great historical events.

On the stage of the world all the major actors contributed to the drama: Great Britain by her prolonged blindness to what was happening in Germany, the United States by their selfish isolation after 1918, Italy by her illusions of grandeur, the Soviet by her Fabian duplicity, even Japan with her ambitions of modernized barbarism.

In France the first fatal germs go back to 1914–18 which by its useless slaughter produced the pacifism of the '*ancien combattant*', the duality of the Foch-Pétain thinking after the war, and above all the narrow conquerors' dogmatism of the Pétain school of thought. From then on, diplomatic wavering, the muddle of internal politics, the general atrophy of the state and all its ingredients could only make matters worse. Neither the French 'fascists' nor the *Front*

Populaire was responsible for our downfall, although they may have contributed to it.

By 1940 there was nothing to be done: fate had stacked the cards too heavily against us. Even had we had a Napoleon to lead us, we might not have avoided defeat but the disaster would have been kept within bounds. This was because there was no one who could make the huge military machine which we had at our disposal move itself, as I have tried to show by describing the events which took place on the Somme between 25 May and 6 June.

How could we have avoided defeat? It is possible that the last chance was thrown away when we refused to make war in 1939. If we had really assaulted the Siegfried Line we would have trained our troops, rejuvenated the high command, tried out our methods of combat and put new life into the war effort. The battle of 1940 would have been fought with a few more cards in our hand. If in addition we had had the great military leader whom we lacked, we might not have won, but we would not have lost. But certain shortfalls—particularly in armament and aviation—were already inevitable and liable to prove deadly dangerous.

This is why the climactic moment of the drama was really long before, before the Russian incident, before Munich. Actually it was in March 1936 that our fate was settled. At that moment we could with the minimum of risk have stopped the German revival in embryo, revised our faulty military ideas, and ensured a long period of peace. Later there was still time to build up our warlike stores, particularly after Munich, but the internal situation in France made this impossible.

Our reaction in March 1936 presupposed the existence of an adequate military instrument; but this we had not got. Palliatives were possible, as we have seen, but difficult. Thus it was in 1932–4, when Germany, the occupation just over, was beginning her revival, that we should have reformed our own organization so that we would be in a position to strike at once if the need arose and then to bring ourselves up-to-date, particularly in armour and aviation. This would have required foresight, which indeed many had at the time—but foresight backed up by an energy which was lacking both in the high command and in the Government, which was too preoccupied with the present to bother about the future.

The lesson of this experience bears out the old saying 'To govern is to foresee'. Nothing is more destructive than a policy of 'wait and see', which is always an excuse for doing nothing. The modern world, because of the time which economic and military plans nowadays take to realize, can no longer afford to think short-term. It is only by a constant reappraisal of the situation and an awareness of incipient dangers, that decisions can be taken in time to keep these future dangers in check. This is undoubtedly a condemnation of any political system which has no guarantee of continuity.

It remains to say something of the men who were involved. I have been particularly hard on Gamelin—the original choice of whom and his maintenance in command were both catastrophic—because he was in control during the decisive time when destiny might still have been turned aside. Instead he allowed an irredeemable situation to arise of which he himself was the first victim. Were there any others who might perhaps have done better? It is possible; but, as I have said, by 1940 it was really too late. In any case, it is not for me to play the dangerous and futile game of apportioning praise or blame in judgement on the leaders of this generation who, whatever their personal qualities, had been heavily scarred by the events which had taken place between the two wars.

This burden was above all the fruit of the long maturation imposed on the Army by the mental attitude of the victors of 1918. But it is difficult to avoid the conclusion that the pre-eminence of this doctrine may well have accorded with the thinking of most Frenchmen at the time.

One is then tempted to go a little further. Why was France, so ardent and resolute in 1914, this time so passive and lulled into taking the easy way out? The evident reason is the terrible exhaustion caused by the First World War which, at the same time, took every vestige of romance out of the test of battle. Patriotism, so firmly implanted in the French spirit, had lost much of its magic. Patriotism may have been in some respects ingenuous, but in recent times it assumed a somewhat tarnished image through the unintelligible contradictions of collaboration, the Resistance and the giving up of our colonies. A similar mental attitude was to be found in Germany after the disasters of 1945, and in this respect even

✳ EPILOGUE ✳

Great Britain, which had suffered neither invasion nor defeat, was not spared.

The inescapable conclusion is that 1940 was but the last step in an inevitable progression. Destiny by certain fortuitous and extraordinary events, such as the command at Sedan losing its head and the accidental death of Billotte, showed clearly that we were lost To use an expression which has become fashionable, we were swept away by the current of history. It is this feeling of inexorable fate which I have tried to describe. It is this which, like a Greek tragedy, dominated our whole dramatic downfall.

But the current of history is merely a synthesis of the natural turn of events to which whole peoples surrender themselves, and from which no one can escape unless he finds a means of constructive reaction. It is the role of great men to escape from the fate of history—or rather, to create another, counter-balancing, fate. Chance, which governs events, dictated that the one man in France who revealed the necessary stature came to the fore too late, when practically all was lost.

The war of 1914–18, which destroyed so much, had nearly destroyed the myth of the great man. The appalling experience of 1940, with the bitter fruits of which we have not yet done, left in its wake one valuable lesson: mankind and nations are but the playthings of destiny if they cannot foresee mounting perils and rise up in time to combat them. This they cannot do unless they discover how to make ready the élite who can grasp the rudder firmly in any storm and can steer a safe course through treacherous waters.

INDEX

✳

Personal names beginning with 'De' or 'D' are indexed among the 'D's' and grouped together.

✳ INDEX ✳

A NOTE ABOUT THE AUTHOR

ANDRÉ BEAUFRE

was born in 1902 at Neuilly-sur-Seine. Upon leaving Saint-Cyr in 1923 he took part in the campaigns of the Rif and Morocco. He then entered the École de Guerre, studied at the École Libre des Sciences Politiques, and was assigned to the Army General Staff. After a mission to the USSR in 1939 he was attached to General Headquarters in Paris. In 1941, while he was Permanent Secretary of National Defense in Algeria, he was arrested and brought before the Conseil de Guerre for having participated in the preparations for the future Allied landing in North Africa. After his release from prison in 1942 he returned to Algeria by submarine with General Giraud and became head of the cabinet of the commander-in-chief in North Africa. He participated in the campaigns of Tunisia, Italy, France, and Germany, and after the war served in Indochina and Algeria before commanding the French troops in the Suez operation. Named Général d'Armée in 1960, André Beaufre is a Grand Officier *of the* Legion of Honor *and holder of the* Croix de guerre *with eleven citations. He was with SHAPE as chief of the General Staff and, in 1960, head of the French delegation to the Permanent Group of NATO in Washington. He is the author of* Introduction to Strategy, Deterrence and Strategy, *and* NATO and Europe.

A NOTE ON THE TYPE

THE TEXT OF THIS BOOK

was set in MONOTYPE BELL, *a copy of the English Monotype face of the same name. The Englishman John Bell (1745–1831) was responsible for the original cutting of this design. The vocations of Bell were many —among a few might be mentioned bookseller, printer, publisher, type-founder, and journalist. His types were considerably influenced by the delicacy and beauty of the French copper-plate engravers. Monotype Bell might also be classified as a delicate and refined rendering of Scotch Roman.*

Printed by Universal Lithographers, Inc.,
Timonium, Md.

Bound by The Haddon Craftsmen, Inc.,
Scranton, Pa.